THE ILLUSTRATED NAPOLEON

DAVID G. CHANDLER

GREENHILL BOOKS   LONDON

THE ILLUSTRATED

NAPOLEON

This edition of *The Illustrated Napoleon* first published
1991 by Greenhill Books, Lionel Leventhal Limited,
Park House, 1 Russell Gardens, London NW11 9NN.

British Library Cataloguing in Publication Data
Chandler, David G., 1934–
1. Napoleonic Wars
I. Title
940.27

ISBN 1-85367-086-3

Designed by Kate Nichols

Printed in the United States of America

Portions of this book appeared in *Napoleon* by
David Chandler (New York: Macmillan, 1973).

CONTENTS

Color illustrations follow page 54.

MAPS

THE ILLUSTRATED NAPOLEON

O N E

THE EARLY YEARS

"I have a presentiment that one day this small island will astonish Europe," wrote Jean-Jacques Rousseau of Corsica in 1762. It was a time when the island's struggle for independence under her leader, General Paoli, had captured the romantic imagination of liberals everywhere. Of less obvious significance, Paoli numbered among his supporters a cultured, kindly, if not particularly notable, Corsican named Carlo Buonaparte.

Corsica—and the name Buonaparte—did indeed astonish Europe, though in a way hardly to be foreseen even by the prophetic Rousseau. Just seven years after Rousseau's famous prediction, Paoli was defeated by the French, and Corsica's dream of independence was destroyed; but on that island, in August of that year, 1769, Carlo's wife Letizia gave birth to a son, Napoleone, who was to become not just an outstanding soldier, nor just a great leader, but one of the most successful conquerors known to history.

Napoleon was not to suffer for his family's association with the Corsican rebel. On the contrary, the influential Baron Marboeuf, a close friend of Carlo and Letizia's, was able to secure places for both Napoleon and his elder brother Joseph at Brienne, a royal school founded by Louis XVI's minister of war, Saint-Germain, for the sons of the nobility. It was not easy to prove, as was necessary, that the Buonapartes had descended from generations of nobility; for although they were an old and prominent Corsican family, with an Italian lineage that could be traced back to the eleventh century, they were scarcely noble in the contemporary sense. However, the formalities were eventually completed and, at the age of nine, Napoleon left the land of his birth for the wider horizon of France.

The first step was a preliminary year at a college at Autun, where the brothers put a little polish on their French; then Brienne, where Napoleon spent five and a half years. The soft-spoken, impoverished and intensely proud Corsican suffered from both loneliness and homesickness, thinking often of his mother, whom he adored, and his

Letizia Buonaparte (1750–1836). Of the long-established Corsican Ramolino family, Letizia married Carlo Buonaparte in 1764 and bore him thirteen children (Napoleone being the second), of whom eight survived. During the Empire, "Madame Mère" retained her sense of proportion: "So long as it lasts . . ." was a favorite saying of hers. After its collapse, she used her careful savings made in the "good years" to help out impecunious members of her family. She died in Rome.

Carlo Buonaparte (1746–1785) (opposite page, upper left). (Engraving by Muller after Girodet.) A lawyer in Ajaccio whose hobby was writing poetry, Napoleon's father was of minor noble descent, the family having originally come from Italy. He died of stomach cancer before Napoleon gained his commission.

Napoleon attacking snow forts at Brienne (opposite page, upper right). (Engraving by M. Haider after Louis Loeb.) This celebrated incident saw Napoleon organize his fellow juniors for a successful attack on snow forts held by the seniors. Clearly, he developed strong leadership traits early.

Napoleon at Brienne (opposite page, bottom). (After Dumas.) The future emperor was educated from 1779 to 1784 at a royal school for young noblemen run by Minim monks. Isolated and mocked for his quaint accent, his nickname being "Paille-au-nez" ("Straw-in-the-nose"), his poverty and his passionate love for Corsica, he made few friends but worked hard, excelling in mathematics, and developed an iron will.

growing family of brothers and sisters, of whom Lucien, Elisa, Louis, Pauline, Caroline and Jérôme, apart from Joseph, survived beyond infancy. At school he was mocked and mimicked by his fellows, and was doubtless developing that sense of being different, of uniqueness, that was to drive him onward throughout his career as a man of destiny.

But Napoleon's school days were not unsuccessful. He began to show his precocious talent for leadership, organizing elaborate war games and, one winter, a snowball fight of heroic and not altogether bloodless proportions in which his fellow juniors outclassed the seniors. He also applied himself to his studies, showing particular promise in mathematics. Toward the end of his schooling, a royal inspector wrote the following report: "Height—five feet three inches. Constitution—excellent health, docile expression, mild, straightforward, thoughtful. Conduct—most satisfactory: has always been distinguished for his application in mathematics. He is fairly well acquainted with history and geography. He is weak in all accomplishments—drawing, dancing, music and the like. This boy would make an excellent sailor: deserves to be admitted to the school in Paris." He was not, however, destined for a nautical career. His ambition was already set on receiving a commission in the artillery.

A vacancy was duly secured, and in late October 1784 he joined the Ecole Militaire in Paris. His formal training lasted less than a year. In the spring of 1785 his father died, and brothers Joseph and Lucien (also sent to train in France) returned home to aid their mother; Napoleon stayed on to complete his training, but he was allowed to graduate early, probably for compassionate reasons. He was ranked only fifty-fifth, but at least he was receiving a pittance of pay from October 31, 1785, no small part of it being transmitted back to Corsica to assist his family. And so it was that probationer *sous-lieutenant* Buonaparte joined La Fère Artillery Regiment at Valence on November 5, 1785. The greatest military career in history had begun.

It was a propitious if dangerous moment. France was heaving under the strains that would shortly dissolve the nation—and Europe—in the tumult of the Revolution. With the Revolution would come internal chaos and external threat: fertile conditions

Target practice, Dieppe. (Painting by François Flameng, 1795.) Peacetime garrison life—which for Lieutenant Buonaparte was interspersed with long periods of leave spent in Corsica—held few attractions, but officers honed their marksmanship and pursued such hobbies as painting and dancing.

for both strong political leaders and strong generals; alternatively, ambitions could just as easily lead to the guillotine. Moreover, the egalitarian nature of the Revolution would mean opportunities for men of lower birth rather than for the traditional French nobility, who had hitherto dominated in church and state. More practically, Napoleon began his career at a time when the French army was technically equipped for the successes he was to achieve. Out of the disasters of the Seven Years' War in midcentury had come new energy and application to modernize the army's weapons, particularly in the field of artillery.

It is therefore significant that young Napoleon began his service by learning in fullest detail the profession of a gunner. He learned how to handle rammer and shot, how to sight a gun and to command a detachment. When he had mastered these matters, his commission was confirmed and, modestly enough, he saw his first active service quelling local food riots at Lyons.

Soon it was time for his first leave, which he managed to extend from February 1787 to June 1788. No doubt he found garrison duty boring, but it is indicative of the easygoing nature of the Bourbon authorities that they countenanced such lengthy absences. Indeed, his first six years as an officer would include no less than thirty-two months of leave. During his first return to Corsica, the ambitious youth started to write a history of the island. He was still inspired with the goal of Corsican independence

Buonaparte at Auxonne, 1788. (By François Flameng.) All his life Napoleon avidly searched after knowledge, and the year he spent at the Auxonne Artillery School was probably the most formative of his adult life. The commandant, Baron Du Teil, recognized the latent ability in the young officer.

and looked upon Paoli, now in exile, as a hero. It was an admiration that would not last much longer.

Following his return to duty, Napoleon spent an important and informative year posted to the Auxonne Artillery School, where he was appointed secretary to a board of senior artillery officers conducting experiments with cannon and shells. This brought him into close contact with the best gunners of the day and, above all, with Baron Du Teil, who took the keen young officer under his wing. The commandant lent Napoleon many books, encouraging him to study the wider spectrum of warfare; from these writings about history and military affairs, Napoleon began to gather those ideas of strategic and grand tactical maneuver that were to form the basis of his generalship. Napoleon was never an original thinker where military theory was concerned; his genius was wholly practical—he made other men's concepts work and improvised upon them. Hence the importance of these months at Auxonne, during which the foundations of future greatness were indubitably laid. He was an avid reader and an apt pupil, and absorbed all that the baron could provide.

The winter of 1788 saw Napoleon seriously ill—possibly because of an inadequate diet, as he sought to save more money to send his family. He recovered, and the following September, as the first waves of the Revolution swept across France, he set out again for Corsica on leave and plunged into the local ferment. Paoli soon returned to Corsica in triumph, and Napoleon, now an ardent revolutionary, saw his hero's patriotism as perfectly compatible with the ideals of the Revolution. He involved himself in local politics, exploiting a new regulation passed by the National Assembly that permitted regular officers to hold additional, elected ranks in the volunteer battalions being raised in various areas. On April 1, 1792, Napoleon became Lieutenant Colonel Buonaparte of the Ajaccio Volunteers, assuring his election by the simple, if unscrupulous, method of arranging for his fellow candidates to be kidnapped for the period

Napoleon at the siege of Toulon. (By Grenier; lithograph by Bianchi.) Captain Buonaparte—through a combination of chance and his well-timed propaganda leaflet, Le Souper de Beaucaire—*was appointed to direct the artillery in the siege of Toulon. As a reward for its recapture, he was promoted to a provisional general of brigade on December 22. His meteoric rise had begun.*

of election day. But the rift with Paoli had come. Paoli was no revolutionary, but a royalist and, in the conflict, pro-British. Napoleon earned his hostility both by his severe repression of local rioting and by his support of a French investigation into Corsican affairs. The Buonaparte family had to flee Corsica to escape Paoli's vengeance and, in June 1793, settled near Marseilles. As for Corsica, it was surrendered in 1794 to the British, who held it for three yers.

For the Buonaparte family, for France and for Europe, 1793 was indeed a critical year. By now the Revolution was entering its bloodiest phase. Louis XVI and his queen, Marie-Antoinette, had been executed. The new French Republic was at war with almost the whole of Europe, the fruit of its absurd boast that it would help "all peoples who rise against their rulers." The Austrian Empire, with its extensive possessions from eastern Europe to Italy, had entered the lists. So too had England, with her command of the seas. Meanwhile, France was torn by internal rebellion, and this gave Napoleon his first great chance—at the siege of Toulon (see page 8).

As a reward for recapturing Toulon, the representatives of the people (political commissars attached as supervisors to every French army in the field) promoted Buonaparte—he continued to spell his name in the Italian fashion until 1796—to brigadier general on December 22, 1793. He was barely twenty-four years old. Napoleon's success at Toulon had stamped him as a promising young soldier of outstanding qualities—qualities sorely needed by the authorities in Paris. The road to preferment seemed open and inviting before him. Under the patronage of Augustin Robespierre (brother of "the Dictator"), he became senior gunner to General Dumerbion's army in Italy, after the German front the most important theater of operations against the Austrians. It was largely because of Napoleon's meticulous planning that the French

captured both Loano, in April 1794, and the area in the Ligurian Alps known as "the Barricades."

Shortly afterward, Napoleon went on an intelligence mission to Genoa, an episode that nearly cost him his head, for in the troubled world of revolutionary France success could prove its own undoing. In July, a *coup d'état* in Paris swept Robespierre and the Jacobin faction from power, all "the Dictator's" closest associates being rounded up by the new regime, the Directory. Napoleon was among those arrested, and he was shut up in the Fortress of Antibes on a trumped-up charge of treasonable behavior in Genoa. His imprisonment lasted only a fortnight, for his skills were needed by the hard-pressed army in Italy, but in the year that followed his release he was alternately dismissed and reinstated as the political pendulum swung in the capital. At times he despaired, contemplating leaving France altogether and placing his sword at the disposal of the sultan of Turkey.

Then, at the beginning of October 1795, came a decisive moment. The Paris mob, in one of its periodic fits of revolt, rose against the Directory. Paul Barras, one of the directors, was charged with organizing the defense of the National Convention, and he turned to former brigadier general Buonaparte to take the necessary measures. Napoleon did not hesitate. Sending Major Joachim Murat, a cavalry officer who happened to be passing, to secure some guns, he drew up his dispositions to isolate the Tuileries Palace, where the mob would make its attempted *coup*. When, on October 5 (13 Vendémiaire), the anticipated attack took place, the rioters, surging forward, were

Thirteen Vendémiaire (October 5, 1795). (Painting after Myrbach.) When a royalist insurrection threatened the Convention, its defense was entrusted to the unemployed general of brigade Buonaparte. He scattered the mob with the famous "whiff of grapeshot" and a grateful government promoted him to general of division in recognition. Napoleon had now arrived with a vengeance.

met with salvos from cannon at point-blank range. Two hundred died instantly; the "whiff of grapeshot" succeeded in crushing the revolt; and the events of 13 Vendémiaire made Napoleon's fortune. Praise and rewards were lavished upon him by a grateful Directory. By October 16 he had been promoted to *général de division*; ten days later he was appointed to command the Army of the Interior.

This astonishing rise had taken Napoleon, at twenty-six, to a pinnacle of professional achievement. At the same time, he began to contemplate a change of a more personal nature; for in the aftermath of Vendémiaire the Paris citizens were ordered to surrender their weapons to the government, and Napoleon was visited by a fourteen-year-old boy who pleaded that his mother might keep her late husband's sword. The general acceded and was visited by the widow herself, Josephine de Beauharnais, who wanted to thank him personally. She was six years older than Napoleon, still very beautiful, with an aristocratic background that had once brought her to the verge of execution before Robespierre's fall had saved her. Napoleon fell passionately in love. Josephine, a former mistress of Barras's, now became mistress to the victor of Vendémiaire. A few months later, on March 9, 1796, they were married.

The honeymoon lasted two days. Already Napoleon had laid plans for his next command, daily bombarding the ministry of war with criticism and advice concerning the feeble campaign being waged in Italy. In the month of his marriage, he was given the appointment he wanted, the senior command in Italy. On March 26 he arrived in Nice with his newly appointed staff, which included Alexandre Berthier as its head and Colonel Murat as senior *aide de camp*. So far, Napoleon's success had resulted largely from good fortune, from being at the right place at the right moment. He had never directed a large-scale military operation. He had studied hard, thought a great deal and was confident in his abilities. Now these abilities would be tested, and Napoleon, and the world, would discover whether the precocious careerist was in fact a military commander of the first rank.

The Siege of Toulon
September 7 – December 19, 1793

Napoleon captured both official and public attention at the age of twenty-four on the south coast of France at the great naval port and arsenal of Toulon. His emergence came at a moment of the greatest crisis for the Revolution. In Paris, the triumph of the Jacobin extreme left and the assumption of power by Maximilien Robespierre's Committee of Public Safety had triggered a series of revolts within France. Of these the most serious was that in the Midi, an area that had strongly supported the deposed Girondin government and contained several pockets of Bourbon royalists. Stung into open rebellion by the new conscription laws and by the repressive legislation passed in late May and early June, particularly the infamous Law of Suspects, the city of Marseilles was the first to rebel, closely followed by Avignon.

This was a development that the government, hard-pressed by external threats, could not ignore: the very survival of the Republic was at stake. A force of three thousand men was hastily assembled at Valence and its command awarded to Citizen-

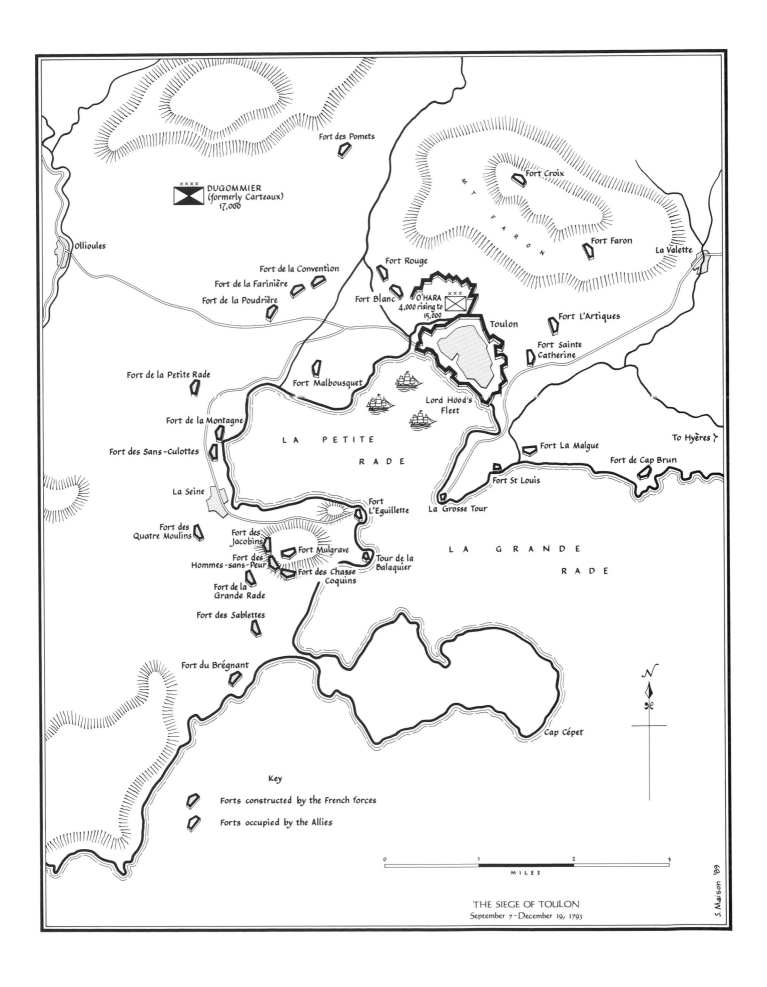

THE SIEGE OF TOULON
September 7 - December 19, 1793

Colonel Carteaux, a sometime painter and policeman, backed (and closely supervised) by a group of all-powerful *députés-en-mission*, political commissars, who included the Corsican Salicetti, Gasparin, Barras and (most significantly) Augustin Robespierre.

Onto this scene of confusion strayed Captain Buonaparte, under orders to escort a gunpowder convoy to the Army of Italy. When his instructions were countermanded, he found himself incorporated into Carteaux's counterinsurgency forces, taking part in an action at Avignon on July 24 that narrowly turned out to be a success for the revolutionary forces. During a lull in operations, Captain Buonaparte penned a propaganda leaflet, *Le Souper de Beaucaire*, a pro-Jacobin plea for loyalty to the Republic and a denunciation of the unpardonable crime of encouraging civil war. This timely document came to the attention of Salicetti, who introduced its author to Augustin Robespierre. Thus was forged an important relationship, one that brought Napoleon's name to the attention of the authorities for the first time. Meanwhile, success—of a sort—continued to bless Carteaux's arms, and on August 25 Marseilles was restored to its republican allegiance. It seemed that the crisis was over, and Captain Buonaparte was ordered to proceed with his convoy-master duties.

However, the heaviest blow was still to fall. The loyalties of the great naval arsenal of Toulon had long been known to be in the balance, but abruptly, on August 27, its twenty-eight thousand inhabitants declared for King Louis XVII and the next day admitted the Anglo-Spanish fleet of Admiral Lord Hood. With his ships came two thousand British and fifteen thousand Spanish and Neapolitan troops, effectively dou-

(After Lecomte du Novy.) In 1793 the young Buonaparte attracted the attention of "Dictator" Robespierre's brother, Augustin, by writing a political pamphlet titled The Supper of Beaucaire. *It centered upon an imaginary conversation at an inn, where a young soldier (Buonaparte) reproves some merchants from Marseilles who are arguing that revolt against the republican government in Paris is justifiable.*

bling the strength of the disaffected garrison and naval personnel. Aghast at this development, which at a stroke threatened France's naval power and her position in the Mediterranean, Paris reinforced General Carteaux to thirty-two thousand men, with five thousand more summoned from Italy. By early September these forces were converging on Toulon from west and east respectively, driving in rebel outposts. In one of these skirmishes Dommartin, commanding Carteaux's artillery and the only regular gunner officer present with the army, was wounded. Napoleon, visiting headquarters at Beausset before setting out for Nice, heard of this mishap and promptly persuaded fellow Corsican Salicetti to put forward his name as Dommartin's replacement. Robespierre and Barras agreed, and so on September 16 Carteaux (who had not been consulted) found himself with a new artillery commander.

Toulon was defended by Vauban-type fortifications supplemented by over a dozen detached forts, which formed an outer ring commanding the landward approaches to the city over Mount Faron from the north, and the coastal plains lying east and west. Two of these positions, forts L'Eguillette and Tour de la Balaquier, overlooked the inner harbor from a promontory to the southwest, while Fort La Grosse Tour was similarly situated in the facing headland across the bay. It was immediately clear to Napoleon that Fort L'Eguillette was the key to Toulon; capture it, and heavy guns could make the inner harbor untenable for Hood's fleet, and if the admiral withdrew he would doubtless take the troops with him. Even Carteaux could see this but was not prepared to allocate the necessary number of troops for the task. Napoleon fumed inwardly and bombarded the *députés* with reports and complaints. His promotion to major on October 19 did little to alleviate either staff obstruction or shortages of munitions. The latter problem he tackled with zeal, and he managed to expand the siege train from a mere handful of guns to 194 pieces of all calibers, manned by sixty-four officers and fifteen hundred men, many of them trained-up infantry volunteers. Requisitions were ruthlessly imposed on the whole region around Toulon. These measures took time to accomplish, but at the outset Napoleon constructed two batteries overlooking the western shores of the inner harbor, which as early as September 20 forced Hood to move his anchorage closer to Toulon. On the twenty-second the French attempted to storm the western promontory, but (despite Napoleon's remonstrations) in insufficient strength.

As a result, the allied command saw how important to their fleet's security were Mount Caire and Fort L'Eguillette at its tip. Almost overnight they constructed Fort Mulgrave, mounting twenty cannon and four mortars, inland from L'Eguillette, in the process greatly improving their defenses on Mount Caire, which was soon nicknamed "le petit Gibraltar" by the French.

These developments so depressed Napoleon that he wrote to Paris requesting the appointment of a gunner senior to him in order to secure proper direction of the siege. After long delays, the aged Chevalier Du Teil was appointed; a sick man, he left everything to Major Buonaparte, backing his subordinate's ideas with his own authority. Still there was a profusion of plans: everybody thought he knew best how to take Toulon, and Carteaux refused to make up his mind which plan to accept. His replacement, General Doppet (a doctor by profession), was no improvement and lasted only three weeks. With the appointment of the veteran General Dugommier to the command on November 16, an experienced soldier at last made an appearance.

Buonaparte massacring fifteen hundred persons at Toulon. (Engraving by R. K. Porter.) When the French revolutionary troops reentered Toulon on December 19, 1793, they wreaked the Republic's vengeance on the townsfolk. There is no proof that Buonaparte took any part in this atrocity, but his later enemies were quick to lay the responsibility for it at his door.

Napoleon had not been idle over these weeks of turmoil. He had set up eleven batteries, eight of them sited to sweep Fort Mulgrave with the fire of thirty-eight guns, two more to bombard Fort Malbousquet, which lay closer to Toulon, and the last, six long-range mortars mounted to bomb the houses of the city. He was confident that these measures would prepare the way for the capture of L'Eguillette; thereafter, if the Allies proved stubborn, all efforts would be turned against Fort Malbousquet, whose fall would doom Toulon. But he was confident that this second stage would not be necessary.

Several French batteries were sited uncomfortably close to Fort Mulgrave. One suffered heavy casualties from fire, and troops eventually refused to reoccupy the exposed position. Napoleon—with his already well-developed awareness of human psychology, particularly that of the French soldier—knew what to do. Aided by young Sergeant Junot, outside the position he set up a notice board that read *"Batterie des hommes sans peur."* Thereafter there was no shortage of volunteers.

On November 25 General Dugommier held a council of war that at last decided, at the commanding general's urging, to adopt Major Buonaparte's plan: a heavy bombardment of Fort Mulgrave followed by an all-out assault on Mount Caire, disguised by a secondary attack against Mount Faron north of Toulon. Once L'Eguillette was in French hands, cannon trained on Hood's shipping would open fire with red-hot shot.

But the Allies were not quiescent. On the twenty-ninth, before the French were ready to attack, General O'Hara (commanding the Allied land forces) made a strong sortie from Fort Malbousquet and overwhelmed the Battery of the Convention. Both Dugommier and Buonaparte took part in the counterattack, which repulsed the Allies with six hundred casualties and captured their wounded commander.

Two weeks later the climax occurred. While the newly arrived *général de brigade* André Massena attacked Mount Faron, a three-day bombardment swept Fort Mulgrave. After some last-minute hesitation occasioned by a gale that was blowing, on December 17 a seven-thousand-man assault of the Allied forts was led by General Muiron through pouring rain. The hand-to-hand fighting was severe; Major Buonaparte was unhorsed and received a bayonet wound in the thigh. But within a few hours "le petit Gibraltar" had fallen, soon followed by forts L'Eguillette and Tour de la Balaquier. At the cost of a thousand casualties, the French were masters of Mount Caire and its defenses— and thus effectively of Toulon itself. By late afternoon on the eighteenth, ten heavy siege guns were ready to pound the British fleet with red-hot shot.

As Napoleon had surmised, this was enough for Lord Hood. He ordered the evacuation of the inner harbor, the blowing up of the arsenal and the burning of the anchored French naval shipping in the harbor. Although the last task was only partly accomplished, the admiral ordered the evacuation of Toulon, packing onto his crowded vessels as many townsfolk as space would allow. At 9:00 A.M. on December 19 the revolutionary forces took possession of Toulon.

All agreed that Buonaparte deserved the major credit for the outcome of the siege. On December 22 the *députés* promoted him to the provisional rank of *général de brigade*. The rank was confirmed by the Committee of Public Safety on February 16. The star of Napoleone di Buonaparte had begun to rise.

T W O

THE GENERAL
IN ITALY AND EGYPT

In Italy, General Bonaparte found himself commanding a neglected, ill-disciplined and largely demoralized force of some 37,600 men. They were hemmed in along the narrow Ligurian Plain by the forces of Austria, under General Beaulieu, and her allies—albeit unwilling ones—the Piedmontese, under General Colli, who were holding the mountains from Cuneo almost to Voltri, while the Royal Navy dominated the Gulf of Genoa. It was a situation to daunt the most optimistic soldier. Napoleon's divisional commanders, Massena, Augereau and Sérurier, treated their new general with barely concealed contemptuous amusement—but not for long. The troops badly needed a victory, and they needed to extricate themselves from their precarious position. Napoleon's solution involved a strategy that was to characterize several of his later campaigns: to concentrate his initial blow against the center of a widely deployed enemy before defeating the left and right by a concentration of superior force against each wing in turn (see page 74). In this instance, knowing that his army must starve and disintegrate if it remained in its present position, Bonaparte planned to break through into the fertile plains of Piedmont without delay, as a preliminary to the conquest of the Po valley, his strategic objective.

A surprise move by the Austrians toward Savona and Voltri precipitated the French offensive. Aiming to divide Colli's twenty-five thousand Piedmontese near Ceva from Beaulieu's widely dispersed twenty-seven thousand Austrians before defeating them in detail, Bonaparte struck north from the coast on April 11, 1796. After repulsing a detachment of Beaulieu's army the next day at Montenotte, the main French force swung west to attack Colli, the primary target. A crisis involving Massena's division, which was holding the right flank at Dego, delayed Bonaparte for three vital days, but by the seventeenth the advance on Ceva had been resumed and the army's communications had been switched, from the exposed route to the coast, to the safer Col di Tende.

Remorseless pressure forced Colli into action at Mondovi on the twenty-second,

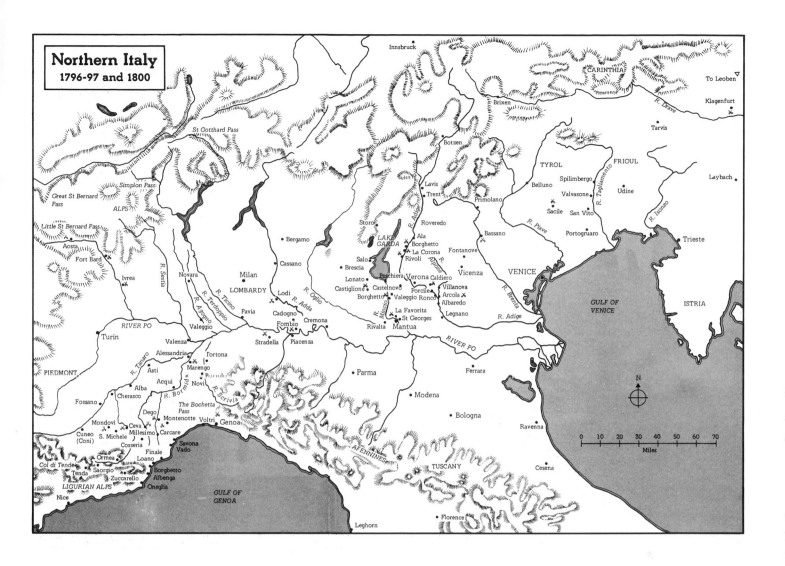

Northern Italy
1796-97 and 1800

St Gotthard Pass

Innsbruck

CARINTHIA

To Leoben

Klagenfurt

Brixen

R. Drave

Tarvis

Botzen

TYROL

FRIOUL

Simplon Pass

Great St Bernard Pass

ALPS

Little St Bernard Pass

Aosta

Fort Bard

Ivrea

R. Sesia

Novara

Milan

LOMBARDY

R. Ticino

R. Agogna

R. Terdoppio

Valeggio

Pavia

Turin

PIEDMONT

Valenza

Asti

Alessandria

Tortona

Acqui

Marengo

Novi

R. Bormida

R. Scrivia

Cherasco

Alba

Fossano

Dego

Mondovi

Ceva

Millesimo

Carcare

Cuneo (Coni)

S. Michele

Cosseria

Finale

Loano

Montenotte

Voltri

Genoa

The Bochetta Pass

Savona

Vado

Col di Tende

Ormea

Saorgio

Tenda

Zuccarello

Borghetto

Albenga

Oneglia

LIGURIAN ALPS

Nice

GULF OF GENOA

Bergamo

Cassano

Lodi

R. Oglio

R. Adda

Cadogno

Fombio

Cremona

Stradella

Piacenza

RIVER PO

Storo

LAKE GARDA

Salo

Brescia

Lonato

Castiglione

Castelnovo

Borghetto

Rivalta

Mantua

Ala

Borghetto

La Corona

Rivoli

Peschiera

Valeggio

Ronco

La Favorita

St Georges

Legnano

Lavis

Trent

Roveredo

R. Adige

R.

Caldiero

Verona

Porcile

Villanova

Arcola

Albaredo

R. Mincio

R. Adige

Fontanove

Vicenza

Primolano

Belluno

Spilimbergo

Valvasone

Sacile

San Vito

Bassano

R. Piave

Portogruaro

R. Brenta

VENICE

R. Tagliamento

Udine

Laybach

R. Isonzo

Trieste

ISTRIA

GULF OF VENICE

Parma

Ferrara

Modena

Bologna

Ravenna

Cesena

TUSCANY

Florence

Leghorn

N

0 10 20 30 40 50 60 70
Miles

APENNINES

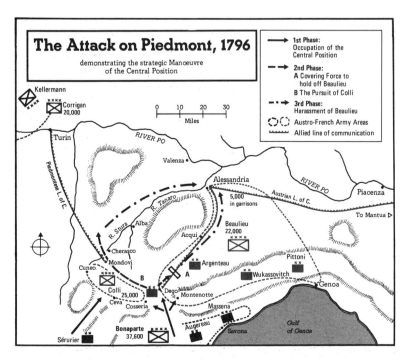

The Attack on Piedmont, 1796

demonstrating the strategic Manœuvre of the Central Position

1st Phase: Occupation of the Central Position

2nd Phase:
A Covering Force to hold off Beaulieu
B The Pursuit of Colli

3rd Phase: Harassment of Beaulieu

Austro-French Army Areas

Allied line of communication

Kellermann

Corrigan 20,000

Turin

RIVER PO

Valenza

Piedmontese L. of C.

Alessandria

5,000 in garrisons

Austrian L. of C.

RIVER PO

Piacenza

To Mantua ▷

R. Tanaro

Alba

Acqui

Beaulieu 22,000

Cherasco

R. Stura

Cuneo

Mondovi

Colli 25,000

B

Dego

Argenteau

A

Wukassovitch

Pittoni

Genoa

Ceva

Cosseria

Montenotte

Massena

Sérurier

Bonaparte 37,600

Augereau

Savona

Gulf of Genoa

0 10 20 30
Miles

N

The cannon at Lodi. (After Myrbach.) The battle at Lodi centered upon the capture of the bridge, and Napoleon earned the nickname "Le Petit Caporal" ("the little corporal") from his troops by personally sitting several cannon along the riverbank to bring effective fire against the foe. In a gun crew of the time this was the duty of the corporal commanding the detail.

and the subsequent French pursuit, pushed to the uttermost, induced Piedmont to sign the Armistice of Cherasco on the twenty-eighth. Thus seventeen days had sufficed for the elimination of one opponent; and Napoleon's underlying strategy of the central position, used here for the first time, had, despite certain imperfections, proved its value.

After a pause to resupply his near-starving troops, Bonaparte swung east down the Tanaro valley in an attempt to envelop the bewildered Beaulieu, but owing to a desperate retreat, the Austrians managed to evade the trap and cross to the north bank of the Po River. With superior forces now at his disposal (some sixty-eight hundred fresh reinforcements had reached him from the Col di Tende), Bonaparte set out to experiment with another of his theories, the strategy of envelopment. Feinting toward Valenza with Sérurier's division, as if presaging a major river crossing at that point (and thus distracting and preoccupying Beaulieu's attention in an irrelevant direction), the main body of the Army of Italy was force-marched down the south bank of the Po to Piacenza, far in the Austrians' rear. Seizing a ferry, the French crossed the broad river there (May 7–9) and set out to occupy the bridges over the tributary River Adda so as to isolate the Austrian army and prevent reinforcement by severing its communications with its base at the great city-fortress of Mantua, the key to Austrian control of north Italy.

The French formations, however, still unused to their youthful commander's blitzkrieg concepts, were too slow in carrying out his orders. Beaulieu realized his peril in the nick of time, and by a second precipitate retreat succeeded in marching his men over the Adda's bridges before they were denied to him by the probing French columns. As a result, the famous Battle of Lodi, fought on May 10, merely mauled Beaulieu's rear guard. Bonaparte sited guns himself and helped storm the bridge. The Austrians had the worst of the encounter (each side losing some two thousand casualties), but Beaulieu's main body of men escaped to Milan. It all amounted to far less than Bonaparte had hoped for, but somewhat paradoxically it was the battle of the bridge of Lodi that set the seal on the troops' confidence in their new general. Henceforward he was nicknamed "Le Petit Caporal," a reference to his personal siting of cannon, a task normally entrusted to the NCO in charge of each piece.

Five days later the French were masters of Milan, and without pause Bonaparte hounded his men on to force the Mincio River line near Borghetto on the thirtieth, affording his opponents no time to recover their balance. The reeling Austrians promptly split their army, part of it retiring north up the Adige valley toward Trent, the remainder seeking sanctuary in Mantua, the key to the famous "quadrilateral" of fortresses (Mantua, Peschiera, Verona and Legnano) guarding the exits from the Alpine passes into north Italy. Garrisoned by twelve thousand men with 316 cannon, Mantua—and Austria's successive attempts to relieve it—was to dominate Napoleon's attention for the next nine months. By June 3 it was closely besieged by the French.

With his main forces investing Mantua, Bonaparte busied himself reorganizing the conquered Milanese, crushing revolts mercilessly as the inhabitants rose in protest against the huge requisitions demanded and the barefaced looting of their towns and villages.

To make matters worse, the Directory by no means attached the same importance to the Italian campaign as Napoleon did. Their ideas were more limited: to pick up, on a secondary front, territorial acquisitions that might be useful bargaining chips in any eventual general pacification with Vienna; to plunder their riches and treasures for the precarious Paris exchequer; and above all to create in Italy a large-scale diversion to assist the planned major offensive under generals Moreau and Jourdan due—indeed long overdue—to move across the Rhine and into the Danube valley. This was very far from General Bonaparte's ambition to establish control over the whole of north Italy and reorganize it into client republics. Hence his chilly reception of the Directory's attempt to divide the Italian army in two, giving half to General Kellermann, presently commanding the Army of the Alps, and restricting Bonaparte to operations and plunder in the south. Napoleon strongly hinted at resignation, retorting, "One bad commander is better than two good ones." In the end he won his point, and the convoys of looted art treasures that he sent off to Paris helped to remind his political masters of his indispensability.

With Mantua under siege, the Austrian hold on north Italy threatened and the French offensives into Germany hanging fire, Vienna could be expected to move against Bonaparte without delay. The Alsatian general Würmser, who had replaced the discredited Beaulieu, was soon massing an army around Trent, using troops from the quiescent German front. In July, Würmser advanced in three columns down each side of Lake Garda and down the more distant Brenta valley, hoping to divide and distract the French. Weaker than his opponent (who had fifty thousand men) in terms of a field army, Bonaparte was set the task of intercepting, and defeating, each enemy force in turn without allowing any of them to relieve Mantua. This proved beyond his capacity, and he was soon speaking of "taking serious measures for a defeat." To gain men for battle, he was compelled to order Sérurier's division to abandon the siege of Mantua. On August 3, Bonaparte rushed twenty thousand men to beat back the westernmost Austrian column at First Lonato, but this enabled Würmser to slip troops and supplies into Mantua from the east. Fortunately for Napoleon, the Austrian general was slow in moving toward the main French army. The French countermarched from Lonato and on August 5 were able to fight Würmser's twenty-five thousand men with twenty-eight thousand at Castiglione. Sérurier's division (under Fiorella) came up from Mantua somewhat early against the Austrian left and rear, and as a result Würmser was able to extricate some twenty thousand men and head back toward Trent. Thus the French had driven off the first Austrian relief army, but not before it had resupplied the Mantuan garrison. On August 10 the siege had to be started all over again.

Meanwhile, away on the Rhine, Jourdan's belated offensive had run into difficulties, but by mid-August Moreau was making substantial progress on the Danube front. The Directory thereupon ordered the Army of Italy to mount a major diversionary attack toward Trent and the Tyrol, despite the complication of leaving an untamed Mantua in its rear. When Bonaparte advanced with thirty-three thousand men up the Adige valley to test the Austrian hold on the Tyrol, he discovered that Würmser was in fact already on the move southward down the Brenta valley, with twenty thousand men, his aim once again being to relieve Mantua and challenge the French hold on the Milanese.

As soon as he realized the new situation, Bonaparte abandoned his Tyrol offensive, left General Vaubois with ten thousand men to mask Trent and rushed the remainder down the Brenta valley behind his adversary. The outcome of this bold and highly unconventional maneuver was the defeat of Würmser at Bassano on September 8. The Austrian survivors were forced to split up, some heading eastward for the sanctuary offered by Trieste, others (led by Würmser) making for Mantua, where they succeeded in breaking through the seige lines on the twelfth to raise the garrison's strength to twenty-three thousand men.

The French reimposed the siege the next day, but were no nearer to capturing the great fortress than they had been in June. Once again, a temporary lull settled over the theater of war, during which Bonaparte busied himself with creating three new republics to consolidate France's grip on its earlier conquests. However, as their demands remained ruthless, the French remained unpopular with the local people.

By October, Moreau's Danube offensive, which Bonaparte had been able to do little to assist, was on the verge of collapse, and this enabled Vienna to find more men for Italy. General Alvintzi, the new commander in Würmser's absence, soon built up an army of forty-six thousand. Leaving eighteen thousand of these to lure the French toward Trent, he marched the remainder via Bassano and headed for Verona, the very linchpin of the French defenses, pushing back Massena's covering division before him. Simultaneously, from Trent, the Austrians applied relentless pressure against Vaubois, forcing him, too, to give ground. Bonaparte was, as he himself admitted, fooled for a time and placed in a considerable quandary. Could he spare troops to reinforce Vaubois without courting disaster at Verona, and vice versa? He was not strong enough to dominate both sectors at the same time, and there was no prospect of reinforcements reaching him.

Deciding that Alvintzi represented the greater peril in view of the size of his army and his closer proximity to Mantua (the Austrians had defeated the defenders of Verona at Caldiero on November 11), Bonaparte reconcentrated his troops to fight the Battle of Arcola on November 15–17 (see page 50). This famous engagement proved to be Napoleon's severest test to date. But against a loss of some forty-five hundred men, the French inflicted seven thousand casualties upon the Austrians over three days' hard fighting and regained the initiative from them. Alvintzi beat a precipitate retreat toward Vicenza.

This boldly handled battle averted the crisis near Verona and, at last, Bonaparte was able to rush troops northward to Vaubois's aid. His opponents were tellingly repulsed on November 21. A degree of stability returned once more, and the siege of Mantua continued unabated.

The Austrian War Council was still determined, however, that Mantua should not fall. Würmser, within the city, was already experiencing serious food problems as well as a heavy incidence of disease amid the unhealthy marshes, which explained his relatively passive role during November; still, he would entertain no thoughts of capitulation. Alvintzi, licking his wounds near Bassano, was soon at work rebuilding his ruffled army to a strength of forty-five thousand men ready for yet another offensive. As for the French, following the failure of Moreau's and Jourdan's campaigns, the Directory was increasingly inclined to make peace, and north Italy remained the only truly active front: it had become, in fact, the major sector of the war. Some reinforcements were sent to Bonaparte during December, bringing his strength up to fifty-five thousand men, but of these one-fifth were permanently assigned to the siege of Mantua, and as many more were needed to garrison the increasingly restive Milanese and keep open the lines of communication with France.

Mantua, like a magnet, was still exerting its baleful attraction upon Vienna, and in early January 1797 Alvintzi was once more on the march through the Alpine passes, this time in no less than five columns, not counting a diversion by nine thousand men approaching from the east under General Provera. Very soon Augereau, from Legnano, and Joubert, from La Corona, were reporting mounting enemy pressures on their various sectors. But Bonaparte continued to wait upon events, seeking clarification of the military situation: he could not afford to be wrong about the main Austrian line of attack.

The French reserve—Massena's and Rey's divisions—consequently were held back near Verona. Would they be ordered north to Lake Garda or east to Legnano? On January 13 Bonaparte realized that the northern sector was the vital one. "The enemy's plan is at last unmasked—he is marching with considerable forces on Rivoli." All but three thousand men (left to garrison Verona) hurried north to reinforce Joubert's hard-pressed holding force.

The battlefield of Rivoli lay on a steep plateau to the west of the Adige, linked to the river by the steep Osteria Gorge. As Alvintzi's five columns, twenty-eight thousand men all together, converged on the area, Bonaparte rode ahead of his hastening columns, joining Joubert's ten thousand men by 2:00 A.M. on the fourteenth. By 8:00 A.M.,

The Battle of Rivoli, January 14, 1797. (By Philipotteaux.) The hard-fought struggle on the plateau centered around the French holding the Osteria Gorge (seen in the background) against Alvintzi's Austrians. At one moment Napoleon's horse was wounded under him, but a staff officer immediately dismounted and the young general was quickly back in the saddle—and back in command of the battle. By nightfall, the foe was in full retreat.

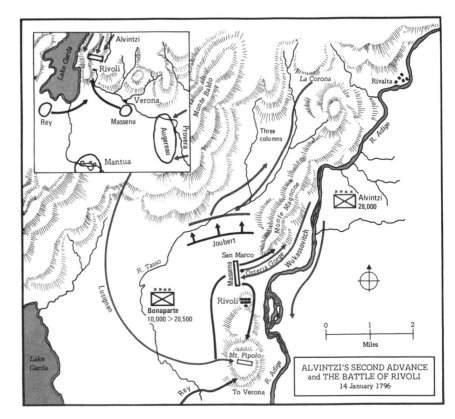

ALVINTZI'S SECOND ADVANCE
and THE BATTLE OF RIVOLI
14 January 1796

with the arrival of Massena, this force had been boosted to seventeen thousand men and eighteen guns, and Bonaparte at once precipitated the battle by launching Joubert and part of Massena's men in a deliberate wasting attack against the first two Austrian columns, some twelve thousand men strong, as they began to breast the Trombalore Heights on the northern edge of the plateau. After a stiff fight, these columns were checked. Meanwhile, one of Joubert's brigades had occupied the head of the Osteria Gorge, while the remainder of Massena's division was held in reserve around Rivoli, with orders to watch the Tasso valley to the immediate west of the plateau.

Simultaneously, the remaining three Austrian divisions appeared from different directions. The easternmost column mounted guns east of the Adige; another, under Wukassovitch, began to storm its way up the Osteria Gorge; and the fifth, under Lusignan, suddenly appeared from the southwest below Rivoli. Desperate fighting ensued, with the French under heavy attack from three directions at once, but nowhere were the Austrians strong enough to achieve lasting success. The main crisis centered around the village of San Marco, where seven thousand Austrians were making considerable headway against the tiring defenders. Suddenly an ammunition wagon exploded in the midst of the Austrians' column. Seizing the fleeting opportunity afforded by the stunned reaction, the French mounted a determined charge by five hundred cavalry and infantry; ten minutes later the gorge was cleared.

It only remained to deal with Lusignan's attack. By midday his four thousand men had been neatly trapped between Massena's troops and the newly arrived advance guard, three thousand strong, of General Rey, coming up from Lake Garda. Three thousand Austrians were taken prisoner.

By 5:00 P.M. the battle was over. The Austrians, having lost fourteen thousand men, were in full retreat for the north, hotly pursued throughout the following day by Joubert. The French, who had lost perhaps five thousand men, pressed on. As Vaubois continued north, Bonaparte hastened south, intent on intercepting the secondary Austrian attack as it forced Augereau back to the approaches to Mantua. Between January 13 and 16, Massena's division covered fifty-four miles of ground and fought three engagements. Provera was narrowly caught on the very threshold of Mantua, at La Favorita, late on the fifteenth. Würmser's attempted sortie from the fortress the next day proved abortive, and Provera, finding himself surrounded, tamely surrendered with six thousand men.

It was the end, at last, for Mantua. On February 2 Würmser and sixteen thousand men formally surrendered; another fourteen thousand were too sick to march out. North Italy, after ten months' fighting, was now almost all French. Yet Vienna still refused to come to terms with the French Republic and sent Archduke Charles— more youthful a commander than Bonaparte himself—to form yet another new army, this time in the Frioul, to the northeast of Venice. The Directory had now fully reversed their strategic priorities, giving Italy precedence over the German fronts, and soon Bonaparte had some sixty thousand men under command to face fifty thousand Austrians. Without the siege of Mantua to prosecute, all his attention and energy could be devoted to an offensive in this, the final stage of the campaign. Employing Joubert to threaten repeated envelopments with his twenty thousand men operating eastward from Trent and into the Tyrol, Bonaparte drove the archduke back from the River Tagliamento on March 16, and then proceeded to press him back from river line to river line as the French swept on devastatingly through the eastern Alps. Eventually, Charles made the dangerous decision to divide his army; as a result, part fell into Massena's hands in the Tarvis Pass, while the rest were pressed back toward Leoben. By this stage, Bonaparte's forward impetus was wholly exhausted, and there was still no news of Moreau's intended—but delayed—diversionary German offensive. And so the French halted on April 7 at the head of the Semmering Pass, only seventy-five miles from Vienna.

Bonaparte turned to the wiles of diplomacy and reached an agreement with his opponents for a five-day armistice to be observed; it was extended on the thirteenth for the same period. Much of this negotiating position was sheer bluff on the part of the French, but on April 17 the Austrian government agreed to sign the Preliminaries of Leoben (which, in October, were formalized in the Peace of Campo Formio). By this treaty, the Austrians ceded control of the Austrian Netherlands (later Belgium), the western Rhine enclaves, the Ionian Isles, and—in Italy—Milan, Bologna and Modena, which were formed into the new Cisalpine Republic under French domination. France returned Istria, Dalmatia and the Frioul, and evacuated the Republic of Venice, thus leaving Austria a contentious foothold in Italy. General Bonaparte had now established his reputation as France's most successful soldier. His stupendous career was well under way. His military ideas had been tried out and adapted in the hard light of experience. Almost every aspect of war had been tested in this year-long campaign, and at its close it could be claimed that Bonaparte's military apprenticeship was over.

After several months spent in reordering the affairs of the new Cisalpine Republic, the successful general returned to receive the plaudits of Paris. Lionized by society, he was mockingly nicknamed "Puss-in-Boots" by the coquettes on account of his lean and somewhat gangling appearance, large hat and even larger footwear. The honor that particularly pleased him was his election to membership in France's most scholarly body, the Institute. Typically, however, an inactive life was not to his liking, and he soon accepted command of the army drawn up along the Channel coast ready to invade Great Britain. Now that Austria had left the coalition (Spain and Prussia had each made a separate peace in 1795), the British were the last foe left in the lists. However, a rapid tour of the Channel ports convinced Bonaparte that the Royal Navy's supremacy ruled out any serious consideration of a crossing.

The Directory had no option but to accept the verdict. It could not risk a fiasco, but it was equally aware of the need to "make war pay for war," and certainly did not wish to have a young firebrand, already a legend to his men, with an idle army standing behind him. It was at the suggestion of the sage and experienced politician Talleyrand that an ancient scheme for attacking England indirectly through an invasion of Egypt was eagerly adopted; such an invasion would destroy the British Levant trade by putting pressure upon the inefficient Ottoman regime and would even create the possibility of mounting a threat to India. Nobody was more enthused than Bonaparte, who had always been fascinated by the East; under great secrecy an expedition of some thirty-

six thousand men was soon massing at Toulon, Genoa and Civitavecchia, together with over five hundred carefully selected *savants* (scholars, civilian engineers, scientists—even a poet, a balloonist and a composer were in the party). Years later, Bonaparte described his motivation:

"In Egypt I found myself freed from the obstacles of an irksome civilization. I was full of dreams. I saw myself founding a religion, marching into Asia, riding an elephant, a turban on my head, and in my hand a new Koran that I would have composed to suit my need. The time I spent in Egypt was the most beautiful of my life because it was the most ideal."

This highly romantic conception—or perhaps misrepresentation—was not to be shared with most of those who accompanied him on his quest, but there is no question that scholarly and civilizing motives as well as military ambitions lay beneath his determination to visit the Orient.

To protect the expeditionary force's journey down the Mediterranean, a cover plan was devised, indicating Ireland as the possible objective. The troops massed at the designated embarkation ports, and naval vessels prepared to escort the forming convoys. On May 19, 1798, the ships put to sea, an offshore gale most conveniently driving away the watchful frigates of Rear Admiral Nelson. Thus the expedition's fears of being intercepted by the Royal Navy's Mediterranean fleet were allayed—at least initially. The convoys made their way to the various *rendezvous*, and on June 9 the combined fleet gathered off the island of Malta, where the token resistance of the Knights of Saint John was quickly overwhelmed; leaving a French garrison behind, the fleet sailed on.

Nelson, by this time, was scouring the seas for the enemy, but his very speed acted to the slower convoy's advantage. The paths of the two fleets crossed late on the twenty-

Imaginary French craft for the invasion of England, February 1798. (By an unknown English engraver.) In command of the Army of England on the north coast of France, Napoleon decided an invasion was impossible. But the British press soon began to draw paddle-driven wind-powered vessels with ramps that went up and down for loading (as here, with cavalry) and unloading (on the British coast). By March Napoleon had set his sights on Malta and Egypt, but invasion scares remained frequent in Great Britain, fuelled by drawings such as this one.

second and again on June 27, but fate remained almost miraculously kind to the French. While Nelson in frustration scoured the coastline of Anatolia, the French sailed southeast for Alexandria, and between July 1 and 3 the transports arrived near Marabout. Little opposition was initially encountered from the Mamelukes, the *de facto* rulers of Egypt, but Alexandria had to be fought for on July 2. Bonaparte did not linger there long. Sending General Desaix to seize Rosetta in the delta and thereafter to operate up the Nile, Bonaparte led the remainder of the army in a desperate and thirsty seventy-two-hour march over the desert toward Damanhur. The near-mutinous force reached the Nile near Rahmaniya on the tenth, and met Desaix's force. There was a sharp skirmish with four thousand Mamelukes under Murad Bey at Shubra Khit and with a Moslem flotilla on the Nile, but the French emerged victorious. Cairo was now Bonaparte's objective, and by July 20 he was within a day's march of the city. Facing him, distantly located by the pyramids, stood massed the forces of the beys, perhaps a hundred thousand in all, although only eighteen thousand, including six thousand gorgeously caparisoned Mameluke cavalry, were drawn up on the west bank of the Nile immediately in the French path.

The Battle of the Pyramids, fought the next day, resulted in a decisive French victory. The feudal Mamelukes stood no chance before the disciplined fire of the French divisional squares, drawn up in a new formation devised by their commanding general himself. Against 390 casualties, the French inflicted some 5,000, occupying Cairo while Murad Bey and his three thousand surviving cavalry fled for Middle Egypt.

The Battle of the Pyramids (or Cairo), July 21, 1798. This victory over the Mameluke rulers, Murad Bey and Ibrahim Bey, and their formidable cavalry (foreground) was won by the large French divisional squares (left) and their superior firepower. Despite the battle's name, the Pyramids were not in sight of the main fighting, which took place near the village of Embabeh.

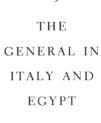

Napoleon crossing the desert on a dromedary. Besides soldiers, the French expedition included five hundred civilian specialists and experts, including Egyptologists who made full studies of the antiquities they found in profusion. Napoleon was equally fascinated by the times of the pharaohs, and founded the Institute of Egypt to coordinate the researches of the savants. Here he passes the Sphinx in the shade of the Great Pyramid of Giza. He also raised a short-lived French camel corps.

Sending Desaix on what proved to be a heroic expedition to conquer Upper Egypt, Bonaparte set himself and his civilian experts to refashion Egyptian life and institutions. The work was interrupted, however, by the arrival of grave news from the coast: on August 2 Nelson's battle fleet had engaged and destroyed Admiral Bruey's squadrons at the Battle of the Nile. The French army was now isolated from France, and the realization sent a shudder of apprehension through the homesick ranks. Work was even more rudely interrupted on October 21, when the people of Cairo rose in revolt. Suppression of the rebellion cost the French three hundred lives, and a brutal retribution was exacted. Outbreaks of bubonic plague added to the misery of the French.

But Bonaparte was soon beset by even graver problems. Encouraged by news of Nelson's victory, the sultan of Turkey declared a holy war against the French infidel, and soon intelligence was reaching Cairo of two large Ottoman armies preparing to

The massacre at Jaffa. (From a design by R. K. Porter.) This bloody killing of some thirty-eight hundred Mamelukes on the beach at Jaffa on March 7, 1799, was ordered by Napoleon when he discovered that many of the town's defenders were freed captives taken at El Arish and Gaza who had given their solemn word not to take part in further hostilities. This barbarism contrasted markedly with the courage General Bonaparte displayed four days later when—to the horror of his advisers—he visited the plague patients in the plague hospital.

invade Egypt. One, under the pasha of Damascus, was gathering in Syria. The other was massing, with shipping, at Rhodes. It was never Bonaparte's style to wait upon events. Deciding that the Army of Damascus constituted the more immediate peril, he determined to attack it outside Egypt before the Army of Rhodes could make its presence felt. Leaving Desaix with some twenty thousand men to occupy Egypt, on February 6, 1799, Bonaparte led four weak divisions from Katia into the Sinai desert. The need to take the fort of El Arish caused an unwelcome eleven-day delay, but by the twenty-third the expedition was in Syria. Gaza was occupied two days later, and Jaffa was stormed on March 7. This success was sullied by the cold-blooded massacre of almost four thousand prisoners, who Bonaparte claimed had broken parole granted them at El Arish and Gaza.

Plague now struck the French in full force, and, at great personal risk, Bonaparte heroically visited the hospitals to restore morale. Then, leaving the sick behind them, the army pressed toward Haifa on March 14, the next important objective being the port and fortress of Acre. At Acre they faced a determined defense by Djezzar Pasha ("the Butcher"), who was in fact inspired and materially assisted by the British naval officer Commodore Sir William Sydney Smith, whose two ships of the line added their crews and guns to strengthen the port's defenses and discourage the French besiegers. After a number of his assaults had been beaten back with losses, Bonaparte

was compelled to resort to time-consuming siege methods; this too was hampered by the Royal Navy, which intercepted and captured half the heavy siege guns being brought up from Egypt by sea. The cannon were promptly used to strengthen Acre's defenses.

As the siege dragged on inconclusively, the number of plague cases grew alarmingly. Then news arrived that the Army of Damascus was approaching. This constituted a challenge more to Bonaparte's liking, and to avert the danger of being ground between the upper and nether millstones, he sent out strong detachments to reconnoiter. One of these, led by General Kléber, ran into the main Turkish army, perhaps thirty-five thousand strong, near Mount Tabor. Kléber's gallant fifteen hundred men gamely engaged the enemy, affording Bonaparte enough time to lead up a division from Acre, twenty-five miles away. In the resultant battle on April 16, a total of forty-five hundred Frenchmen inflicted seven thousand casualties and routed the foe, with a loss of fewer than a hundred men. Thus the strategic purpose of the invasion of Syria had been achieved; one threat to a French-controlled Egypt had been driven back.

Acre, however, remained an intractable problem, and on May 20, after further attempted assaults had proved fruitless, Bonaparte decided to cut his losses and abandon the siege. A traumatic withdrawal toward Egypt began, but at last, on June 3, the half-starved survivors limped back into Katia. By the fourteenth, the battered army, perhaps one-third smaller than when it had set out, was back in Cairo; a flamboyant victory parade fooled nobody. Soon renewed revolts against French rule were springing up everywhere, but these were ruthlessly repressed in the customary French fashion. Then, in mid-July, the news arrived that the Army of Rhodes had been sighted off the coast

Saint John of Acre. (By J. Jeakes.) Called "the Key to Palestine," Acre stands on the Mediterranean coast upon a small peninsula. In 1799 it was defended by Djezzar Pasha, supported by Commodore Sir William Sidney Smith, RN, and his small naval squadron. Also present was the Bourbonist French engineer, Phélippeaux, an old foe of Napoleon's from school at Brienne.

Saint John of Acre. (Colored lithograph after Grenier.) Napoleon's campaign in Syria (as Palestine was then called) came to a full halt before the outdated but strong defenses of this coastal fortress. Despite repeated storming attempts carried out under Napoleon's gaze, the defense held firm, and on May 20, his army riddled by plague, Napoleon was forced to order a retreat back to Egypt.

and was landing near Alexandria. Bonaparte rushed north with every available man, and on July 25 routed the new foe at the hard-fought Battle of Aboukir. The survivors lost little time in reembarking and sailed away. But this success had cost the French some 970 killed and wounded—losses that the rapidly dwindling army could ill afford, being without hope of reinforcement.

Bonaparte was now becoming increasingly aware of, and worried by, his isolation. The trickle of news from France was bad—the Directory's armies appeared to be falling back on every front—and Commodore Smith deliberately had newspapers sent ashore to keep his foe informed of the rapidly worsening international situation. It was clearly no time for a man of ambition to be away from the center of affairs, where, in the prevailing climate of alarm and uncertainty, careers could be furthered or broken with every shifting wind of fortune. Bonaparte determined not to be overtaken by events and, in the greatest secrecy, he laid his plans to slip away from Egypt and return to France through the naval blockade.

And so, on August 22, he set sail, accompanied by only a handful of confidants and key staff officers, leaving the deserted Army of the East to the command of the enraged Kléber. For propaganda purposes Napoleon declared that he had left Egypt to seek reinforcements and a new fleet, but few were fooled for long. The adventure of Egypt and Syria was a gamble that had failed to come off, and it was never Bonaparte's way to be personally associated with failure even when he was in large measure responsible for it. This was the first, but it would not be the last, occasion on which he would leave a defeated army to its fate.

The Battle of Arcola
November 15 – 17, 1796

November 1796 brought General Bonaparte one of the most critical situations he had been called upon to face. With powerful Austrian forces pressing south from Trent under Davidovitch, Würmser's strong garrison of Mantua threatening to break out through the siege lines to his rear and General Alvintzi with almost twenty-three thousand men pressing on the gates of Verona, the French commander (with barely eighteen thousand men under his immediate orders) faced a difficult series of decisions. It was true that the advantages of the central position were his, enabling him to march rapidly to reinforce a particular sector, but the problem was how to select the correct course to pursue. Vaubois was appealing for reinforcements as he fell back before Davidovitch's stronger force and Kilmaine was warning that he could not hold in Mantua's twenty-three-thousand-man garrison if it attempted a major sortie, while Massena and Augereau were far from optimistic about their ability to deny Alvintzi the fortress of Verona. To reinforce all pressure points was impossible; to reinforce just one was to court disaster on the two remaining sectors. "We are abandoned in the depths of Italy," Bonaparte declared. His pessimism appeared justified.

This atmosphere of strategic crisis formed the background to the famous three-day struggle for Arcola, a period that revealed some of Bonaparte's brightest talents— opportunism, calculation, clarity of thought and speed of both decision and action.

His decision was to deal first with Alvintzi, the most immediate target, but to retain the freedom of action to break off and head for one of the other sectors should events absolutely demand that he do so. At best this constituted a dangerous gamble, but he was playing for high stakes: nothing less than the continued French presence in north Italy. One major miscalculation and all that had been achieved since April would be laid in ruins, and his reputation shattered.

His plan was an adaptation of the strategy of envelopment already employed at Lodi and Bassano. Taking all but a skeleton garrison from Verona, he would force-march every available man east along the southern bank of the Adige toward Arcola and Albaredo, then sweep north to threaten the capture of Villanova (a town on the Verona-to-Vicenza highroad) and take Alvintzi's lines of supply, severing his lines of communication and thus forcing a battle on ground of the French army's choosing. To overcome his numerical disadvantage and wholly neutralize the Austrian superiority in cavalry, Bonaparte intended to fight on the marshy, uneven ground forming a large triangle at the confluence of the Adige and the River Alpone. It would be hard for Alvintzi to come at him in such a restricted area, and the French had already displayed a talent for coming to terms with difficult terrain. But, at best, as with so many of Napoleon's battles, it was a calculated risk.

To be a complete success, the plan called for the mounting of a credible threat against Villanova before the Austrians could realize that most of Verona's defenders were marching elsewhere. Surprise was therefore of the essence. Accordingly, leaving General Macquard with barely three thousand men (part of Vaubois's command) to hold Verona, Bonaparte set off with eighteen thousand men during the night of November 14–15 and marched hard for the village of Ronco. By dawn on the fifteenth, Andréossy's detachment had thrown a pontoon bridge over the Adige at this spot, and the French moved over the river onto the causeways traversing the marshes adjoining the north bank.

Augereau's division was the first to cross, followed by Massena's. Obeying Napoleon's orders, Massena marched northwestward for Belfiore di Porcile, on the edge of the marshland, to create a defensive flank in the direction of Verona. On the village's outskirts Massena ran into part of General Provera's command, but a brisk fight drove the Austrians back and Porcile was safely occupied. Although Alvintzi was now aware that something unusual was afoot, Bonaparte still hoped to see Augereau capture the bridge over the Alpone leading to Arcola, then press on up the local road for San Bonifacio and Villanova—the ultimate objective. Unfortunately, Augereau ran into difficulties. As the French approached the bridge, they were suddenly raked with fire by two battalions of Croatian infantry and a number of guns from the farther bank of the Alpone. The French advance died away as the troops jumped for cover into some nearby dykes.

This check alarmed Bonaparte. He at once sent off Guieu's brigade of three thousand men to seek a ford near Albaredo, southeast of Ronco, in the hope of finding an alternative crossing place. But the element of surprise was now lost, and time was passing. Every hour that went by was now operating in the Austrians' favor. Soon Provera brought up four thousand reinforcements against Massena at Porcile, while Metrouski arrived with a similar force to strengthen the Croatians holding Arcola. In the meantime, Alvintzi was moving back with half his available men from before Verona to Villanova. All French hopes of severing the Austrian communications were fast dissolving.

In desperation Bonaparte seized a *tricolor* and attempted to lead a renewed charge over the bridge into Arcola. But a zealous officer seized him around the waist, exclaiming, "General, you will get yourself killed!" and they both fell into a canal. The commander in chief's *aides de camp* narrowly extricated him from under the bayonets of a sudden Austrian counterattack and moved him to safety. But the French had still failed to shake the Austrian defenders of Arcola.

The fighting continued all afternoon, but it was now obvious that Alvintzi had eluded the proposed trap. At 7:00 P.M. the village of Arcola was at last taken from the Austrians by Guieu's force, which had succeeded in crossing the Adige at Albaredo and was thus able to take the Austrians in the flank from the south. But this was at least six hours too late. Half the Austrian army was now drawn up east of the Alpone ready to defend any thrust toward Villanova. True, this meant that there was no threat to Verona's security for the time being, and the likelihood of Alvintzi being able to link up with Davidovitch in the near future was more remote. On the other hand,

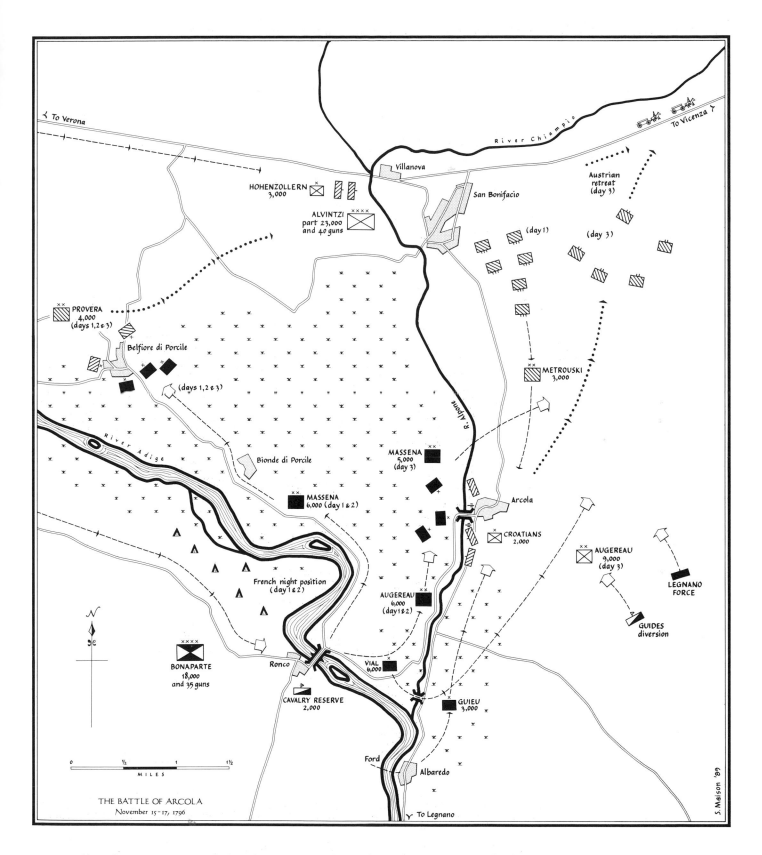

To Verona

River Chiampio

To Vicenza

Villanova

HOHENZOLLERN 3,000

San Bonifacio

Austrian retreat (day 3)

ALVINTZI part 23,000 and 40 guns

(day 1)

(day 3)

PROVERA 4,000 (days 1, 2 & 3)

Belfiore di Porcile

METROUSKI 3,000

(days 1, 2 & 3)

River Adige

Bionde di Porcile

MASSENA 5,000 (day 3)

R. Alpone

Arcola

MASSENA 6,000 (day 1 & 2)

CROATIANS 2,000

AUGEREAU 9,000 (day 3)

French night position (day 1 & 2)

AUGEREAU 6,000 (day 1 & 2)

LEGNANO FORCE

GUIDES diversion

N

BONAPARTE 18,000 and 35 guns

Ronco

VIAL 6,000

CAVALRY RESERVE 2,000

GUIEU 3,000

0   ½   1   1½
MILES

Ford

Albaredo

THE BATTLE OF ARCOLA
November 15–17, 1796

To Legnano

S. Maison '89

bad news had reached French headquarters in the early evening: Vaubois had been forced back to Bussolengo and was not sanguine concerning his ability to hold the Austrian advance much longer in the northern sector.

This was very much what Bonaparte had feared would take place. Accordingly, he had no choice but to abandon all the hard-won gains of the fifteenth and recall his

The Battle of Arcola, November 15–17, 1796. (By unknown artist.) One highlight in this difficult, protracted battle saw General Bonaparte seize a tricolor to inspire a hesitant assault force to storm a vital bridge. Moments later he was knocked into a water-filled canal and might have drowned but for the devotion of Colonel Jean Lannes, who rescued him. The two men remained close friends until Lannes's death in 1809.

weary troops to the south bank of the Adige near Ronco in case it proved imperative to force-march his men to Vaubois's assistance. The only thing that could be said for the activities of the fifteenth was that they had attracted all of Alvintzi's attention.

A tense night passed. The next morning, however, as no more alarming tidings had arrived from the north, Bonaparte ordered a resumption of the previous day's attack. The French swarmed over their pontoon bridge into the marshes, and renewed onslaughts were launched against Provera at Porcile and Metrouski at Arcola. Every yard gained the previous day had to be exhaustingly refought. Massena became master of Porcile once more, but Augereau proved incapable of taking the Arcola bridge again. Worse, by midafternoon some seven thousand of Alvintzi's main force had reinforced Arcola's garrison to almost eleven thousand men, and there were therefore Austrians to spare to block General Vial's attempt to place a new pontoon bridge over the Alpone just above its confluence with the Adige.

But now the Austrians were suffering severe casualties, and Alvintzi sent messengers to warn Davidovitch that the main army could only hope to repulse one more French attack. The grinding battle of attrition that Arcola had now become was working in Bonaparte's favor, although he had scant means of knowing it. As the evening shadows lengthened, he once again recalled his men over the Adige so as to be prepared for any new emergency on Vaubois's sector. This time, however, a small force remained on the north bank holding a bridgehead to protect the pontoon bridge. A second uneasy night passed.

In preparation for a possible third day's fighting, Bonaparte had sent an urgent order to the forces containing Würmser's garrison at Mantua. As a result, after a hard day's march three thousand men under General Kilmaine reached the French camp overnight. Bonaparte had now assembled some twenty thousand men, and it was unlikely that Alvintzi would be able to field more than seventeen thousand for the resumed conflict. But on each of the two previous days, the French had enjoyed superiority in overall numbers actually engaged: numbers alone would not assure victory on so restricted a battlefield.

Once again there was no alarming news from Vaubois: he appeared to be holding his ground while Davidovitch weighed the implications of the warnings he had received from his chief. Bonaparte accordingly ordered a third onslaught against Alvintzi. The Austrian force at Arcola was now split into two separate parts. Provera had been reinforced to six thousand men by the arrival of the general Hohenzollern, near Porcile; so a full third of Alvintzi's available strength was tied down on the northwest corner of the marshes. Bonaparte had decided to change the form of attack radically for the third attempt. He judged that one *demi-brigade* of Massena's division—perhaps three thousand men—would suffice to keep the reinforced but restricted Provera in play. The remainder of Massena's command could be used to take over Augereau's position of the two previous days, with orders to engage the enemy's attention opposite Arcola; meanwhile, the whole of Augereau's division was to head for the east banks of the two rivers—part crossing the Alpone by way of Vial's bridge of the sixteenth, part over the crossing opposite Albaredo, and the rest, after a lengthy detour, by way of Legnano. In this way, Bonaparte calculated, he would be able to complete the demoralization of Alvintzi's command by rolling its left flank up toward Arcola and thence back toward Villanova.

In the event, matters turned out rather differently than Napoleon had intended— an indication of how his battle plans were infinitely adjustable in the light of circumstances: "One engages, then one sees." The greatest honors of the day were won by Massena. His third crossing at Ronco was unexpectedly strongly contested, the Austrians having pushed forward a force to occupy part of the marshes during the night. In the severe fighting that ensued, the bridge collapsed, making the French army's situation even more precarious. But Massena was always at his best in a crisis, and eventually the bridge was repaired and the Austrians were beaten off. Massena then pressed on to carry out his orders. A single brigade went off toward Porcile and another toward Arcola, while the remainder of his division concealed itself among the neighboring willows and dykes. The Austrians duly fell for the bait. The garrison of Arcola, able to see only the single brigade on the causeway, launched a strong attack against it over the bridge. The exposed French force fell back by stages, drawing their jubilant pursuers into the prepared ambush. Judging his moment finely, Massena suddenly revealed his remaining troops, who charged out of their cover to attack the flank of the astounded Austrians. In no time they were in full flight, and in the prevailing confusion Massena's men were able to pour over the long-contested bridge and retake part of Arcola itself as they exploited their success to the limit. The Austrians lost many men.

Massena's unforeseen success offset Augereau's equally unanticipated problems. Although the part of his force diverted toward the bridge at Legnano made excellent progress, the troops ordered over the rivers at the earlier crossing points found strong Austrian detachments in position to contest them. A series of French efforts failed to dislodge these opponents. Bonaparte, equal to this serious challenge, devised a stratagem to solve the impasse. A small party of his personal escort, the Guides, was sent off with four cavalry trumpeters to pass over the Adige unseen, with orders to create a diversion in the enemy's rear. The party crossed the river in secret, rode unnoticed over the plain beyond and then, swinging in behind the Austrians, began to create enough din to impersonate a large-scale cavalry attack. The trick worked. Metrouski, in great alarm, believing his position had been turned, ordered his men to retreat at once. Sensing his opportunity, Augereau flung every soldier over the bridges and followed the retiring Austrians back toward Arcola, where he made common cause with Massena's men.

These developments coincided with the arrival of the detatchment from Legnano from the south. This was too much for Alvintzi's wavering resolve. Believing himself to be threatened from three sides at once, he ordered an immediate retreat toward Vicenza. At dawn on the eighteenth, French patrols reported no sign of Austrian troops in the vicinity of Villanova.

Bonaparte had won the three-day Battle of Arcola. Having lost forty-five hundred men, the French had inflicted at least seven thousand casualties on the enemy, and in the process ended all chance of Alvintzi joining up with Davidovitch before breaking through toward beleaguered Mantua.

The jubilant army returned to Verona on the eighteenth. There was no time for rest for the weary troops. Their general at once force-marched them north to aid Vaubois—in the nick of time, as Davidovitch had at last resumed his attack and driven Vaubois back again to Castelnovo. But now the tables were turned, and the Austrians, after being defeated at Dolce, headed for Trent on the twenty-first, in the process losing their trains and baggage together with nine cannon. Alvintzi's first attempt to relieve Mantua now lay in ruins. The crisis of Arcola had tested Bonaparte severely, but he had risen to the challenge magnificently. Some commentators, indeed, rate it among his greatest achievements. But it would still be over two months before Mantua was forced to surrender.

THREE

EMPIRE

Napoleon's journey home took six weeks. On October 9, 1799, he landed at Fréjus and at once headed for Paris. There his first crisis was not a public but a private affair, for Josephine had made little secret of her infidelities during his absence. At one point the jealous husband wanted a divorce, but in the end he relented, won over by Josephine's entreaties. He himself had not been blameless; in Egypt he had found consolation with Madame Fourés, the wife of one of his lieutenants. And so the marriage was saved, though it became one of detached tolerance on both sides.

Meanwhile, the Directory greeted Napoleon's unexpected return with reserve. Some spoke of charging him with desertion, though his popularity was such that no one spoke very loudly. It was a critical time for the government. Administrative incompetence and financial weakness had combined to undermine its authority. Moreover, a new war, that of the Second Coalition, had broken out earlier in the year. Encouraged by the Battle of the Nile, Great Britain had persuaded other powers to join her against the French, and now Russian and Austrian armies were in the field.

The result was a political *coup* against the regime, one that, for the first time, brought Napoleon to political power. One of the directors, the aging, subtle Sieyès, laid the plan. He chose Napoleon to be his "sword," and the general agreed. It was a confusing affair, in which Napoleon himself played a muddled and undistinguished part. At one point, he narrowly escaped death when he descended on the Council of Five Hundred, one of the main constitutional assemblies. He was saved only by the timely intervention of his soldiers and by the presence of mind of the council's president, his own brother Lucien. Yet, by the evening of November 9, 18 Brumaire by the revolutionary calendar, the *coup* had been accomplished. A new constitution was created, dominated by three consuls: Sieyès; another former director, Roger-Ducos; and Napoleon himself. It was a victory for authority against the Jacobin left-wing politicians.

There quickly followed a second victory: that of Napoleon over his new colleagues;

for if the inspiration had belonged to Sieyès, the power belonged to the armed forces and their leader. There could be no opposition once Napoleon, urged on by his growing belief in his destiny, had maneuvered his fellow consuls into retirement within a few short months. Two nonentities replaced them, and the Constitution was once again rewritten to place all real authority in the hands of the first consul, Napoleon. In February 1800, in a national plebiscite on this new constitution, three million voted in its favor, fifteen hundred dissented. France had chosen a dictatorship in all but name.

A period of frantic activity began. Rewards were showered on the faithful; the opposition was either won over or made to disappear. The first consul also embarked on a series of major reforms that began the remodeling of French life. But he knew that he could set the seal upon his exalted position only by giving the French people what they craved most: peace through victory in the field. This he set out to obtain, and under cover of peace negotiations he began to prepare a new campaign against Austria. Moreau would attack on the upper Rhine. A new army, called the Reserve, began to collect around Dijon under the nominal command of General Berthier; its intended destination was Italy, its real commander Bonaparte himself.

Napoleon was helped when Prussia, which had failed to field an army, backed out of the coalition, and by Russian disagreements with Vienna, which effectively left only Austria to deal with on the Continent. Austria had two main armies in the field: 120,000 men under General Kray in Germany, and some 97,000 under General Melas in north Italy. The former was to be used defensively while the latter exploited Italian discontent with French rule, consolidated earlier gains, marched on Genoa and ultimately threatened Toulon.

Bonaparte was determined to avert any such possibilities. He intended to launch a rapid attack to snatch a quick victory, making the fullest use of the advantages offered by French-dominated Switzerland, its passes and rivers, to move a force into the rear of one or the other major Austrian field army. Moreau, commanding some 120,000 men on the Rhine, was not eager to have the first consul operating in his sector and obstructed plans for the Reserve, 50,000 strong, to be employed in this direction. Meanwhile, in north Italy, Melas launched his offensive on April 5, and General Massena and the 40,000 men of the Army of Liguria were soon sundered in two, half being driven back beyond the Var, the rest tightly besieged in Genoa.

With commendable flexibility, the first consul adjusted to circumstances. The Reserve would now sweep south over the Alps, reinforced by a single corps from the Rhine, to force a decisive battle with Melas's troops. While Massena in Genoa attracted Melas's attention, the Reserve would appear over the Alps to cut the enemy's links with Mantua and Austria, and fall upon Melas's rear. By early May, as the siege became ever more desperate for the defenders, the Reserve had moved into Switzerland, ready for its bold advance. Executive orders had been issued to both Moreau and Berthier on April 24; the next day Moreau crossed the Rhine, and by May 13 the Austrians were in full retreat eastward, abandoning their links with Melas.

This was the moment Bonaparte had been waiting for. On the fourteenth, he ordered his army into the Alpine passes despite snow and icy conditions. The summit of the Great Saint Bernard was safely passed, the first consul crossing over on muleback. But on May 19 the French encountered a determined Austrian garrison in Fort Bard,

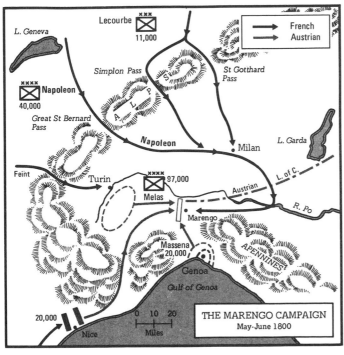

THE MARENGO CAMPAIGN
May-June 1800

The crossing of the Great Saint Bernard Pass. (A contemporary lithograph by Muller.) The French army had great difficulty crossing the Alps, and cannon placed in split and hollowed-out tree trunks (right)—a bright idea of General Marmont's—had to be hauled over by manpower. At the top of the pass was the Hospice of Saint Bernard. A few years ago monks there produced a receipt and an IOU (never redeemed) for requisitioned supplies, signed by Bonaparte, first consul. With interest, this was worth many millions of modern francs—which were no more forthcoming in the late 1980s than they were in the early 1800s.

The Battle of Marengo, June 14, 1800. (By Lejeune.) This celebrated defeat of General Melas's Austrian army was almost a cataclysm for Napoleon. General Desaix arrived with his division to save the day—only to be killed at the moment of victory. The mounted figure in the right foreground is not Napoleon but General Berthier, who was technically in command: according to the constitution, a consul was barred from leading the army.

blocking the only road. Finally, on May 25 and 26 six cannon were spirited past the fort in the dead of night to rejoin the infantry that had already avoided the obstacle by goat tracks—and so Bonaparte pressed ahead to Ivrea.

The immediate objective of the French was to find cannon to replace those bottled up beyond Fort Bard (which held out until June 6), so they headed for Milan, arriving on June 2. Here Lecourbe also arrived with his eleven thousand men. The Reserve next crossed the River Po near Piacenza between June 7 and 9.

Melas, meanwhile, had been about to abandon the siege of Genoa when Massena, despairing of relief, surrendered on June 4. The news reached the first consul on June 7 in captured dispatches. He was deeply disturbed, for his foe could now use Genoa as a refuge if need be. Bonaparte's solution was to press ahead past Stradella toward the town of Alessandria, where a large part of the Austrian army was reportedly massing. After a brisk action at Montebello on June 8, by the thirteenth the French had crossed the River Scrivia and had also been joined, at last, by most of their guns from Ivrea. They pressed on toward Marengo through heavy rain.

Still fearing that Melas might escape over the Po or toward Genoa, and never for a moment anticipating an attack, the first consul detached Lapoype's division northward, and early on the fourteenth, he sent off Desaix to block the road to Genoa. These decisions reduced the Reserve's frontline strength to barely 24,100 men and fifteen guns, and almost led to a major catastrophe. For, far from seeking to escape, General Melas decided to attack, with 31,000 troops out of Marengo over three concealed pontoon bridges. By 7:00 A.M., the battle had burst into violent life.

Napoleon at first thought that the Austrian advance was a feint, but by nine o'clock, he had realized his error, and sent off urgent orders of recall to Lapoype and Desaix. By midday, the outnumbered divisions of Lannes and Victor were being forced back from Marengo toward San Giuliano. Even worse, there were threatening signs that seventy-five hundred men under General Ott were about to outflank the Reserve's right wing.

Soon the danger became stark reality, and Bonaparte was forced to send in his last reserves—Monnier's division and the Consular Guard. This earned Napoleon a brief respite, but Victor's troops were now running out of ammunition. The first consul was tireless in his efforts to rally his men, but by 2:30 P.M. the Austrian center and right had re-formed into a huge column, ready to crash through the weary French.

But help was at hand. About three o'clock, a mud-spattered General Desaix rode up ahead of his men. Fortunately for the Reserve, Desaix's progress toward Novi had been delayed by a flooded river when the urgent message of recall found him. "This battle is completely lost," commented the newcomer cryptically, "but it is only two [in fact, it was three] o'clock; there is time to win another."

By 5:00 P.M., General Boudet's fifty-three hundred foot-sore but battle-fresh men, with their eight guns, had arrived, and were drawn up behind the exhausted Victor. At this point, the aged Melas handed command of the Austrian army to his second-in-command, General Zach, and the massive column began to advance. To meet it came Desaix's force, left flank forward. Suddenly, a lucky shot exploded several Austrian ammunition caissons. As had happened at Rivoli, the Austrians hesitated. The French snatched at the fleeting opportunity; Marmont rushed up eight guns to the front and opened point-blank fire; Kellermann wheeled four hundred cavalry into line, and plunged into the Austrian flank, while Desaix and his infantry charged. Desaix fell, mortally wounded, but the impact of his attack was irresistible, and by 6:00 P.M. the Austrians were in full flight for the safety of Alessandria. For a loss of seven thousand casualties, the French had inflicted fourteen thousand casualties (which included eight thousand prisoners) and captured forty guns. The next day, Melas sued for an armistice, and in return for leave to retire east of the River Ticino abandoned Genoa and the Milanese.

"Marengo was a lesson," Bonaparte once admitted in an honest moment. Defeat had been very near; but for Desaix's timely arrival the outcome would have been grim. Over the years, Napoleon was continually taking pains to represent Marengo as a major success, its various phases deliberately planned in advance. In successive rewritings of the official account, he fabricated the idea of a deliberate withdrawal by the French left, designed to draw the Austrians toward an approaching Desaix, who was carefully placed so as to outflank them at the moment when they were farthest from their bridges. Such was the gist of his account in 1803. Two years later, Napoleon was prepared to claim that the French right had never lost control of Castel Ceriolo but had used it as the anchor for the controlled swing of the French line toward San Giuliano, at the same time setting up a new line of communications, or of retreat, toward the River Po and General Lapoype. These developments in the story were almost wholly bogus, but the ideas upon which they were based would be built into La Grande Armée's devastating system of grand (or operational) tactics. The outcome that June, however, was almost wholly due to the first consul's subordinate commanders, and most especially to the loyal Desaix, rather than to his own efforts. Nevertheless, he could still learn from his errors, though he already found it hard to admit to them. Thus Marengo became part of the legend.

The universal toast: the Peace of Amiens. The nations of Europe, illustrated by representational archetypes of the day—England, with pipe in hat (it was not yet the age of "John Bull"), France, standing, the hatted Prussia, turbaned Turkey, beplumed Italy, fur-capped Russia—drink to "Bonaparte and Peace for Ever." The peace was short-lived; in August 1802 Le Moniteur *accused London of bad faith, counter-accusations soon followed and an Anglo-French war (mainly naval) began on May 16, 1803.*

Marengo regained much of north Italy for the French, but it did not win the war. Three more campaigns had to be launched by generals Moreau, Brune and Macdonald before victory was assured. Napoleon, in the meantime, returned to Paris (a constitutional rule technically barred the first consul from taking command in the field, and throughout the campaign he had posed as Berthier's adviser). The struggle dragged on as inconclusive peace negotiations continued at Leoben. But the French were remorseless in applying pressure, which culminated in Moreau's victory at Hohenlinden on December 3 and Murat's drive into Tuscany and the Papal States. On February 8, 1801, hostilities came to an end in the Peace of Lunéville, which effectively restored the situation brought about by the Peace of Campo Formio, with the French adding the duchy of Parma to the Cisalpine Republic, compensating the duke with Tuscany. Further territorial adjustments were made along the Rhine, but in many ways it was a moderate peace.

Once again, a coalition had collapsed around England's prime minister, William Pitt, who was forced to resign in March 1801. Since the beginning of that month, however, a British expeditionary force had been in Egypt, and by September Bonaparte's former comrades were driven to accept a negotiated capitulation, by which they were to be allowed repatriation. The first consul, meanwhile, had been negotiating for some months with British representatives at Amiens, and before the final news from Egypt had broken, the Preliminaries of Amiens were signed, on October 1, 1801. A formal

In the engraving, on the sign:

CONSTITUTION ITALIENNE

TITRE PREMIER

La religion Catholique
Apostolique et Romaine
est la religion de l'Etat.

peace treaty followed in March 1802, and the first consul could claim that he had honored his promise to bring peace through victory. For a brief spell, Europe was not at war, and a grateful French people voted on August 2, 1802, to appoint Bonaparte, "the Peacemaker," consul for life. A crown and throne now lay only one step away.

Some time before the signature of peace with Great Britain, Bonaparte had launched the great series of reforms—legal, economic, social and constitutional—that together make up his most constructive and lasting work. As great a statesman as he was a soldier, he daringly carried through a concordat with the pope in 1801 whereby France returned to the Catholic fold, and the following years saw the emergence of the great codes that refashioned almost every aspect of French life and many parts of which remain the basis of French civil law—and that of the E.E.C.—to the present day.

Sensing a need for some system of rewarding the deserving, Bonaparte instituted the Légion d'Honneur in 1802, creating military and civil branches. Rewards were showered on loyal and able generals, culminating in the establishment of the marshalate in 1804, the year during which the first steps were taken toward the creation of a new nobility. At the same time, remaining centers of opposition, whether die-hard republican or convinced royalist, were steadily eliminated by the secret-police apparatus wielded by Fouché. Censorship of the press, spying and "tuning the pulpit" (using the churches for spreading propaganda) remained in force. On the other hand, such

Bonaparte, President of the Italian Republic, January 25, 1802. This propaganda engraving by an unknown artist shows the first consul as president of the Cisalpine Republic, "elected" following a congress, held at Lyons, of 452 carefully selected Italian notables. In the new constitution, the name was changed to the Italian Republic. The president is shown declaiming the first article of the constitution—a declaration of faith in the Roman Catholic church. This was a long way from the atheistic and deist declarations of earlier years, and was a reflection of Napoleon's bold reestablishment of the Catholic faith in France by the secret concordát with the Pope.

The Infernal Machine. *This print by an unknown artist shows an assassination attempt that narrowly missed its target as Napoleon rode to the opera on Christmas Eve. Because his half-drunk coachman was driving faster than usual, the bomb exploded just after the first consul's coach turned the corner. Over fifty people were killed or wounded. Napoleon's propagandists used this and similar incidents to justify the proscription of remaining pockets of resistance—Jacobin and extreme royalist alike—and to prepare the way for the introduction of first the consulate for life and then the Empire to stabilize and institutionalize Napoleon's position.*

unpopular instruments as the infamous Law of Suspects were repealed, and *émigrés* who would return to serve the new regime were restored to at least part of their estates.

Of course, the consul became the target of much bitter criticism—and of several assassination attempts by both royalists and left-wing Jacobins. He escaped a bomb explosion in December 1800, and 1804 saw the exposure of the notorious Cadoudal conspiracy, which had been planned with British connivance. These incidents were used by his propagandists to prepare the way for the suspension of the Constitution. Already consul for life, Napoleon now took the next logical step, nominally to safeguard the regime, by founding a new dynasty. And so in 1804, the proposal to replace the Republic with an empire modeled upon Charlemagne's of the ninth century was put to the test in a national plebiscite. The outcome was never in doubt (the official tally was 3,524,254 in favor and only 2,599 against), and on May 18 Napoleon was proclaimed emperor. The coronation was held on December 2, 1804; although the pope was brought to Paris for the ceremony, Napoleon insisted on placing the crown on his own head before crowning Josephine in her turn. This was all a far cry from the impecunious days of his Corsican childhood. "If only our father could see us now," Napoleon remarked to Joseph. He was a little over thirty-five years old, and his career had indeed been meteoric.

Yet already France was at war again. Europe's short-lived peace had lasted only until May 16, 1803, when France was once more fighting with Great Britain over their colonial and commercial rivalry. During the next year, Napoleon massed two

Napoleon's coronation, December 2, 1804. (A sketch by David for his famous painting.) Napoleon crowns himself, his left hand symbolically grasping the sword that gave him a "right" to the imperial throne, before an astounded Pope Pius VII. The finished painting showed a more muted scene.

hundred thousand men along the Channel coast in the camp of Boulogne but, as in 1798, his navy could never gain the necessary control of the sea to permit an invasion to be launched. Meanwhile, friction steadily grew between France and the Continental powers. The established monarchs would not accept Napoleon's titles or position and absolutely distrusted his ambitions in Germany, where he was building alliances within the southern states, a traditional sphere of Austrian influence. His ruthless methods climaxed with the execution in 1804 of the duc d'Enghien, an alleged though unproven conspirator, who was kidnapped from neutral territory. The general repugnance caused by this crime played its part in helping William Pitt, once again prime minister, to form the Third Coalition. British gold persuaded the Francophile tsar of Russia, Alexander I, to join in April 1805; Sweden agreed to make war on the French; and in June Emperor Francis II of Austria followed suit. It was indeed a coalition of the "European establishment" against the emperor, and of the great powers only Prussia remained aloof. Thus Pitt called into being a force of 200,000 Russians and 250,000 Austrians; in round numbers the Alliance could field half a million men, subsidized by Britain. Following the anticipated Allied victory, France was to be restricted to the frontiers of 1791.

By mid-August 1805, Napoleon had got wind of these developments and began to transfer troops from the Channel toward the Rhine. He was determined to get his blow in first in central Europe and rechristened his Armée d'Angleterre: henceforth, it would be known as La Grande Armée. Napoleon's intention was to forestall the Allied offensive and if possible to destroy Austria's armies before the Russians could arrive in central Europe.

The Austrians were preparing three field armies: in north Italy, on the Danube and in the Tyrol. Archduke Charles was to initiate the offensive in the Tyrol, while Archduke Ferdinand and General Mack occupied Bavaria pending the arrival of the

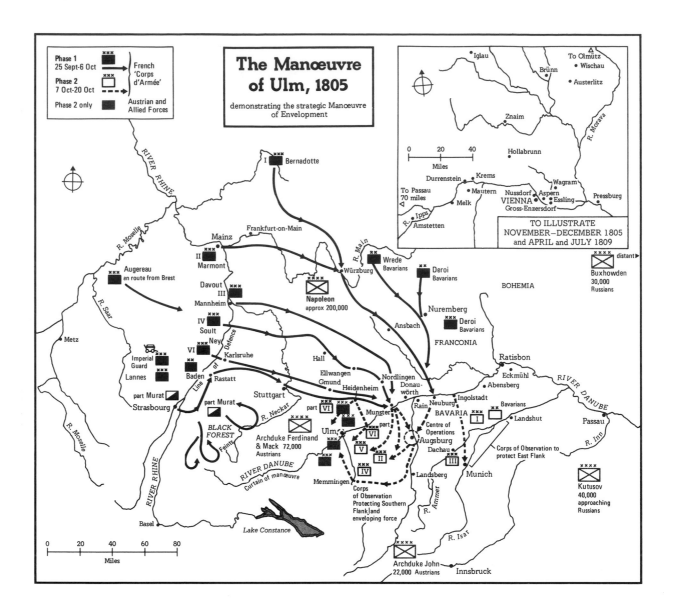

The Manoeuvre of Ulm, 1805

demonstrating the strategic Manoeuvre of Envelopment

Phase 1 25 Sept–6 Oct — French 'Corps d'Armée'

Phase 2 7 Oct–20 Oct

Phase 2 only — Austrian and Allied Forces

TO ILLUSTRATE NOVEMBER–DECEMBER 1805 and APRIL and JULY 1809

tsar's forces. Then, massively reinforced, the Austrians would launch a major onslaught through the Black Forest and cross the Rhine into the heartland of France.

Matters were to prove otherwise. The Austrians were courting a great risk by moving in Germany and Italy before the Russians arrived. Incredibly, the Austrian staff failed to take into account the ten days' difference between the German and Russian calendars, a fatal error, as it was to prove.

Meanwhile, Napoleon was massing 210,000 men and 396 guns along and near the Rhine. Subdivided into five *corps d'armée*, the Imperial Guard and the Reserve Cavalry, they quietly lined the west bank from Mainz to Strasbourg; a further corps under Bernadotte was ordered to join the Bavarian forces at Frankfurt and Würzburg, and Augereau to transfer his VII Corps from Brest as a reserve. The defense of Italy was entrusted to Massena with 50,000 men; he was ordered to keep Archduke Charles in play while La Grand Armée wheeled through central Germany, pivoting on Stuttgart to cross the Danube and thus sever the Austrian army's communications with Vienna. Once Mack was destroyed, Napoleon intended to tackle the Russians and then occupy Vienna. Such a bold plan called for brilliant staff work, but Napoleon had every confidence in his finely honed army, with its young marshals and eager rank and file; above all, he now fully controlled a centralized war machine.

War was declared on September 2, and eighteen days later the Austrian army occupied the city of Ulm on the Danube. On the 25th, Murat's cavalry launched a feint attack into the Black Forest region, which, as intended, served to distract Mack's attention. Then, during the night of September 26–27, the main body of the French army crossed the Rhine and set out on its long march through Germany. The web of self-sufficient corps swept on with devastating speed. By October 3 they had occupied a line between Stuttgart and Ansbach, and four days later the leading elements were crossing the Danube east of Ulm before the startled Austrians realized what was happening.

General Mack made a series of attempts to break out along the Danube's north bank, on October 11. Dupont's outnumbered division miraculously survived an attack at Haslach. Napoleon blamed Murat for allowing this error to develop, and launched Ney, followed by Lannes over the key bridge at Elchingen on the thirteenth. A sharp action ensued. Then, remorselessly, the French closed in on the city of Ulm. Archduke Ferdinand, after a bitter quarrel with Mack, broke out with the Austrian cavalry, but for the remainder of the troops there was no escape. While Murat's cavalry pursued the archduke, a desperate Mack, still hoping for the arrival of Kutusov from Russia, tried to win time by negotiation—but Napoleon was able to provide incontrovertible proof that the Russians were still far away to the east. Mack was a beaten man, and on October 20 he agreed to surrender with his twenty-seven thousand troops. Soon a

The combat at Elchingen, October 14, 1805. (Contemporary print.) As La Grande Armée closed in upon the hapless General Mack around Ulm, a sharp engagement was fought by Marshal Ney at Elchingen. The struggle eventually centered on possession of the large abbey and its enclosure standing on the summit of a steep ridge above the River Danube. Ney triumphed, and in 1808 was created duc d'Elchingen in recognition of his achievement.

Entry of La Grande Armée into Vienna, November 15, 1805. (Engraving after J. Ziegler.) Following the surrender of Mack at Ulm, Napoleon turned to catch the Austrian's approaching Russian allies under General Kutusov. Misunderstanding his orders, Prince Murat allowed the Russians to escape to the north bank of the Danube while he rode hell-for-leather to occupy the Austrian capital.

further thirty thousand (including all Ferdinand's troops) were also rounded up. Although Napoleon was well on the way to mastering central Germany, far away beyond Cape Trafalgar in Spain, October 21 had seen Admiral Nelson's great naval victory over the Franco-Spanish fleet, and the war at sea was irretrievably lost.

It still remained for Napoleon's army to defeat the approaching Russian forces. The wily Kutusov lost no time in retreating, and successfully escaped to the north bank of the Danube on November 9, where part of Mortier's newly created corps was almost trapped at Durrenstein while Murat, to Napoleon's fury, headed for the irrelevant prize of Vienna. He redeemed himself on the twelfth by capturing intact a major bridge by a superb piece of bluff. This assisted La Grande Armée's move on Hollabrunn, where Murat, without the emperor's leave, agreed to an armistice. This was broken off on the sixteenth, but Kutusov had eluded his pursuers and on November 20 at last joined up with Buxhowden at Znaim, bringing their joint strength up to some eighty-six thousand men. The chance of defeating the Russians in detail, column by column, had thus eluded the French.

The French army, reduced to only fifty-three thousand men, stood exhausted and hungry near Brünn, but that did not deter its chief. Napoleon at once determined to lure the Russians and Austrians into a precipitate battle near Olmütz by feigning even greater weakness. He chose a battle position, to the west of the town of Austerlitz, and then, with consummate skill, lured the Allies toward its southern flank on December 1. The suspicious Kutusov advocated caution, but the tsar demanded action.

Napoleon, meanwhile, in great secrecy summoned up Bernadotte's I Corps (thirteen thousand men) from Iglau, and then Davout's III Corps from Vienna. Late on December 1 he thus had over seventy-two thousand men in, or near, the proposed battle area. He was still at a serious numerical disadvantage, but his situation was far better than the enemy knew. That night, the anniversary of his coronation, Napoleon walked among his ragged troops, receiving a great ovation and an impromptu torchlight procession in his honor.

Twenty hours later, Napoleon had won the great Battle of Austerlitz (see page 56), and in doing so had completely reversed the strategic position. Against a loss of some nine thousand men, he had killed fifteen thousand Allies and taken eleven thousand prisoners, besides 180 cannon and forty-five colors. Even more important, he had broken the enemy's will. On December 3 Emperor Francis sued for peace, and the tsar lost no time in heading back toward Poland. Thus, the Third Coalition, in its turn, lay in ruins, and Napoleon's new empire had emerged triumphantly from the acid test of battle. By the Treaty of Pressburg, signed on December 26, Austria ceded Venice, the Tyrol and Swabia to France and her German allies, Bavaria and Württemberg.

Pitt was prostrated by the news of this new disaster, and died in January of the new year. Frederick William III of Prussia, so near to joining the Allies himself, hastened to send an envoy to Napoleon with a letter of congratulation on his victory. The emperor was not fooled, remarking to the envoy that the letter seemed to have been redrafted. He was well aware of Prussia's earlier intentions and was not going to forget them.

The news of Austerlitz was received ecstatically in France, and Napoleon's popularity reached new heights. Early hopes that a lasting peace would result proved ill-founded, however, as Great Britain remained doggedly in the struggle and Russia did not agree to a formal treaty. Napoleon, moreover, was not finished. He lost no time in exploiting his success by seizing Naples, and then turned his attention to reordering German affairs. In July 1806 the diffuse and anachronistic Holy Roman Empire was formally abolished—a further humiliation for Austria—and to fill the power vacuum in central and western Germany Napoleon created the Confederation of the Rhine, basically a grouping of pro-French princelings.

The reforms he introduced into the confederation were resented and feared in nearby Prussia, but Napoleon had no trouble bullying the weak-willed Frederick William III. His power seemed limitless. His brother Joseph was appointed king of Naples; stepson Eugène Beauharnais was made viceroy of Italy; the loyal ruler of Bavaria was elevated to a throne; brother Louis became king of Holland.

Napoleon still retained some lingering hopes of reaching an agreement with Great Britain. As an olive branch, in June 1806 he suddenly offered to return the electorate of Hanover to George III. Only months earlier he had awarded Hanover to Prussia, in compensation for ceded territory along the Rhine; now this *volte-face* caused Prussia's smoldering resentment to burst into flame.

On August 7, driven by the strong-willed Queen Louisa, the king and his vacillating government secretly decided on war against France, encouraged by promises of immediate aid from the tsar. For once a secret was kept, and it was only in September, when Prussian preparations were well advanced, that Napoleon learned what was in the wind. At his disposal were some 160,000 men, most of them veterans of the previous campaign, stationed from the Danube to the Main, but the emperor did not at this stage discount the prowess of the Prussian army, which was capable of putting perhaps 170,000 troops into the field; he recalled and revered the memory of that army's creator, Frederick the Great, and his martial achievements. However, since Frederick's death, his army had moldered under aging generals; its regiments were subject to endless ministerial red tape and its officers were overconfident and idle. Of the executive generals, Blücher was among the youngest, and he was sixty-four years old. The senior commanders ranged up to eighty years of age; this gerontocracy was not going to prove very successful against Napoleon and his energetic young marshals.

Only when news arrived on September 18 that Prussia had invaded Saxony, and that Russia had finally rejected France's offer of a treaty, did Napoleon take the omens seriously. Reassured that Austria was in no condition to take the field, the emperor set out to destroy the Prussian army before the Russians could intervene. By the nineteenth he had selected the method—a daring advance on Berlin through Saxony, via the difficult Thüringer Wald area, using three unconnected mountain roads. One hundred and two instructions were dictated in thirty-six hours as Napoleon proceeded to divide his army into three columns for the crossing, trusting in surprise and speed, together with a feint offensive by Louis Bonaparte over the Rhine, to see his army through. The emperor assumed command of the army from Berthier at Würzburg on October 2—the very day Prussia presented an ultimatum in Paris. Napoleon's reply would be the invasion of Saxony six days later, although he had scant idea of the Prussians' exact whereabouts.

On October 8, La Grande Armée entered Saxony. The Thüringer Wald was safely crossed, a Prussian detachment being defeated at Schleiz on the ninth, and another the next day at Rudolstädt. Late on the tenth, the French army had reached the River Saale; the Prussian high command started to collect thirty-five thousand men near Jena under Prince Hohenlohe, with the Duke of Brunswick; and General Rüchel massed at Weimar to the west of the River Ilm.

Still seeking exact news of his enemies' positions, Napoleon marched northeast toward Leipzig, adopting the flexible *bataillon carré* formation (see page 80). Questing cavalry found no sign of the Prussians between Gera and Leipzig, and Napoleon called for reports from the west. Suddenly, vital news came in from Lannes near Jena: the enemy was in strength west of the Saale. Napoleon rode to join V Corps just beyond Jena, ordering the whole army to march for the Saale ready to fight on the sixteenth. With complete precision, his *corps d'armée* swung westward.

After joining Lannes near Jena, late on the thirteenth, Napoleon deduced that he was facing the full Prussian army and that consequently the battle would take place the next day. New orders were galloped to his converging columns, summoning most to Jena, but Davout's III Corps and Bernadotte's I Corps were to cross the Saale through Naumburg, farther north (or, in the event that I Corps was not in contact with the Third, it was to move instead through Dornburg to the south), in order to sever the Prussian communications. In fact, however, Napoleon was only facing Hohenlohe's thirty-five thousand men, backed by Rüchel's fifteen thousand still near Weimar. The remaining fifty thousand were already moving north toward Auerstädt. This miscal-

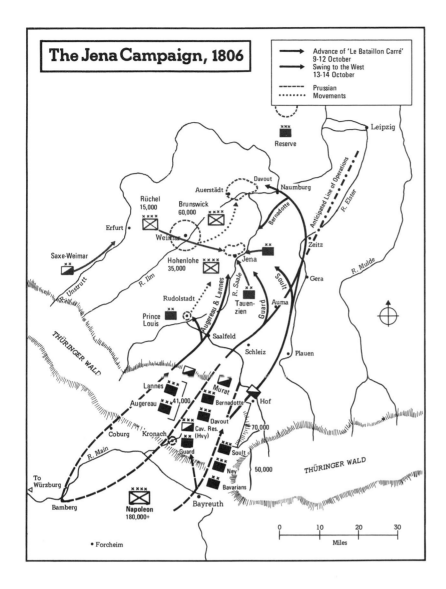

culation, together with Bernadotte's deliberate misinterpretation of his latest orders, would soon place Davout's twenty-seven thousand men in the utmost peril.

By dawn on the fourteenth, the emperor had issued his battle plan; in the event, matters worked out very differently. By 10:00 A.M., Napoleon had secured the plateau, and by 12:30 P.M., ninety-six thousand French troops were in the field with more arriving. Hohenlohe's outnumbered forces could not withstand the French pressure and began to scatter. The same fate awaited Rüchel's men as they arrived from Weimar about 1:00 P.M. All was over by 3:00 P.M., and within an hour Prince Murat was in the streets of Weimar. The French had lost five thousand men but had inflicted casualties perhaps five times greater.

Then dramatic news arrived from III Corps. An astounded emperor learned that Davout had fought—and beaten—Brunswick's fifty thousand men near Auerstädt, accepting unfavorable odds of two to one. A combination of French valor and Prussian confusion and errors had resulted in a dazzling success for Davout—but at a high cost. A full third of Davout's men were casualties, but so were thirteen thousand Prussians.

The battle of Auerstädt, October 14, 1806. (Painting by G. Gobaut.) Napoleon faced a strong Prussian rear guard at Jena; at Auerstädt, eight miles north, a force commanded by the great Marshal Davout was out-manned three to one. After a heroic battle (below) Davout triumphed over the main Prussian army, which the king of Prussia accompanied. To nobody's surprise, in 1808 Davout was made duc d'Auerstädt in honor of a superb feat of arms, achieved at a cost of almost a quarter of his force killed and wounded.

But why had Davout fought alone, without Bernadotte's aid? The prickly Gascon had no desire to fight under Davout, and had exploited a minor ambiguity in his orders to march on Dornburg, thus taking no part in either battle. The emperor almost had Bernadotte court-martialed, but relented.

The pursuit after Jena proved a military classic. Berlin was occupied on the twenty-fifth, and the hue and cry continued remorselessly to the Baltic, with mounting Prussian surrenders all the way. By the month's end, of the Prussian field forces only Blücher's remained, but on November 6 his force of twenty-two thousand laid down its arms to Bernadotte at Lübeck, a fate shared by a disembarking Swedish division arrived too late to participate in this whirlwind campaign. Finally, on November 10, the twenty-two thousand Prussians taking shelter within Magdeburg surrendered to Ney, while Mortier took possession of Hamburg. Thus, in less than a calendar month, Napoleon and his lieutenants had accounted for 125,000 out of the original 160,000 Prussian troops in the field. Prussia had been brought to her knees. King Frederick William was a fugitive seeking safety in east Prussia, and not one Russian soldier had entered the fray. Never had the meaning of Napoleonic blitzkrieg been more convincingly demonstrated, and rarely had a military power been reduced to impotence more rapidly or effectively.

Yet Jena and Auerstädt did not bring peace. Prussia might have been humiliatingly defeated, but the tsar's forces had still to be encountered, and Russian assurances of

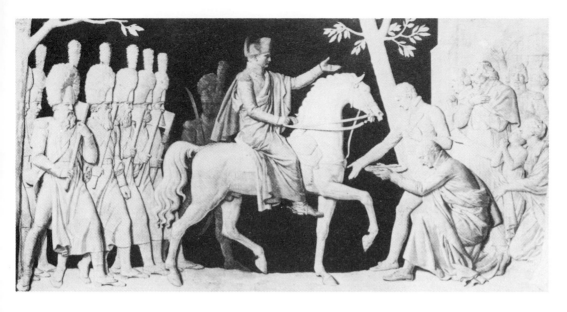

Just twelve days after Jena-Auerstädt, Napoleon entered the Prussian capital. In a staged ceremony, the keys to Berlin were presented to the conqueror by a kneeling Prince Hatzfeldt, whose wife had to beg Napoleon to spare his life. Behind Napoleon stands a rank of pioneers of the Imperial Guard, distinguished by their white aprons and axes. Both the theatricality—and the classical bust-relief—show the imperial legend in formation.

immediate aid fortified Frederick William's shaky resolve to remain at war. To this extent, the campaign of 1806 had an unsatisfactory conclusion. The Fourth Coalition still remained in being, and, as always, British hostility remained unshakable.

Napoleon's immediate problem in late 1806 was twofold: to force Prussia to make peace and to defeat the Russian armies. The approach of winter was a major complication, but in the hope of snatching a quick success against generals Kamenskoi, Bennigsen and Buxhowden, he decided to advance deep into Polish territory, at that time largely divided between Prussia and Russia. There was also a possibility of attracting recruits for his armies, for Polish patriots had long dreamed of regaining a semblance of independence for their historic nation. By mid-November the French were halfway to Warsaw, and on the twenty-eighth Murat occupied the Polish capital unopposed.

After reordering his forces, Napoleon strove to trap the Russians at Pultusk, on the River Narew. By mid-December much fighting was taking place, but by early January 1807, General Kamenskoi had made good his escape, and the French offensive ground to a halt amid appalling weather.

The corps were dispersed over French-occupied Poland to find shelter, but in late January, Marshal Ney, seeking better conditions, moved his men without permission. In midjourney, he brushed with a large Russian force en route to surprise Bernadotte at Mohringen. The news was rushed to Warsaw, where Napoleon abandoned the charms of his current mistress, the countess Marie Walewska, and ordered his army back into the field despite the weather.

But a copy of his orders to Bernadotte fell into Russian hands, making General Bennigsen aware of Napoleon's plans. The Russians at once fell back to Allenstein, and then, after an indecisive combat on February 3, back toward Eylau, abandoning two depots to the hungry French pursuers.

At Eylau Bennigsen turned at bay with sixty-seven thousand troops and 470 guns, and a Prussian force still to join him with ten thousand more. Napoleon captured Eylau late on February 7, and the next morning accepted battle, but with only forty-five thousand men and 210 guns present, he relied upon Davout and Ney arriving

The capture of Magdeburg, November 10, 1806. (Engraved after Martinet.) As Napoleon advanced remorselessly upon Berlin, he of necessity bypassed the great Prussian fortress-city of Magdeburg on the River Elbe, detaching a force under Marshal Ney to besiege it. Ney had eighteen thousand men against General Kleist's garrison of twenty-five thousand, but the Prussians were demoralized, and after a heavy bombardment by cannon and mortars (colorfully depicted here), Kleist agreed to an armistice and to surrender.

General Gebhard Leberecht von Blücher (1742–1819). (Watercolor by William Heath.) Blücher commanded the Prussian cavalry at Auerstädt and was eventually forced to surrender to Marshal Bernadotte at Lübeck on November 6, 1806. Denied active employment until Prussia joined the Sixth Coalition, and with a hatred for Napoleon that was both personal and intense, he had his revenge during the campaigns of 1813–14, and above all at Waterloo-Wavre in 1815. Despite his age he inspired his young conscripts, who called him "Papa Blücher" or "Alte Vorwarts" ("Old Forward") after his favorite, much-repeated command.

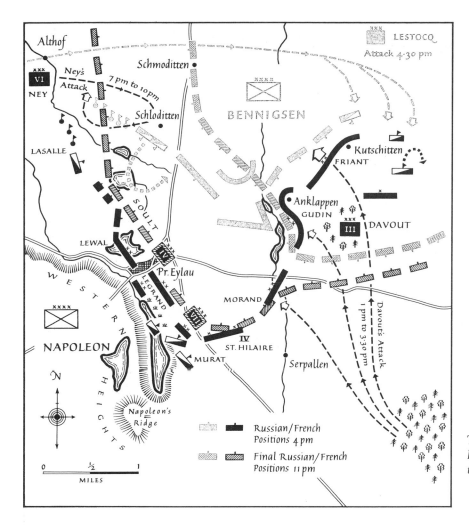

Within the map:

Althof

Schmoditten ●

LESTOCQ
Attack 4.30 pm

VI
NEY

Ney's
Attack
7 pm to 10 pm

Schloditten

BENNIGSEN

LASALLE

Kutschitten ●
FRIANT

SOULT

Anklappen ●
GUDIN

III   DAVOUT

LEWAL

IV

W E S T E R N

Pr. Eylau

LEGRAND

MORAND

NAPOLEON

VII

IV
ST. HILAIRE

MURAT

Serpallen ●

Davout's Attack

1 pm to 3.30 pm

N

Napoleon's
Ridge

H E I G H T S

Russian/French
Positions 4 pm

Final Russian/French
Positions 11 pm

0   ½   1
MILES

*The Battle of Eylau,
February 8, 1807:
the afternoon battle*

during the day with thirty thousand reinforcements. As Bernadotte had received no orders, he was unlikely to appear.

After a bitter night, the battle opened across a frozen plain. Napoleon held back his attack, awaiting the arrival of his outlying formations to threaten both Russian flanks. By 9:00 A.M. Soult was under heavy Russian attack, and to relieve him the emperor ordered Augereau's VII Corps to attack the Russian left. A heavy snowstorm caused Augereau to veer into Bennigsen's center, where his corps was all but destroyed by the massed Russian guns.

Following up this success, Russian columns fought their way into Eylau and almost captured Napoleon. In desperation, Napoleon ordered his last uncommitted troops to attack—namely Murat's 10,700 cavalry.

The celebrated charge that ensued retrieved the fortunes of the day, winning a breathing space for Davout to arrive from the southeast. By 1:00 P.M. III Corps was pressing back the Russian left remorselessly—but then the Prussians under Lestocq arrived to reinforce the threatened sector and pushed back Davout in his turn.

Only at 7:00 P.M., when dusk had already fallen, did Ney make his tardy appearance. It was too late to use the VI Corps for anything more than a demonstration, but it sufficed to persuade the Russian high command to abandon its plans for renewing the conflict the following day. This was a relief to the French, who had fought to a

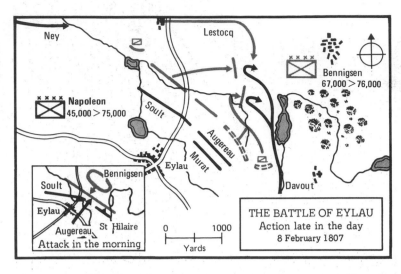

Ney

Lestocq

Bennigsen
67,000 > 76,000

Napoleon
45,000 > 75,000

Soult

Augereau

Murat

Bennigsen

Soult

Eylau

Eylau

Davout

Augereau   St Hilaire

Attack in the morning

THE BATTLE OF EYLAU
Action late in the day
8 February 1807

0   1000

Yards

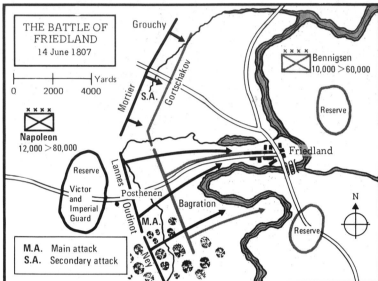

THE BATTLE OF
FRIEDLAND
14 June 1807

Grouchy

Bennigsen
10,000 > 60,000

Yards

0   2000   4000

Mortier

S.A.

Gortschakov

Reserve

Napoleon
12,000 > 80,000

Reserve

Friedland

Victor
and
Imperial
Guard

Lannes

Oudinot

Posthenen

Bagration

N

M.A.

Reserve

M.A.   Main attack
S.A.   Secondary attack

Ney

standstill amid atrocious conditions. Napoleon took pains to disguise his losses, but they may have been in excess of twenty thousand men; the Russians lost perhaps fifteen thousand. Both sides claimed a victory, but there was no disguising the fact that for the first time in his career Napoleon had failed to win a decisive battle. Furthermore, the problem of defeating the Russians remained, as they had retreated in good order on Königsberg. There was scant attempt at a pursuit, and soon the exhausted French were gratefully returning to their winter quarters. So ended the indecisive winter campaign of 1806–1807. Napoleon vented his wrath on Bernadotte, in this case wholly unjustly. If anyone had bungled the Battle of Eylau, it was the emperor himself, who had summoned Ney to the field far too late. The fate of the campaign, therefore, was undecided, and would wait through the harsh winter until spring made further operations possible.

Napoleon's enemies had no intention of allowing him long to recover. On April 26 Prussia and Russia signed a new agreement at Bartens, reaffirming their determination to remain in the field. Nor had the emperor any intention of withdrawing: Lefebvre besieged and captured Danzig (May 27). The year 1807 would see a decisive campaign.

Napoleone Buonaparte in 1785, age sixteen (in the earliest known sketch from life), at the Ecole Militaire in Paris, where he trained for less than a year. By this time his cadaverous face and general leanness were apparent, as were the penetrating eyes upon which so many contemporaries commented.

Marie-Josèphe-Rose Tascher de La Pagerie, called Josephine. (By Jean-Baptiste Isabey.) Josephine (1763–1814) was a Creole born in the French West Indies. In 1779 she married Vicomte Alexandre de Beauharnais (guillotined in 1794), by whom she had two children: Eugène and Hortense. She was for a time mistress in turn to directors Tallien, Gohier and Barras, and a member of the frivolous Parisian set. She first met Napoleon in 1795, and he at once fell passionately in love with her. Whether she fully reciprocated his feelings is arguable, but on March 9, 1796, she married him. Since she was unable to bear him an heir, they were divorced on December 15, 1809. Josephine died at Malmaison on May 29, 1814.

General Napoleon Bonaparte. (By Gros, 1797.) The artist chose the moment at Arcola depicted in the illustration on page 32 for this effective but idealized picture.

The Battle of Aboukir, July 25, 1799. (Colored engraving by Berinet.) After crushing a revolt in Cairo, Napoleon rushed north to the coast to intercept the landing of a large Turkish army from Rhodes, whose fleet was convoyed by the Royal Navy. The French gained a complete victory, and the Turks were driven back into the sea, where many drowned. Soon after this, Napoleon secretly left Egypt for France.

KEY TO THE JOMINI ATLAS PLATES

On each map, the sequence of battles is built up as follows:

	FRENCH	OPPONENTS
Original positions	light blue	pale yellow
Second positions	dark blue	dark yellow
Third positions	light red	orange
Fourth positions	dark red	green
Fifth positions	violet	n/a

AUTHOR'S NOTE

Baron Antoine-Henri Jomini (1779–1869) was born in Switzerland but spent much of his early adult life as a staff officer attached to French headquarters—most notably those of the emperor and (from 1805 to 1813) of Marshal Ney. He wrote several influential studies on the Napoleonic Wars and together with the Prussian Carl von Clausewitz (1780–1831) became regarded as a major interpreter of those dramatic campaigns and battles. The maps have been selected from his Atlas Portatif, which was produced to illustrate his various works, especially his Vie de Napoléon, and published in Brussels in 1840. Jomini's influence on several generations of West Point officer cadets was considerable, and many U.S. Civil War commanders attempted to model their conduct of operations upon his precepts. In August 1813, after a major disagreement with Marshal Berthier (who prosecuted a feud against him), he transferred his services to Tsar Alexander I and remained in Russian service until 1848.

The first consul crossing the Alps, 1800 (left). (By David.) This famous painting was a propaganda exercise intended to portray Napoleon as a great leader following in the steps of Hannibal and Charlemagne, whose names are seen here along with Bonaparte's (though they are far less prominent than his) carved on boulders. David had to paint several versions of this dramatic scene before his patron was satisfied. Some half-dozen versions still survive.

The first consul crossing the Alps, 1800 (right). (By Delaroche, painted during the Bourbon restoration.) This version is far closer to the truth. Huddled on the back of a mule, led by a mountain guide, Napoleon passed over the mountains in far less dramatic style than that depicted by David. Indeed, he fell off his mule at least twice during the crossing.

The coronation, December 2, 1804. (By David.) Napoleon is shown raising the crown more reverentially than in David's early sketches, while the pope (without miter) raises his hand in symbolic blessing. Napoleon's mother—"Madame Mère"—is shown seated in the box (background), although in fact she was not present at the ceremony, whether from illness or pique is still a contentious subject.

Bonaparte, first consul, at Marengo (left). (By Gros.) Wearing the gold-laced red coat of the first consul, Napoleon is shown inspecting the Consular Guard. In later years he had the "official" history of the battle rewritten twice to ensure that his role was sufficiently impressive.

Bonaparte, age thirty-four, as first consul in 1803 (opposite page). (By Ingres.) This painting, presented to the citizens of Liège after a state visit, shows Napoleon striking the pose that was to become almost his hallmark, although it was common artistic convention in portraits of the period. Symbolically, his other hand rests upon one of his many legal achievements while his sword remains peacefully sheathed. By this time he had adopted the short hairstyle that caused his soldiers to nickname him "le Tondu" ("the Shorn One").

At the Battle of Jena (By H. Chartier.) Prince Murat leads a charge at the head of several thousand horsemen, defeating them and pursuing the Prussian reinforcements brought up by General Rüchel. Scornfully wielding his riding crop instead of his saber, the flamboyant Gascon chased the enemy all the way to Weimar. Napoleon regarded his brother-in-law as "in battle probably the bravest man in the world."

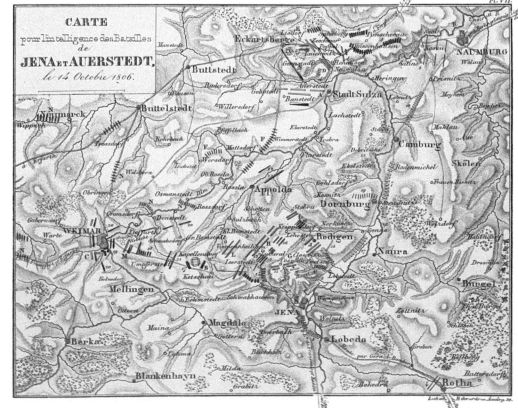

CARTE
pour l'intelligence des Batailles
de
JENA et AUERSTEDT,
le 14 Octobre 1806.

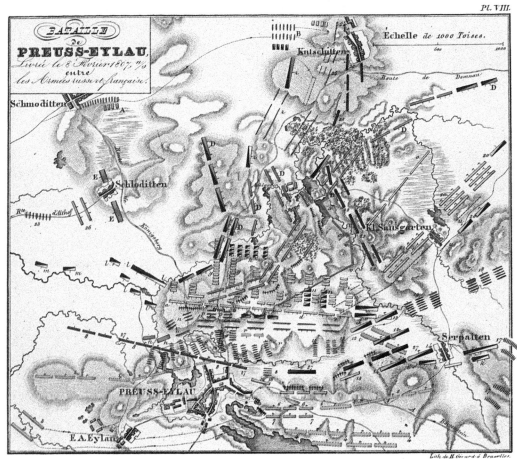

Eylau. (By Gros.) One of the most terrible battles fought by Napoleon, Eylau took place amid a freezing blizzard. Although technically the victors because General Bennigsen conceded the field, the French lost at least twenty thousand men.

*Napoleon at the Battle of Fried-
land, June 14, 1807 (this page,
top). (By Vernet.) If Eylau was
only a technical victory, Friedland, fought four months later
on the "happy day" of the seventh anniversary of Marengo,
was truly decisive. Napoleon
reinforced Lannes's seemingly
isolated advance guard and by
dusk had smashed Bennigsen's
army beyond repair. Soon after,
Tsar Alexander I declared an
armistice. The famous summit
conference at Tilsit followed.*

*(Engraving by Johann Otto.)
The first meeting between emperor and tsar took place on a
raft in the center of the River
Niemen on June 25 (this page,
bottom). After two weeks of talks
interspersed with parades and
lavish entertainments, the two
peaces of Tilsit—one public, one
secret—were signed on July 7
and 9 respectively. France and
Russia became firm allies. Prussia, practically dismembered,
was the only state to suffer.*

*General Antoine-Charles-Louis
Lasalle (1775–1809) (opposite
page, upper left). (By Gros.)
Lasalle was the epitome of the
leader of light cavalry, and
second only to Murat as a beau
sabreur in La Grande Armée.
He served with great distinction
at Austerlitz, Jena and its pursuit, Golymin, Heilsberg and in
Spain (where he led the Twenty-
sixth Dragoons to break a Spanish square at Medellin). He was
killed at the Battle of Wagram
in early July 1809.*

*Dos de Mayo (Second of May)
(opposite page, bottom). (By
Goya.) The abrupt rising of the
people of Madrid against the
French on May 2, 1808, was
the signal for growing revolts
throughout Spain. Although the
rising was suppressed by Murat,
it forced Napoleon to take personal command of an army of
conquest and also provided
Great Britain with the chance
to intervene militarily on the
continent of Europe.*

Sir Arthur Wellesley, later duke of Wellington (1769–1852) (this page, top right). (By Lawrence.) At the head of a small British army, Wellesley landed in Portugal in July 1808 and soon forced General Junot to capitulate. But the terms were deemed too generous, and Wellesley and two other senior generals were recalled to London to face the Cintra Enquiry. In mid-1809, completely cleared, he returned to Lisbon, and resumed the series of campaigns known as the Peninsular War, which by late 1813 had driven the French out of Spain. Two years ahead lay Waterloo.

The Battle of Somosierra, November 30, 1808. (By Lejeune.)
As Napoleon's conquest of northern Spain swept inexorably toward Madrid, one last range of mountains divided the French from the Spanish capital. Somosierra Pass was held only by a weak Spanish force, but Napoleon's patience snapped, and he ordered the Polish Light Horse (forming his escort) to take it at the charge. After two attempts, and at heavy cost, the gallant Poles succeeded. Four days later Napoleon entered Madrid.

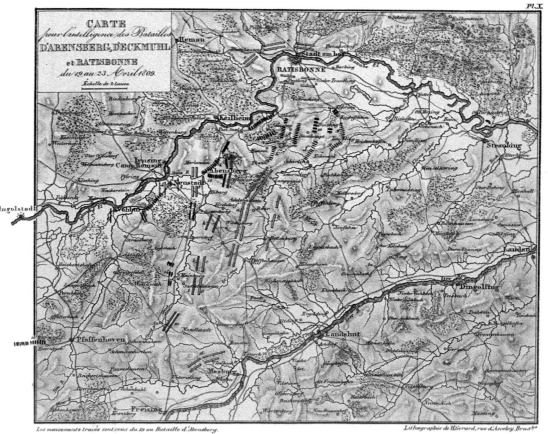

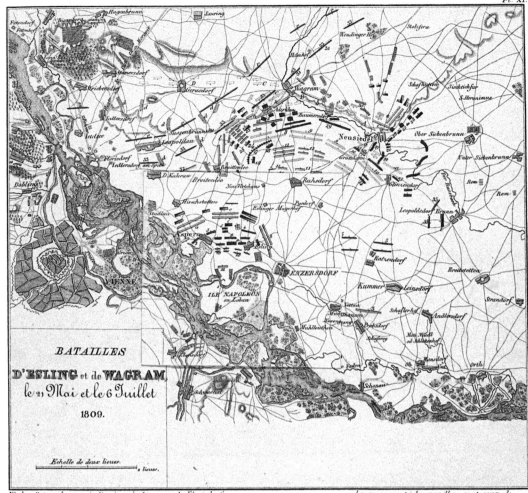

Pl. XI.

BATAILLES
D'ESLING et de WAGRAM
le 21 Mai et le 6 Juillet
1809.

Echelle de deux lieues.

NB. *Les Retranchemens indiqués près des ponts de Florisdorf*
ne furent construits qu'après la Bataille de Wagram.

Les mouvements du papillon sont ceux de
la Bataille d'Essling.

The death of Marshal Lannes (1769–1809). (Contemporary print.) One of Napoleon's few real friends, Lannes was mortally wounded on the second day of the Battle of Aspern-Essling, his legs smashed by a cannonball (although he did not die on the field, as depicted here). Napoleon visited him several times and openly wept at his death on May 31.

Almost 200,000 Frenchmen (with seven hundred cannon) fought 342,000 Allies (with fifteen hundred cannon) at the Battle of Leipzig (this page, top). No less than 122,000 men of all nations had become casualties by the close. It was the largest battle in history before the First World War.

1814. (By Meissonier.) This picture, commonly but erroneously called The Retreat from Moscow, shows Napoleon and his staff riding through the snow and slush during the campaign of France in early 1814 (opposite page, top). In many ways this proved to be a virtuoso performance by the emperor, who achieved marvels with his small army made up mainly of "Marie-Louises" (schoolboys) and pensioners. But time was not on his side.

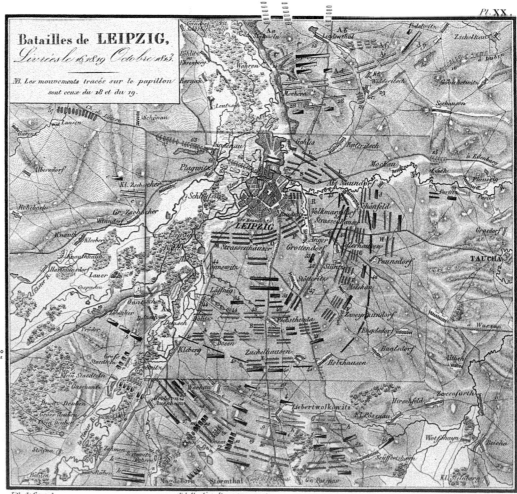

Batailles de LEIPZIG,
Livrées le 16, 18, 19 Octobre 1813.
N.B. Les mouvements tracés sur le papillon sont ceux du 18 et du 19.

Pl. XX.

Lith. de Gerard.

Echelle de 2 lieues communes.

The Duelling Lesson, *1814. (By J. G. Schadov.) While a British Jack-tar looks on, Blücher,
with a Cossack and German peasants as his seconds, duels with Napoleon, seconded by a group
of caricatured French generals. The propaganda war waged in the press and through the sale of
prints was a novel feature of the Napoleonic Wars.*

The return of Napoleon. (By Karl Stenben.) As he moved inland from the coast, Napoleon was intercepted by the Fifth Regiment of the Line at the defile of Laffrey. For several anxious minutes it seemed that firing might break out, but the old magic proved too great for Louis XVIII's soldiers, who flocked forward to cheer the emperor.

Napoleon escaping from Waterloo. (By Crofts.) Napoleon wished to stay with the Old Guard, but his staff persuaded him to join the flight. At one stage, near Gennape, his traveling coach became trapped in the rout, and he was forced to transfer to his horse as the Prussian cavalry pursuit came thundering over the horizon.

Napoleon on board HMS Bellerophon. (By Orchardson.) Accompanied by his immediate staff, Napoleon takes a last look at the coast of France. His charm soon won over Captain Maitland, RN, and his crew. At first the fallen emperor hoped that the prince regent would afford him sanctuary in England. Instead he was transferred to HMS Northumberland in Torbay and shipped down to the island of Saint Helena in the south Atlantic.

(By Meissonier.) Wearing his gray overcoat and distinctive bicorne hat, mounted on one of his favorite Arab horses, Marengo—this was the image of Napoleon that was sedulously fostered by many paintings throughout the nineteenth century. The myth was already being propagated before his death on Saint Helena in 1821.

Napoleon visiting the plague hospital at Jaffe, 1799. (By Gros.) There was no denying his personal and moral courage. The visit to the hospital during his campaign into Syria was a sublime moment, given the dread reputation of the disease. It did nothing to diminish his standing with his contemporaries—or with posterity.

The return. (By Jean-Baptiste Isabey.) In 1840, the British government agreed that Napoleon's remains should be returned to France. In this dramatic painting his triple coffin is being loaded on board the French frigate L'Inconstant.

Early in June, on the tsar's insistence, Bennigsen resumed the offensive toward the Baltic coast. Napoleon responded by rushing to sever the Russian communications. Two actions ensued at Güttstadt and Heilsberg, between June 8 and 10, against parts of the Russian army, inducing Bennigsen to retreat up the River Alle as far as Friedland, where he turned at bay on the thirteenth after crossing to the west bank, thus unwisely placing the river to his back. This rash action was due to the arrival of Lannes's small *corps d'armée*, all alone—seemingly inviting destruction. But as usual, appearances could be deceptive, for soon Napoleon had neighboring French corps converging overnight on Bennigsen's fifty-three thousand men.

At dawn on the fourteenth—the anniversary of Marengo in 1800—the skirmishing opened. By 9:00 A.M., the French strength had only grown to seventeen thousand men, but problems of deployment in the bend of the river caused the Russians to delay their attack. An hour later forty thousand French were in the field, and Napoleon arrived at midday. With three corps still to arrive, the emperor's staff advised him to postpone the battle until the fifteenth. But when his strength had risen to eighty thousand men by 4:00 P.M., he ordered the attack, intent on capitalizing on the problems Bennigsen was still having in the cramped space bisected by the Millstream.

At 5:30 P.M., a twenty-gun battery fired a signal salvo, and Ney advanced from the cover of Sortlach Wood. Caught unawares, Bennigsen stopped his army from retiring over the Alle. But aided by cavalry, Ney made rapid progress northward. As the Russian left wing recoiled, Napoleon sent in Victor's corps to reinforce Ney's tired formations, and maintained the impetus of the advance. The Russian Bagration, commanding the left, was forced back in growing chaos, hotly pursued by Dupont's division and Brigadier General Sénarmont's thirty boldly deployed cannon. In vain, Russian cavalry charged bravely, only to be decimated by case shot. At 7:00 P.M., Bennigsen played his last card and sent in the Russian Imperial Guard supported by General Gortschakov to attack the French left and center. But Lannes and Mortier stood their ground, and the attacks foundered. By 8:00 P.M., the Russians were in full retreat, even if Grouchy's bungled cavalry attack allowed many to escape over the Alle.

Nevertheless, Napoleon had won a decisive victory. With eight thousand casualties, he had inflicted almost twenty thousand on the Russians, and captured 80 of their 130 cannon. Retreating through Allenburg, Bennigsen strove to reorder his demoralized army, but the fall of Königsberg to Soult on the sixteenth deprived the Russians of their depots, and by the nineteenth Murat's cavalry had reached the Niemen near Tilsit. The tsar promptly sued for an armistice, and on June 23 a four-week cessation of hostilities became effective. Well might Napoleon declare: "My children have worthily celebrated the anniversary of Marengo." The setback at Eylau had been avenged, and everything now pointed to a favorable peace with Russia.

On June 25, 1807, Tsar Alexander and Emperor Napoleon met on the famous raft anchored in midstream of the Niemen. During the two weeks of negotiations that followed, Napoleon lost no opportunity to dazzle and impress Alexander, but behind the façade of reviews and banquets, hard bargaining was taking place. Inevitably, the only real victim was unfortunate Prussia. Frederick William was summoned to attend the conferences, and despite Queen Louisa, who tried every feminine wile to gain more favorable terms, Prussia was virtually dismembered. By the treaty ratified on July 12, Prussia was returned to her frontiers of 1772. All possessions west of the Elbe were to be incorporated into a new kingdom of Westphalia, and all Prussia's Polish provinces were incorporated into the new grand duchy of Warsaw. Prussia's army was to be restricted, and a huge war indemnity paid. Pending the fulfillment of these terms, French troops would remain in occupation of Prussian soil. Russia, predictably, escaped more lightly. In return for the tsar's cession of the Ionian Isles, Napoleon agreed to Russian claims for freedom of action against European Turkey and Finland. Alexander also agreed to join the Continental System (see page 108) and to induce Sweden and Denmark to follow suit. Recognition was accorded to Joseph as king of Naples, Louis as king of Holland and Jérôme as king of Westphalia, while the rulers of Württemberg and Saxony were also to receive crowns. Thus the two potentates agreed to a virtual partition of Continental Europe between them.

Napoleon's triumph appeared complete. His international prestige seemed to have reached a new height and his power extended ostensibly from the Pyrenees to the Niemen. However, behind his success lay weakness. The Continental System was already highly unpopular in western Europe, as was the "blood-tax" of conscription and the heavy taxation. In France itself there were murmurs against the extension of Napoleon's ambitions. The French empire, many said, had been Napoleonic.

His popularity, therefore, was brittle. As for La Grande Armée, although it had reestablished its reputation at Friedland, its composition, no longer exclusively French, was becoming increasingly multinational. There was friction between the marshals, the line troops distrusted the staff and the infantry was critical of the cavalry. While Tilsit has been widely regarded as the high watermark of the First French Empire, it was also to prove the turn of the tide.

The Battle of Austerlitz
December 2, 1805

Napoleon's overall strategic position in late November 1805 was far from favorable. Since his important success at Ulm, the needs to pursue the retiring Kutusov down the Danube valley, to occupy Vienna and then to follow the Russians northward through Hollabrunn toward Olmütz had placed great strains on La Grande Armée's resources. No less than 450 miles lay between the French and their bases along the Rhine, and the ceaseless marches and the need to protect the flanks of the army's advance had greatly sapped Napoleon's fighting power. His original 210,000 men had shrunk to 55,000 under immediate command. Furthermore, the threats he faced were multiplying alarmingly. To his front the reinforced Austro-Russian army (Buxhowden had now joined Kutusov) numbered at least 85,000 men; archdukes Charles and John were closing in from the south with 122,000 Austrians, but were still distant; and now, to cap it all, there were ominous signs that to the north Prussia was considering joining the Third Coalition, which could mean a further 200,000 opponents threatening his already tenuous links with France. To advance farther or to halt was unthinkable; retreat could spell catastrophe. Small wonder that the emperor desired a major battle without delay: it would be a gamble at best, but the alternatives were even grimmer.

Napoleon, however, was often at his best when disaster seemed to loom. With

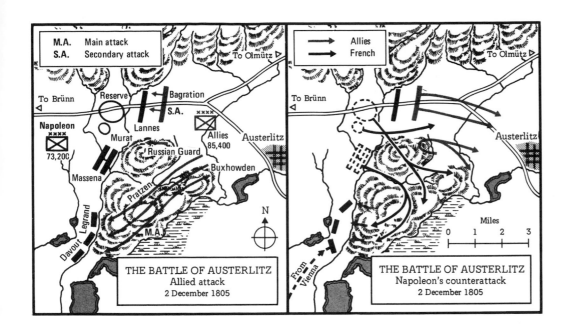

THE BATTLE OF AUSTERLITZ
Allied attack
2 December 1805

THE BATTLE OF AUSTERLITZ
Napoleon's counterattack
2 December 1805

great skill he dangled the bait of an easy victory before his opponents. French cavalry patrols retired in apparent panic when they brushed Cossack patrols near Olmütz. La Grande Armée then evacuated the town of Austerlitz and, even more significantly, the high ground around Pratzen. When the Allies offered armistice talks (to gain time for Archduke Charles to draw closer), Napoleon went out of his way to be pleasant to the bombastic Russian envoy, Count Dolgourki. These assorted deceptions had their intended effect. Despite Kutusov's repeated cautions, Tsar Alexander and Emperor Francis became ever more confident of success, and on December 1 their deep columns marched west from Olmütz, occupying the Pratzen Heights. Their cocksure advisers claimed that the French were at their mercy.

Meanwhile, Napoleon's countermoves were being executed. Hidden behind an impenetrable cavalry screen, Bernadotte's I Corps and Davout's III Corps were hastening east from Iglau and up from Vienna respectively. Bernadotte arrived on November 30, and as a result of herculean marching (the men covered sixty-four miles in just forty-eight hours), Davout's leading division and corps cavalry were close by late on December 1. Unknown to the Allies, Napoleon's strength had grown to 73,200; but with 139 cannon the French were seriously outgunned by their opponents' 278 pieces.

The battlefield of Austerlitz stretched south for five miles from the Santon Hill and the Brünn-Olmütz highroad to the frozen meres near the village of Telnitz. The valley at the confluence of the Goldbach and Bosenitz streams, with its cluster of villages, formed the front of the French position, although sixty-five thousand men were deliberately massed in the northern sector, many of them concealed behind the Zurlan feature, leaving only one and a half divisions (which were joined with Davout's corps) to hold their extended right. As for the Allies, the bulk of their imposing array was encamped on, or adjoining, the Pratzen Heights; a secondary force was preparing to move up the Brünn highway; the Russian Imperial Guard, the main cavalry force and Allied headquarters were situated near Krenowitz. By 3:00 A.M. on December 2 the whole area was blanketed in a thick curtain of freezing mist.

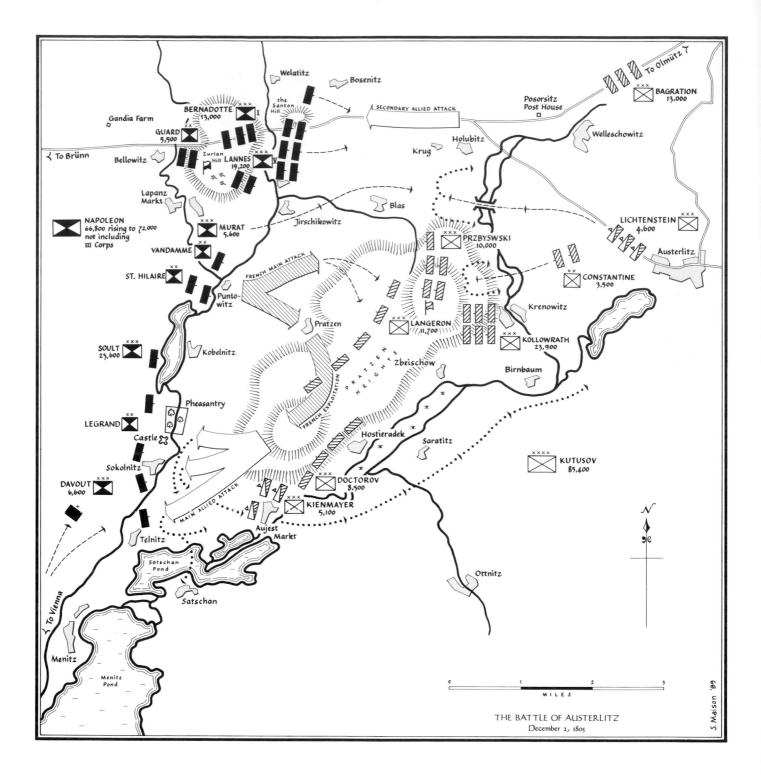

THE BATTLE OF AUSTERLITZ
December 2, 1805

Not only the battle itself but the form it took was important to Napoleon. He wanted to lure the Allies into making their main attack against his right flank in the general direction of the Vienna road, which seemed to constitute the sole French line of retreat. In fact, the emperor had already designated a safer route if the French had to retreat running west through Brünn, but this was carefully concealed from the enemy. To lure them southward, the French right, entrusted to General Legrand of Soult's IV Corps, was kept deliberately weak along the Bosenitz. His orders were to hold for as long as possible but to withdraw northward if necessary. However, he was

assured that he would be joined at dawn by General Friant's division of the III Corps.

Napoleon entrusted Marshal Lannes's V Corps, supported by parts of Bernadotte's I Corps and Murat's Reserve Cavalry, with holding the Santon sector, the hill having been fortified. Lannes's role was also mainly defensive. Meanwhile, in the vicinity of the Zurlan, Napoleon deployed the two remaining divisions of the IV Corps, the Imperial Guard, Oudinot's division of grenadiers, the Reserve Artillery and the rest of Murat's cavalry and Bernadotte's infantrymen. His plan was to lure the strength of the Allies against his right and then to unleash Soult against the Pratzen Heights before using the reserve formations to envelop either the enemy left or right, according to circumstances.

Meanwhile, the Allied Council of War, meeting at 1:00 A.M. on December 2, had been pleased to approve General Weyrother's plan of attack. Some forty-five thousand Allies in four columns under Buxhowden were to sweep down from the Pratzen to cross the Goldbach, expel the French from the area and cut the Vienna road. As this movement unrolled, a fifth column of fifteen thousand men under General Kollowrath was to descend to take Puntowitz, thus destroying the hinge of the buckling French line. Meanwhile, Bagration and Lichtenstein would advance on the Santon. The Imperial Guard would be held in central reserve. Napoleon could not have hoped for a better plan.

Both armies were astir by 4:00 A.M., but the Allies found the fog a grave inconvenience. By seven o'clock, however, their leading formations were attacking Telnitz and Sokolnitz with eventual success. This, however, coincided with Friant's arrival from Gross Raigern, a timely reinforcement that permitted Legrand to check the enemy advance. This in turn induced Buxhowden to summon Kollowrath into the fray. Thus, by 8:30 A.M., the last major Austro-Russian forces were leaving the Pratzen.

This had not gone unnoticed by Napoleon atop the Zurlan, Soult at his side. At 9:00 A.M. Napoleon ordered the attack on the Pratzen to commence, and out of the

Napoleon at Austerlitz. (After Gérard.) On December 2, 1805, "the Battle of the Three Emperors" took place, Napoleon, Tsar Alexander I and Emperor Francis II all being present. Here General Rapp presents to the emperor prisoners of the Russian Chevalier Garde. Fought amid the frosty fields of Moravia near Brünn, Austerlitz ended in a great Napoleonic victory—the first of the Empire and of La Grande Armée. It effectively destroyed the Third Coalition, sealing once and for all Napoleon's reputation as a commander of genius.

Napoleon meeting Francis II of Austria. (By Gros.) At the Austrian emperor's request, Napoleon granted an armistice after Austerlitz, and two days later the rulers met in a rural setting to discuss a possible pacification. On December 26 the Treaty of Pressburg was signed. Although neither man guessed it, a future son-in-law and future father-in-law had met for the first time. Francis was the father of Princess Marie-Louise.

foggy valley rose the divisions of Vandamme and Saint Hilaire. Taken aback, Kutusov urged the recall of Kollowrath, but the latter was already too distant. By the time parts of his column returned, the French had become masters of Pratzen village and much of the summit, after a tough struggle in which the intervention of Bernadotte on the left was required to clinch the capture of Blasowitz.

All this time a fierce battle had been raging around the Santon. Lannes had been sustained by Murat's cavalry, which engaged Lichtenstein's massed squadrons near Jirschikowitz and eventually defeated them. Meanwhile, Napoleon had moved Oudinot southward to sustain his tiring right wing, where 10,800 Frenchmen were pinning over 35,000 Allies.

Back in the center, the crisis of the day was at hand. By 10:30 A.M. the IV Corps was under heavy counterattack from three directions as Kutusov strove to regain the Pratzen; the arrival of Soult's corps artillery stabilized the position to some degree as the French Imperial Guard moved nearer. At 1:00 P.M. Vandamme and Saint-Hilaire were assailed by the Russian Imperial Guard. Their front line was scattered and two battalions fled. Fortunately Napoleon was at hand to send in Bessières and the French Guard cavalry, and a second charge led by General Rapp soon routed the Russians, who left five hundred dead and two hundred prisoners behind them.

It still remained to convert victory into triumph. Napoleon ordered Soult and the Guard to move south to envelop Buxhowden's isolated wing in the valley below. "Let not one escape" was Soult's grim order. By 3:30 P.M. all was nearly over. Many Russian troops were forced to surrender, and those who tried to flee over the frozen meres were thwarted when French cannonballs smashed the ice. Numbers drowned. Away to the north, Bagration beat a hasty retreat, accompanied by the tsar. Murat's cavalry, followed by Bernadotte's infantry, swept forward to occupy Austerlitz and capture the enemy wagon convoys. By 4:00 P.M. the last guns had fallen silent as the "sun of Austerlitz" began to set.

Napoleon had gained his decisive victory. With a loss of nine thousand casualties, he had inflicted twenty-six thousand (including prisoners) and taken 180 guns and 45 colors. The next day Emperor Francis appealed for an armistice while his erstwhile Russian allies headed for Poland. A few days later the Prussian government hastened to offer its congratulations to the victors. In sum, the Third Coalition had been shattered.

The brilliant campaign of 1805 and its great climax at Austerlitz had proved the power of the year-old French Empire, its Grande Armée and its chief. Napoleon's military genius had been convincingly displayed. More successes lay ahead, but none would surpass the achievements of December 2, 1805, the "Battle of the Three Emperors." As Napoleon proclaimed with good reason: "*Soldats, je suis content de vous.*"

THE INSTRUMENTS
OF POWER

"Men of genius are meteors destined to be consumed in illuminating their century," wrote Napoleon as a young man in 1790. His own career—from his emergence at Toulon to the final cataclysm at Waterloo—spanned twenty-two action-packed and dynamic years of European history, the results of which are still very much part of the pattern of life and institutions over a century and a half later. Napoleon was more than a remarkable soldier and an outstanding statesman: he was a born leader of men. This quality is fundamental to any understanding of his generalship and, indeed, lay at its foundation. It made his troops follow him where they would have followed no one else; it made his marshals accept orders they would have questioned from a lesser man; it made his adopted countrymen fight as they had never fought before—and would never fight again.

Napoleon's magnetism was certainly not physical. Of small stature, inclined to stoutness from early middle age, he was a sitting target for hostile caricaturists such as Rowlandson, Gillray and Terebenev. Nothing could have been further from reality than Canova's celebrated classical statue of Napoleon, which portrays him as a godlike being of more than human size. Nevertheless, all who met him were instantly struck by his natural authority and above all by his large, grayish-blue, almost hypnotic eyes. In manner he could be charming, considerate, crude or vulgar, and was almost invariably outspoken; yet he had the power to enthrall the soul of most any man or woman he encountered. "So it is that I, who fear neither God nor the Devil, am ready to tremble like a child when I approach him," confided the war-hardened General Vandamme.

This hypnotic fascination undoubtedly accounts for much of the mastery he exerted over all his subjects, both military and civil. It could transcend both time and space, though Napoleon learned in 1812 that the loyalty it produced was limited to his person alone; the Malet conspiracy, based upon an announcement that the emperor had perished in Russia, threw the French government into confusion for several days, and hardly any ministers or high civil servants rallied to Napoleon's heir, the infant king of Rome. Nevertheless, this magnetism formed a powerful weapon in his armory, and Napoleon made deliberate and systematic use of it to obtain his way. "If I want a man sufficiently badly," he remarked during the Consulate, "I would kiss his arse." The easy familiarity he permitted the rank and file made him highly popular. Many of his methods were deliberately theatrical. He encouraged his men to present in person their claims to promotion or a decoration, and used his knack for remembering the faces and records of old soldiers to spread a little more of his charisma during his unending inspections. The lightest rebuke could reduce a veteran grenadier to tears; the merest passing word would be treasured for life. The ultimate accolade for a soldier was to have the emperor seize his earlobe between thumb and forefinger and give it a good tweak.

Tales of personal recognition of this type were legion; if many an old soldier exaggerated his own greatest moment, there is no need to doubt the truth of most of the stories. Within hours of boarding the British man-of-war HMS *Bellerophon* in 1815, Napoleon had completely won over both officers and crew. In the sad, final years of exile, only one man proved wholly unsusceptible to the former emperor's charm—the oafish Sir Hudson Lowe, governor of Saint Helena, an undistinguished soldier who exasperated his fellow countrymen almost as much as he infuriated his distinguished captive. Few other foreigners who met him were so resistant, so there is small wonder that his effect on his own men was so electric.

Just as his personality set him apart from other men, so did the incredible range and sheer power of his intellectual capabilities. The historian Octave Aubry wrote that Napoleon possessed "the greatest personality of all time, superior to other men of action by virtue of the range and clarity of his intelligence, his speed of decision, his unswerving determination, and his acute sense of reality, allied to the imagination on which great minds thrive." The emperor's interests were not restricted to purely professional matters; they were many, embracing the arts and sciences, jurisprudence and economics, education and industry. (See pages 104–107.)

His fertile mind was rarely at a loss for a valuable idea on practically any subject. His grasp of detail was phenomenal, his powers of concentration daunting; yet he could switch from one avenue of thought to another at a moment's notice without in the least clouding his incisive mind. He once summarized his mental agility: "Different subjects and different affairs are arranged in my head as in a cupboard. When I wish to interrupt one train of thought, I shut that drawer and open another. Do I wish to sleep? I simply close all the drawers, and there I am—asleep." When dictating letters in those days before shorthand, he was capable of keeping four secretaries hard at work on as many different subjects, pacing from one to the next to rattle off a sentence without once confusing his various trains of thought. He could assimilate information at a glance and retain it in his near-photographic memory, which was particularly receptive to statistics. Many a minister and secretary of state was astounded by his mastery of departmental business, and it was practically impossible to conceal errors or shortcomings from his razor-sharp mind and ruthless scrutiny.

Behind everything lay Napoleon's phenomenal capacity for hard and unremitting toil. "Work is my element," he once asserted. "I was born and made for work. I have recognized the limits of my eyesight and of my legs, but never the limits of my working

power." A twenty-hour day was nothing extraordinary for him, and he worked his perspiring teams of secretaries and servants almost to death. Even in the boiling-hot baths that constituted one of his few luxuries, he would hold interviews, liberally splashing his impeccably attired visitors as they sweltered amid the clouds of steam. Alternatively, he would summon one of his intimates to read to him from state papers or, more rarely, some novel.

On campaign his routine was arduous in the extreme. He was a hard taskmaster but drove no one harder than himself. He habitually retired to his camp bed at 8:00

or 9:00 P.M. for four hours' sleep. On rising he would read the latest reports from the corps commanders on the previous day's events, dictate the necessary replies, issue any changes of orders and then retire shortly before dawn for another hour's sleep. By six in the morning, he had dressed and breakfasted, and the main work of the day would begin. First he would summon General Bacler d'Albe with his maps, and together they would crawl over them on all fours, measuring distances and driving in marking pins, red and black, as they considered future movements. Next, the emperor would often grant interviews to important personages either summoned to his presence or desirous of seeing him. Sometimes they had to wait in an antechamber for days before receiving an interview. With these matters completed, Napoleon would enter his office and go to his desk. There stacks of sorted documents would be awaiting his attention; the emperor would scrawl brief minutes in the margins of reports, dictate a quick letter to one of his secretaries or simply fling papers onto the floor if he deemed them unworthy of his attention. More dictation and brief interviews followed, and by ten o'clock the new letters and dispatches would be back on his desk awaiting his signature. A hasty glance through their contents, and a scrawled N at the bottom was sufficient to send most of them on their way. But when a matter of grave importance was involved, Napoleon would place the document on one side with the remark "Until tomorrow; night brings counsel."

After completing his routine business, the emperor would call for his horse and

Napoleon in bivouac at Wagram, the night of July 5–6, 1809. The emperor never expected comfortable quarters on the eve of, or during, a major battle. Here he is napping in a chair near the customary bonfire while his staff anxiously waits for him to awake and give orders for the second day's fighting against Archduke Charles.

set off accompanied by his "little headquarters" to inspect a unit or visit a senior headquarters. He was firmly convinced of the importance of a commander in chief seeing and being seen, and the incessant inspections, reviews and parades gave him the opportunity of assessing the morale and mettle of his men. On days of battle, he would issue the grand tactical orders to his generals and then let them get on with the job, leaving him free to watch the crucial timings, the positioning and deployment of reserves and the correlation of messages and reports from the various sectors. He would also ride among the ranks waiting to move into action, cheering and inspiring them with his words, and so heedless of his own safety that at one critical moment of the Battle of Aspern-Essling in 1809 the Imperial Guard threatened to ground arms *"si l'empereur ne se retire pas."* On other, rare, occasions, when feeling off-form or ill, as at Borodino, Napoleon would spend the entire day in the rear taking scant interest in the action, merely doubting the authenticity of every report and refusing to release reserves.

Back from the day's ride, Napoleon would return to his desk to read the latest news and digests, taking action as necessary. For information he drew upon his *carnets* (notebooks of carefully updated information), Savary's spy reports and the *résumés* prepared by Berthier's staff.

Meals were at the best of times haphazard affairs. A frugal luncheon was normally taken in the saddle or with the officer of a unit he was visiting, but the timing of the evening meal was rarely consistent. Nevertheless, the emperor expected food to be ready the moment he decided to eat, and the imperial cooks often found themselves preparing and discarding endless meals while awaiting their master's pleasure. Napoleon rarely dined alone; he usually sat down with Berthier or, in his absence, with other close associates or distinguished visitors to his headquarters. His servants recorded that Napoleon ate quickly—twenty minutes being the average time for a meal—and as often as not in silence; he ate little, and drank even less, but was partial to an occasional glass of his favorite Chambertin.

After-dinner relaxation was rare, but sometimes the emperor would call for cards and play pontoon or whist, cheating extensively and consequently always emerging the winner. After a final conference with Bacler d'Albe, the emperor would retire to his camp bed, but even then the harassed "household" could hardly relax, for at any moment the well-known voice would be heard calling for an aide or a secretary to take dictation.

Napoleon believed that the way to screw the maximum effort out of his officers was to keep them in a state bordering on nervous anxiety. Normally his mood was fair and just, but nobody could ever be sure that one of those redoubtable rages or fits of severity was not imminent. He rationed his smiles and jokes, and had few favorites. He often played his subordinates—particularly the marshals—against one another, adopting the maxim of Caligula: *"Divide et impera."* He expected instant obedience and would tolerate nothing less. Even Berthier, who was permitted more familiarity than anyone else, was occasionally driven to near-despair by his ever-critical master. "I am being killed by hard work," he once lamented in 1812, "a mere soldier is happier than I."

"I am today at Gera, my dearest love," Napoleon wrote to Josephine in October 1806, shortly before Jena-Auerstädt, "and things are going very well. . . . My health remains excellent, and I have put on weight since my departure. Yet I travel from 20 to 25 leagues a day, on horseback, in my carriage etc., I retire to rest at eight o'clock and rise at midnight. I sometimes imagine that you will not have yet retired to bed." Yet we know that Napoleon's endurance was not as great as it has sometimes been represented. While he never seems to have suffered from insomnia, he needed regular sleep, according to his valets, even if the amount was limited. He had the happy knack of being able to catnap; even amid the din of Wagram in 1809, he stretched himself out on his bearskin rug for a short sleep. He was quite frequently ill, with ill-health having a bearing on his showings at Borodino and Waterloo. His irregular eating habits affected his digestion, and he suffered persistently from both piles and bladder trouble.

At a time of crisis, he could work from two to three days without real pause, although he felt the toll later on. Between September 18 and 19, 1806, for example, Napoleon is known to have dictated no less than 102 orders and letters, in effect launching a complete campaign in all its planning and administrative aspects. Clearly, he possessed immense reserves of nervous energy to make such feats possible; but beneath the calm surface great passions lurked, which sometimes led to tearing rages. He would not hesitate to use his riding crop on the heads and shoulders of officers and servants, and at least once he kicked a minister in the crotch. On another occasion, he seized Berthier by the throat and hammered his head against a stone wall until the paroxysm subsided. Normally, however, he retained strict control over his emotions, using them as instruments of his will. Nevertheless, there are those who subscribe to the belief that he suffered from hystero-epilepsy, the so-called conqueror's syndrome.

Whatever the views of enemy propaganda or critics, he was no monster. He probably wielded more power than any man who lived before the twentieth century, but it is amazing how much time elapsed before he succumbed to its temptations. Throughout his career, he was more interested in the accumulation of the *means* of power than in its unbridled employment.

He always stressed that he was a realist, but there was also a strong streak of fatalism in his makeup. "All that is to happen is written down. Our hour is marked and we cannot prolong it a minute longer than fate has proclaimed." In the end his "sense of destiny" affected his judgment as a realist and led to the irrational obstinacy of the last years of his decline and fall.

This, then, was the personality that captivated a generation of Frenchmen. (For a fuller analysis of his charismatic appeal, see chapter 7.) Added to it was an extraordinary military talent that ensured his immortality as one of the truly great generals of modern history.

Napoleon once listed the three basic requirements for successful generalship: concentration of force, activity and a firm resolve to perish gloriously. "They are the three principles of the military art that have disposed luck in my favor in all my operations. Death is nothing, but to live defeated is to die every day"—which, indeed, was destined to be his own fate. A fourth principle might be added to these three, and occurs repeatedly in the emperor's letters and dispatches: the importance of surprising the enemy at both the strategic and tactical levels of warfare.

Utilizing his great mental powers, he was in the habit of thinking through any military problem days, even months, in advance. This analysis was no light affair, and Napoleon once likened the effort involved to that of a woman bringing a child into the world. He invariably thought a problem through to the very bottom and examined it from all sides, making allowance for every conceivable complication. Even then he was not satisfied, but left some space for pure chance, which he gave a mathematical value in his calculations. Thus many of his seemingly inspired and opportunistic adjustments of plans in midcampaign were in fact preconsidered concepts, and it was rare for a situation to find him completely at a loss.

Napoleon was positive that "a military leader must possess as much character as intellect—the base must equal the height." He was liberally endowed in both respects. He was also convinced that "a general's principal talent consists in knowing the mentality of the solider and in gaining his confidence." He mastered most of the psychological aspects of man management early in his career. Battle honors, swords of honor, promotions, titles, decorations and financial rewards were lavishly bestowed on the deserving. Those who let him down without good reason were mercilessly castigated. "Quartermaster General," the young general declaimed before two recalcitrant units in 1796, "let it be inscribed on their colors: 'They no longer belong to the Army of Italy.' " Such penalties were bitterly regretted by the recipients, who would take any steps to persuade the emperor to restore them to favor. He was thus preeminent in the skills of practical generalship as well as in the theoretical planning of great concepts.

Centralization of supreme authority was another vital tenet of Napoleon's command philosophy. "In war men are nothing; one man is everything"; and "better one bad general than two good ones." The degree of centralization he required—and achieved—was impressive. Practically every decision was taken, or at least approved, by the emperor in person, and his contemporaries marveled that he continued to run a war and a continental-sized empire at the same time. So long as his armies remained of manageable proportions, his unique command methods functioned surprisingly well; the French corps marched over Europe in a well-coordinated pattern, the whole being directed by a single master intelligence. In later years, however, his desire for rigid centralization became a snare and a delusion.

Behind everything else lay Napoleon's boundless ambition. This, allied with great and ruthless ability, formed a fertile breeding ground for both achievement and disaster. For many years Napoleon followed a worthy inspiration; only later in his life did the ideal he set himself become tarnished.

Every human quality unfortunately has its perversion, and with the years of near-limitless power, Napoleon's abilities began to atrophy or produce sad distortions. Censorship, police terror, and the very growth of the empire's boundaries—all were evidence of incipient megalomania. The emperor's ambition became increasingly self-centered. The unscrupulous treatment of the Spanish royal family at Bayonne, the earlier execution of Enghien, the humiliation of Prince Hatzfeldt at Berlin in 1806, the shoddy treatment of the king of Prussia at Tilsit—all were indications of growing tyranny. Even his allies were treated with condescension and without tact. This lack of what Bismarck called "the golden quality of statesmanship" made it impossible for

Napoleon to convert a former enemy into a convinced ally, however great the personal charm he could exert when he chose. Every ally was forced to accept the status of a vassal; every defeated foe became a resentful satellite.

The same lack of tact contributed to his illogical and extreme vendettas. The struggle with Britain took on all the irrational overtones of a Mafia feud, which led Napoleon into making his cardinal error of grand strategy: the declaration of all-out economic warfare in late 1806, which rebounded upon his own head with a vengeance, and ultimately drove him toward those fatal military involvements with Spain and Russia. As one minister of the Empire remarked: "It is strange that though Napoleon's common sense amounted to genius, he never could see where the possible left off. . . ." Here, if anywhere, lies one major clue to Napoleon's ultimate defeat. Even his military talents declined in certain respects. There were still flashes of the old genius—as at the Beresina and in 1814—but moral and physical bankruptcy warped his grand strategic judgment on a number of critical occasions.

As a military theorist, Napoleon was neither original nor revolutionary. His major contribution to the "bless'd trade" lay in the executive aspect, the acid test for any commander. The gulf between precept and practice is immense, and a soldier's mastery of great strategic concepts is often less important than his ability to overcome the myriad practical difficulties encountered day to day; but Napoleon was highly skilled in both areas. At the root of his success lay "an infinite capacity for taking pains"—one definition of genius—rather than immense original thought.

His largely undeserved reputation as a theoretical innovator springs from several sources. Napoleon was only too pleased to have his contemporaries believe him to be a unique military phenomenon. His main means to this end was steadfastly *not* to explain his methods in any great detail, or even in outline, thus fostering an illusion of sublime and unique abilities incapable of comprehension by ordinary mortals. It is notable that he never instituted a staff college or institution of higher training for his more senior officers, an omission he came to regret after 1812, when his detached commanders were left very much on their own—a responsibility they were neither eager nor trained to assume. Napoleon's reasons were, as ever, complex. If he liked to bask in a reputation of almost magical personal skill, he was also from first to last a wily opportunist. Aware that he had climbed to power by ruthless means, he always had that sneaking fear known to every dictator that he might one day be replaced by an able subordinate; he therefore saw little sense in imparting his innermost military secrets to men who might come to be his rivals.

His enemies were for many years prepared to be dazzled by Napoleon's image as the super-general, for this at least helped excuse their own proven shortcomings as commanders. Eventually, the Allies began to catch glimmerings of what Napoleon was about, and this enabled them to institute organizational reforms and to devise countermeasures that, added to the atrophy and distortion of Napoleon's ambitions and military systems, served ultimately to bring him down. Even then, their success left them surprised. A few foes, however, were capable of learning from their mistakes—and those of others—Archduke Charles of Austria, General Gneisenau of Prussia and the great duke of Wellington being of this select number. Wellington clearly discovered part of Napoleon's secret before he set out for the Peninsula in 1808, for he once said:

I have not seen them [the French] since the campaign in Flanders, when they were capital soldiers, and a dozen years of victory under Bonaparte must have made them better still. They have, besides, it seems, a new system of strategy which has out-manoeuvred and overwhelmed all the armies of Europe. . . .

My die is cast, they may overwhelm me but I don't think they will out-manoeuvre me. First, because I am not afraid of them, as everybody else seems to be; and secondly, because if what I hear of this system of manoeuvre is true, I think it a false one against steady troops. I suspect all the continental armies were more than half-beaten before the battle was begun—I, at least, will not be frightened beforehand.

Here we have two clues to the basic ingredients of Napoleonic warfare. First, the emperor dominated his opponents psychologically, keeping them acutely apprehensive, bewildered and off balance. The second and related tenet was to gain, and retain, the initiative. There are no truly defensive campaigns fought by Napoleon before 1814, and even then he clearly believed that "the best form of defense is attack." Napoleon employed speed, deception and surprise to mount blitzkrieg attacks of great energy. "I may lose ground, but I shall never lose a minute," he once claimed; and "Ground we may recover, time never."

By 1804, and possibly from 1800, he had one immense advantage to aid him. As early as 1796 he had stressed the primordial importance of true unity of command. As head of state, he alone decided policy or "grand strategy"; he selected objectives, decreed alliances, adopted or rejected plans. As senior commander in the field, he directed the "grand tactics"—the day-to-day movements, broad plans of battle and disposition of reserves, which were equally vital ingredients of success. The only military area in which he did not actively intervene after 1799 was that of minor tactics; he left the details of fighting techniques to his subordinates, but he made clear to one and all his preference for *l'ordre mixte* and massed batteries. In sum, Napoleon had a firm finger on the pulse of the French war machine, and though the system would ultimately develop grave weaknesses, this high degree of centralized authority, fully developed from 1804, was one major secret of his shattering successes.

Napoleon's innate conservatism as a soldier can be illustrated by several telling examples. Many of his military concepts were drawn directly from his study of history and military affairs, and then improved upon and made to work by that ruthless, practical *daemon* that was the hallmark of his genius. To the end of his life, he paid tribute to the seven commanders he believed great—Alexander, Hannibal, Caesar, Gustavus Adolphus, Turenne, Eugene and Frederick the Great. The last-named had a particularly strong influence over him. Many of Napoleon's maxims and military sayings have parallels in Frederick's writings, and he freely borrowed (before transforming) Frederick's strategic concept of the central position and adapted the oblique order for part of his grand tactical system. Others who conditioned his thought were Guibert (the prophet of the nation-in-arms and near-total war), Bourcet, Turpin de Crissé, the Welshman Lloyd and the chevalier de Folard. As for the theory and employment of artillery, he followed the work of Gribeauval as interpreted by the Du Teil brothers.

Napoleon benefited greatly from the reforms introduced into the French army following the humiliating defeats of the Seven Years' War in the mid-eighteenth century. Under the supervision of the duc de Broglie, some effort was made to tackle the abuses associated with the purchase of commissions, and the development of experimental mixed divisions of all arms began again. Infantry tactics were also being reconsidered, the proponents of fighting in the traditional linear formations being challenged by the champions of the column. The outcome was the *ordre mixte*, whereby formations in column were linked by others in line, thus combining the advantages of shock and fire action. Also, the year 1777 had seen the introduction of an improved flintlock musket, destined to remain in French service until the 1830s. Meanwhile, the whole art and science of gunnery had been transformed by Gribeauval, who lightened cannon by superior casting and design, improved trails and limbers, introduced interchangeable equipment and for field use standardized the calibers into four types—twelve-, eight- and four-pounders and six-inch howitzers. He also organized the guns into *compagnies*, or batteries, of eight pieces and greatly improved training schedules for artillery personnel. By the 1780s, these reforms were beginning to take effect, particularly in the artillery, and it was, of course, into that arm of the service that the young Bonaparte was commissioned. But it would be wrong to represent the situation as too favorable, for in other respects the forces of aristocratic, hidebound conservatism remained strongly entrenched (even Broglie was forced into exile) and only the Revolution would effect the sweeping changes still required.

From 1792, the Revolution began to transform the French services. The disappearance of much of the officer corps, either purged or fled, caused confusion in the infantry and cavalry. Nevertheless, under the inspired leadership of Lazare Carnot, the "organizer of victory," the revolutionary armies managed to survive the perils of the first years of the war and rapidly began to put their house in order. A rudimentary general staff organization made greater control of the war effort possible, while the adoption of various measures leading to conscription in 1798 provided a reservoir of soldiers, making larger armies available.

Two other developments of great significance were the concept of the nation-in-arms—the wholesale mobilization of the state's resources to support the war effort—and the extemporized doctrine of making war pay for war. In the area of supply, this meant requiring the troops to "live off the countryside" for all but the most rudimentary rations. It was a doctrine of sheer necessity rather than deliberate design, for to support the vastly increased numbers of troops sent to the frontiers at the crisis of the Revolution in 1792 was simply beyond the capacity of the administrative machinery. Surprisingly the new idea worked, at least in the relatively fertile and productive areas of Italy and central Europe, and the increased mobility that the lack of huge convoys and prestocked magazines afforded the armies of republican France would, under Napoleon, transform the conduct of campaigns.

The Revolution also produced, by natural selection, a whole class of leaders, Napoleon himself being, of course, the most conspicuous example. Early experiments with the election of officers proved unsatisfactory, but from 1793 promotion to even the highest ranks became based solely on talent (and political reliability). The proverbial *bâton* was "in every soldier's knapsack" if he could prove his ability, and the very real prospects of advancement served as an invaluable inducement to valor and meritorious service. A number of Napoleon's future marshalate were already soldiers of distinction and officer rank under *l'ancien régime*—Berthier, Davout and Sérurier being among the most notable examples. Others were sergeant majors or noncommissioned officers, including Massena, who earned rapid promotion during the Revolution. The "career open to talent—the tools to him who can use them," as Carlyle wrote, became a reality and resulted in a dynamic leadership of young men who proved more than a match for the more experienced but generally older and more hidebound generals of their opponents. (See also pages 89–93.)

Napoleon was also able to make use of, and to heighten, the morale of the French army. The average conscript tended to be more intelligent than his equivalent "walking musket" in the older armies, and he demanded to know what he was fighting for. Once again, the Revolution provided ideological inspiration. Danton's famous "the Motherland in danger" served to rally national sentiment behind the *tricolor* in the desperate days of 1792, and the heady slogans of the Revolution, among them "Liberté, Egalité, Fraternité," provided inspiration thereafter, as the soldiers became imbued with the idea that they were leading a worthy crusade to liberate the oppressed peoples of Europe. As the years passed, these slogans became a trifle outworn and faded, but they were replaced by an almost mystical reverence for the emperor's person; his charisma extended its magic over both officers and rank and file. As Wellington observed many years later, "I used to say of him that his presence in the field was worth 40,000 men."

Thus Napoleon was not called upon to create a new army from first principles or to reorganize his adopted country for war. The weapon was ready-forged; it required only fine tempering and then wielding with skill. He would improve the operation of many aspects of his war machine, adding a taste for *la gloire*, and institute a system of rewards for outstanding service. For the rest, he would make the most devastating use of his resources. As has been well said, "Napoleon gave nothing to the French army—except victory"; and, it is only fair to add, ultimate defeat.

Napoleon's operations, from first to last, were directed toward short, decisive campaigns. Wars of attrition (as in 1796, 1812 and 1813) were not to his liking and were contrary to his military convictions. His basic formula for success, the quick destruction of the enemy's army, engendered his most original contribution to the art and science of war—the fusing of marching, fighting and pursuing into one continuous process. There was no pause in a Napoleonic campaign. This was in contrast to his eighteenth-century predecessors—and contemporary opponents—who marched in one formation and fought in another after time-consuming conversion.

Napoleon once claimed that he never employed a "system of operations," but this statement was, at best, a half-truth. It is true that no single plan or group of principles dominated, for aspects of every campaign, operation and battle were unique. At the same time, however, a close study of the campaigns does reveal a number of basic underlying patterns or broad systems.

At the level of strategy—the movement of forces to obtain a favorable battle situation—Napoleon employed three methods, either singly or in combination. Again, they were not unique as concepts, but only in the way in which they were applied. First, and least important, was the strategy of *penetration*, often employed at the opening of a campaign when a frontier's defenses had to be pierced or when a major obstacle, such as a defended river line, had to be tackled by direct means. The aim of penetration was to induce the enemy to overextend his forces into a long cordon by mounting feint or secondary attacks before achieving a crash concentration of force to make a decisive breakthrough at one selected point, giving the enemy scant chance to offer major opposition. Examples of this operation in use include the crossing of the River Mincio at Borghetto in late May 1796 and the crossing of the Niemen into Russia in June 1812. In every such case, surprise was important to enable bridges to be thrown across a river and a bridgehead developed on the farther bank to cover the transfer of the main forces. Penetration operations of this type could be perilous if improperly prepared, as Napoleon learned to his cost at Aspern-Essling in 1890, when half his army became isolated over the River Danube in the presence of a powerful and aggressive-minded enemy army. On the other hand, the crossing of the Sambre at Charleroi on June 15, 1815, was highly successful. This maneuver was often associated with a more complex strategy based upon either of the two remaining methods.

The second method often employed was that of the *central position*, which was commonly used when the French faced a superior opponent or series of opponents. Its aim, simply described, was to divide the enemy into several parts before achieving superiority over each in turn and thus gaining a cumulative victory. For this purpose the French army was usually divided into four parts: an advance guard whose role, together with the cavalry screen, was to discover and occupy the central position, a left wing, right wing and reserve. Both wings, generally at a numerical disadvantage, would attack the neighboring enemy forces, while the reserve maneuvered to join one of the wings to build up a local superiority. If possible, part of the second wing would also be brought into the battle. Then, with the defeat of those troops who had been attacked first, the reserve would march without delay to reinforce the second wing to gain a second success, leaving part of the victorious first wing to pursue the original enemy.

This system was used, with variations, many times. The first was at Montenotte and Ceva in April 1796, shortly after Napoleon had taken over command of an army for the first time. The last was in June 1815, following the successful crossing of the Sambre. On this one occasion, Napoleon revealed his strategic intention on paper for the benefit of Marshal Ney, who was leading the left wing to engage Wellington's Allied army while Grouchy (commanding the right wing) pressed back Blücher's leading corps of Prussians. "For this campaign I have adopted the following general principle— to divide my army into two wings and a reserve: the Guard will form the reserve, and I shall bring it into action on either wing as circumstances may dictate. . . . Also, according to circumstances, I shall draw troops from one wing to strengthen my reserve."

Of course, this method had its disadvantages. Even if the strategy was successfully carried through, the outcome would rarely be total victory; at least one enemy force would survive to fight another day, as the French did not possess the strength to overwhelm both opponents, and timings were critical if the second foe was to be caught at a decisive disadvantage. Moreover, a discerning enemy might execute a straight-forward countermove; while it might not prove possible to prevent his forces from being divided, at least he could strain every nerve to keep the various components within supporting distance of one another, even after a defeat. Thus, after Ligny on June 16, 1815, Blücher's army drew off north (partly by chance, it is true) and kept

THE STRATEGY OF THE CENTRAL POSITION

A ADVANCE TO CONTACT

Base

L. of C.

A
60,000

Cavalry screen

①

Advance Guard

One day's march

②

Two-three days' march

Left Wing

Right Wing

GQG

Reserve

L. of C.

N 100,000

Base

L. of C.

B
60,000

1 On contact, the forward corps occupies the central position.
2 The main French army advances in *le batallion carré*.

B THE DOUBLE-BATTLE

Base

L. of C.

A
60,000

SA

Advance Guard

Detachment

③

25,000 for secondary attack

Forced march

GQG

③ 75,000 for main attack

MA

Base

L. of C.

B
60,000

Left Wing

Reserve

Right Wing

3 Both French wings engage; the forward corps and reserve reinforce the main attack.

C THE COUP DE GRÂCE

Base

L. of C.

A
60,000

⑥

75,000

⑤

④

Base

L. of C.

B

Overnight forced march

4 After winning the main attack, the French right wing pursues Army B, whilst
5 the French reserve and forward corps reinforce the outnumbered left wing, to
6 force a battle of annihilation against Army A with superior numbers.

within marching distance of Wellington instead of retreating along its communciations to the southeast, as Napoleon had assumed it would do. As a result, Blücher was able to afford vital assistance at the Battle of Waterloo two days later. Nevertheless, the method achieved considerable successes for the French on many earlier occasions.

Neither of these strategic methods, however, was as important as the third—the maneuver of *envelopment*. When it succeeded—it required a substantial superiority of force, at least during the critical period—the *indirect approach* (as it can also be termed) could produce the total victory that was ever Napoleon's objective. While the method could be varied infinitely in detail, its basic principles were that at the opening of a campaign, a small but highly integrated part of the French army would tempt the enemy army to make the first advance toward it. Once the enemy's attention had thus been focused on an objective, Napoleon would suddenly unleash his pre-positioned major force and rush it down the flank of the theater of operations, using any natural cover such as rivers, forests or a mountain range, supplemented by a screen of light cavalry operating in irrelevant as well as relevant areas to confuse the foe even more. The intention was to swing a substantial force across the enemy's lines of communication far to the rear of his army. A lateral river line with its bridges was the best strategic barrier to occupy in order to achieve this purpose, as the enemy's rein-forcements and supply convoys would inevitably be channeled to the available, and thus readily identifiable, crossings. Then, leaving sizable corps of observation to seal off the sector and preclude the arrival of aid for the victim, the main force would advance toward the enemy army from its rear and seek out a promising battle position.

The blow was shrewdly intended to strike at the Achilles heel of such armies—their supply and administrative systems. All contemporary armies, except for the French, were dependent on the establishment of depots and magazines and the arrival of regular supply convoys at the front. If the flow of these supplies was interrupted, and at the same time the line of retreat was severed, many a foe would be compelled to drop all further thought of advance in favor of a desperate retreat in an attempt to reestablish the lines of communication. The enemy would thus be robbed of all initiative and at the same time made psychologically uneasy. Moreover, waiting for the foe, in a preselected battle position, ready to spring, was the main French army. If the battle went well for the French, the enemy's position was likely to be almost impossible. Defeated, he had nowhere to go: the victorious French would still be blocking the line of retreat, and in front of him the original French secondary force would be pressing forward to complete his discomfiture. This method, therefore, held the prospect of annihilation for the enemy: he was left with the choice between total destruction and surrender on the best terms obtainable.

This system was ideal for the new French army with its simplified logistical ar-rangements. Without complete reliance on wagon convoys, the corps could move quickly and decisively. For the same reason, the communications of the French were not nearly as vulnerable or exposed as the enemy's, especially as Napoleon insisted that the rear lines of his army be kept close to the front, and his munitions and hospitals were moved forward regularly as the advance continued. Thus the enemy's nerve was likely to break before that of the French, and under such circumstances the foe was more than half beaten before the first shot was exchanged.

This method, in varied form, Napoleon employed at least thirty times between

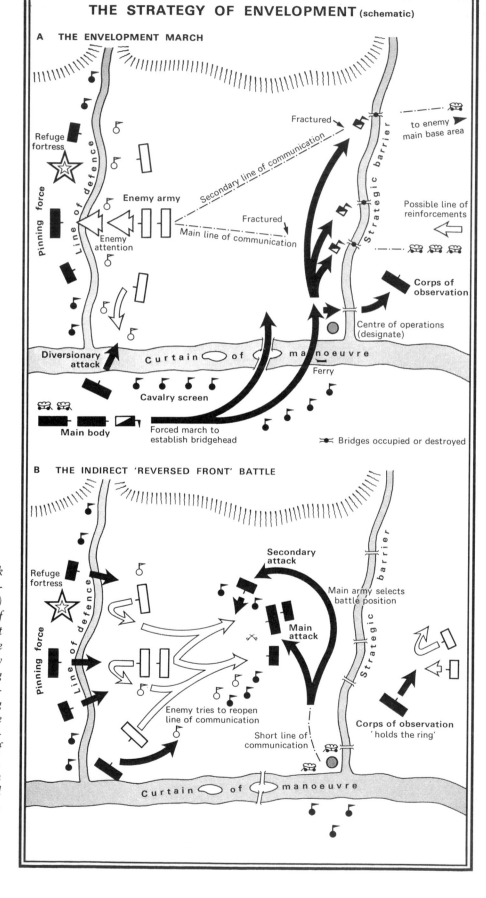

THE STRATEGY OF ENVELOPMENT (schematic)

A THE ENVELOPMENT MARCH

Refuge fortress

Pinning force

Line of defence

Enemy army

Enemy attention

Secondary line of communication

Fractured

Fractured

Main line of communication

to enemy main base area

Strategic barrier

Possible line of reinforcements

Corps of observation

Centre of operations (designate)

Diversionary attack

Curtain of manoeuvre

Ferry

Cavalry screen

Main body

Forced march to establish bridgehead

Bridges occupied or destroyed

B THE INDIRECT 'REVERSED FRONT' BATTLE

Refuge fortress

Pinning force

Line of defence

Secondary attack

Main army selects battle position

Main attack

Strategic barrier

Enemy tries to reopen line of communication

Short line of communication

Corps of observation 'holds the ring'

Curtain of manoeuvre

The surrender of General Mack at Ulm, October 21, 1805 (opposite page). (By Thevenin.) This culminating moment of perhaps Napoleon's greatest maneuver of envelopment—the surrender of the Austrian army without a major battle having been fought—shows the Austrian commander introducing himself to his conqueror, while behind and below some twenty-seven thousand men file out of Ulm to lay down their arms. Rarely has an opponent been more effectively dominated psychologically.

1796 and 1815. It was not uniformly successful, of course, for many things could go wrong to spoil the effect, but it brought off some astounding victories. Its first use, at Lodi in May 1796, failed to achieve the destruction of the Austrian army because the French timings were not perfect; as a result, Beaulieu slipped out of the trap—but at the price of surrendering control over the Milanese. It also failed at Allenstein in 1807, when the Russian Bennigsen learned from a captured message what was afoot before the net had closed around him, while the atrocious Polish weather further hampered French moves. Nevertheless, the major successes represented by the great campaigns of 1800, when Napoleon swept over the Alps to confront Melas in north Italy, using as the bait a French force bottled up in Genoa, and the first part of the campaign of 1805 (see the map on page 44), when Murat distracted Mack's attention while Napoleon swept from the Rhine to the Danube to encircle Ulm from the rear and induced the enemy to capitulate without a major battle, demonstrate the potential of the concept. So does the campaign of 1806, when Napoleon distracted the Prussians by having his brother Louis mount demonstrations toward Hamburg from the Rhine while the mass of La Grande Armée traversed the defiles of the Franconian Forest to penetrate deep into Saxony, there ultimately to find a great double victory at Jena-Auerstädt.

Once again, however, there were effective countermeasures available once the enemy had learned what to expect at the hands of Napoleon and his armies. A decade of defeat taught some hard lessons, but these were assimilated, and once Napoleon

became more predictable, much of the hypnotic effect of his devastating maneuvers began to wear off. To call Napoleon's bluff (for that, after all, was what lay at the base of his methods) required the massing of large quantities of ready-to-use supplies immediately behind the army—to lessen the practical effects of Napoleon's appearance in the more distant rear—and a steady determination to press ahead against the smaller French force to the fore and the targets beyond, leaving the French to do their worst in the rear. Thus Blücher aborted Napoleon's rush up the River Mulde to attack his rear before Leipzig in 1813, and the following year the Allies called the emperor's bluff for the last time by ignoring his seizure of Saint-Dizier and pressing ahead for the ultimate goal of Paris. They became aware that the secret of success was to avoid Napoleon in person and to concentrate on his lieutenants, thus robbing him of initiative and control by compelling him to repair the damage inflicted on his outlying detachments. Nevertheless, if Napoleon does stand accused of becoming predictable and lacking originality, there is also no denying the fifteen years of triumph his methods afforded him.

It would be erroneous to claim that each campaign was based on only one of these maneuvers, for Napoleonic warfare was highly complex, an ever-shifting kaleidoscope of moves and intentions that as often as not left the foe completely bewildered. Thus one strategic maneuver often led into another of a different type. The Italian campaign of 1796 started on the Ligurian coast as a maneuver of the central position designed to separate the Piedmontese and Austrians, developed into a strategy of envelopment in the Po valley, became a strategic penetration on the River Mincio and was then transformed into a whole series of maneuvers based upon the central position to defeat successive Austrian attempts to relieve Mantua. Similar patterns are equally detectable in later campaigns.

Napoleon's strategy would not have worked had his grand tactics and organization not complemented his overall designs. The concept of the strategic battle was one of Napoleon's most telling contributions to the art and science of warfare. His fusion of maneuver, battle and pursuit into one devastating process has already been mentioned, and the strategic battle was the climax of the process. "It is often in the system of campaign that one conceives the system of battle," he once wrote, and there was often a close similarity between the grand tactical plan of a number of major battles and the strategies of envelopment and central position. This is what made the fusion of marching and fighting a reality.

Before describing these combinations, it is important to examine the means that made possible both the strategies and the battles. Both were built on the *corps d'armée* organization and the Napoleonic doctrine of "concentration and dispersal."

The *corps d'armée* grew out of the experiments of de Saxe, Broglie and Dubois-Crancé. It was the descendant of the "legion" of 1745, the "grand divisions" of the 1770s and the "mixed divisions" of the Revolution. It was not a Napoleonic idea as such, though Napoleon fostered and expanded its development to the logical limits; the first real corps per se were those employed by General Moreau in Germany in 1800. However, on occasion, Napoleon made use of ad hoc groups of divisions in both 1796 and 1800 in north Italy, but his ideas on the subject came to full practical fruition only between 1803 and 1805.

In the simplest of terms, a *corps d'armée* was a miniature army, containing elements

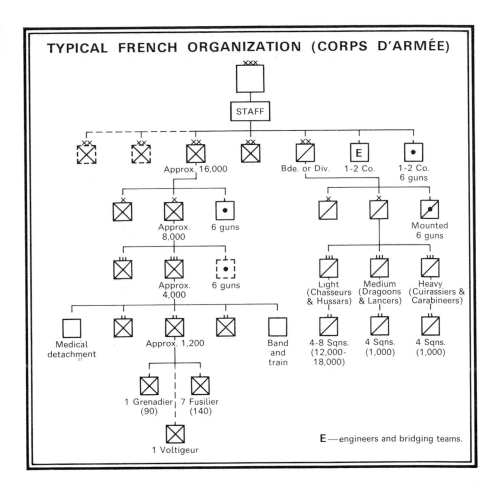

TYPICAL FRENCH ORGANIZATION (CORPS D'ARMÉE)

STAFF

Approx. 16,000

Bde. or Div.   1-2 Co.   1-2 Co.
6 guns

Approx. 8,000   6 guns

Mounted
6 guns

Approx. 4,000   6 guns

Light (Chasseurs & Hussars)   Medium (Dragoons & Lancers)   Heavy (Cuirassiers & Carabineers)

Medical detachment   Approx. 1,200   Band and train   4-8 Sqns. (12,000-18,000)   4 Sqns. (1,000)   4 Sqns. (1,000)

1 Grenadier (90)   7 Fusilier (140)

1 Voltigeur   E—engineers and bridging teams.

of infantry, cavalry and artillery besides medical and supply services, together with a staff. Their command was generally entrusted to a senior general or, from 1804, to a marshal. In size they varied enormously, some comprising barely fifteen thousand men, others as many as thirty thousand or even more, depending upon the intended role of the formation and the emperor's estimation of the capabilities of the commander. Their composition often fluctuated even in midcampaign or on the very eve of battle, as Napoleon would move a division from this corps to that or even create a completely new formation from transferred components, as his restless mind devised subtle solutions to strategic problems. The fluidity of the system was a feature that time and again hopelessly confused enemy intelligence as it tried to assess French strengths and intentions.

In addition to unsettling enemy intelligence, the corps afforded Napoleon a number of other important advantages and opportunities. Perhaps the most important of all was the fact that a corps, a miniature army, was capable of fighting alone for a time against considerably superior enemy forces until help could be brought its way. Napoleon wrote to his stepson, Eugène, in 1809:

Here is the general principle of war—a corps of 25,000–30,000 men can be left on its own. Well handled, it can fight or alternatively avoid action, and maneuver according to circumstances without any harm coming to it, because an opponent cannot force it to accept an engagement, but if it chooses to do so it can fight alone for a long time. A division of 9,000–17,000 men can be left for an hour on its own without inconvenience; it will contain a foe several times more numerous than itself, and will win time for the arrival of the army.

This ability to face substantial odds without courting complete destruction had another important implication. A corps could be safely routed through the countryside along its own axis of advance. This ability often increased both overall range and mobility because the available roads would be reserved for the use of only a single major formation in any one sector; moreover, it also assisted "living off the countryside," as each corps would be provided with its own area of subsistence. Thus, the French army habitually moved over large distances in a web of scattered (but carefully coordinated) *corps d'armée*—as in the great sweep from the Rhine to the Danube in 1805— that could completely fox the enemy concerning the army's ultimate intentions, as reports would arrive from every quarter indicating enemy columns on the march toward unspecified objectives. These characteristics of mobility, subsistence and security were advantages that old-fashioned armies, moving along a single set of roads in a narrow area, unit behind unit, could never enjoy. Equally important, the system often enabled the emperor to leave open his strategic and tactical options until the last moment. The secret was to ensure that each corps was always within twenty-four hours' marching distance of one or more of its neighbors and within thirty-six to forty-eight hours' march of the greater part of the army so that any particular formation could be reinforced, or diverted elsewhere as a reinforcement, as circumstances might dictate.

This organization may have reached its ultimate refinement in 1806, in the *bataillon carré* that swept into Saxony. Operating in a vast diamond-shape formation, the French army proved capable of changing its direction of march from north to west with a minimum of delay and dislocation. All this was made possible by the flexibility and fighting capacity of the individual *corps d'armée*, which may be said to constitute the secret weapon of the Napoleonic Wars.

The corps system was the basis of Napoleon's tenet concerning "march dispersed, fight concentrated." The wider the strategic web of corps could be spread, the more likely was the army to contact the enemy. Once the contact had been established, every unit would "march on the sound of the guns" to join their embattled colleagues in a full trial of strength. By "assembly" of an army, Napoleon meant the placing of sufficient forces within range of the battlefield but not necessarily within sight of it. This was replaced by "concentration" of force as the crisis approached, and time and again Napoleon produced far more men on the battlefield—as at Austerlitz and Bautzen—than the enemy anticipated.

Napoleon's plans for fighting battles were, of course, varied. No two were exactly the same, but they fit into three broad patterns or types. As we have seen, he liked least the straightforward *battle of attrition*, with the two armies facing up to each another on equal fronts, with their respective lines of communication stretching away behind them (as for example, at Borodino). In the second type, the *double battle*, the emperor would designate a double struggle, as at Quatre Bras and Ligny on June 16, 1815, or would find himself unexpectedly committed to one, as at Jena-Auerstädt in October 1806. His favorite form of grand tactics was the *strategic battle*, which promised almost total success if it was controlled with sufficient skill. He once likened this type

NAPOLEONIC GRAND TACTICS: THE STRATEGIC BATTLE

'the scheme of campaign often contains the plan of battle:
none but superior minds can appreciate this....' (Napoleon).

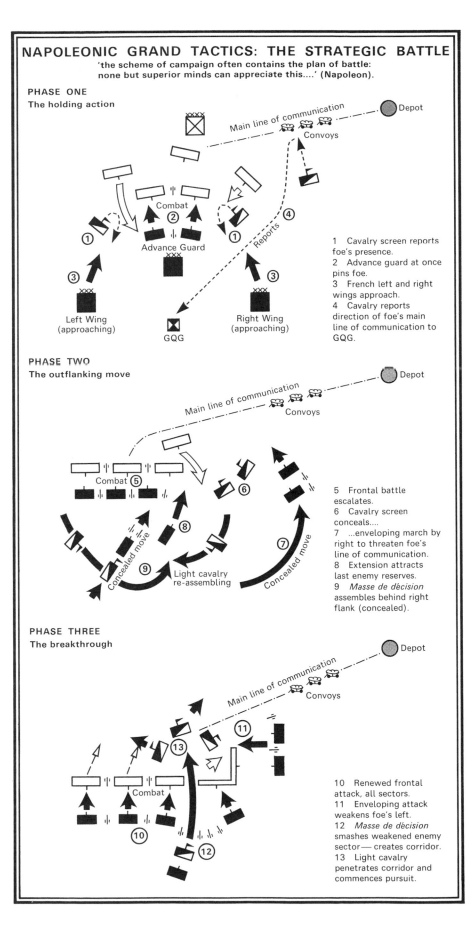

PHASE ONE
The holding action

Depot

Main line of communication

Convoys

Combat

②

Advance Guard

①

①

④

Reports

③

③

Left Wing
(approaching)

Right Wing
(approaching)

GQG

1 Cavalry screen reports
foe's presence.
2 Advance guard at once
pins foe.
3 French left and right
wings approach.
4 Cavalry reports
direction of foe's main
line of communication to
GQG.

PHASE TWO
The outflanking move

Depot

Main line of communication

Convoys

Combat ⑤

⑥

⑧

⑦

Concealed move

⑨

Concealed move

Light cavalry
re-assembling

5 Frontal battle
escalates.
6 Cavalry screen
conceals....
7 ...enveloping march by
right to threaten foe's
line of communication.
8 Extension attracts
last enemy reserves.
9 *Masse de décision*
assembles behind right
flank (concealed).

PHASE THREE
The breakthrough

Depot

Main line of communication

Convoys

⑪

⑬

Combat

⑩

⑫

10 Renewed frontal
attack, all sectors.
11 Enveloping attack
weakens foe's left.
12 *Masse de décision*
smashes weakened enemy
sector — creates corridor.
13 Light cavalry
penetrates corridor and
commences pursuit.

of engagement, which he only rarely managed to bring off, to a *pièce de théâtre* "of several acts," each leading on to the next.

Theoretically, in the sequence of a strategic battle, the French corps, preceded by their cavalry, would scour the country seeking out the enemy; as they did, news reached headquarters that one part of the army had at last found the foe. The standard order given to the formation that ran into the enemy was to engage, heedless of odds, and then alert headquarters and neighboring corps, providing them with a fixed point upon which to march. The neighboring corps would march to its assistance, thus escalating the struggle, while the emperor decided upon the form of his grand tactical plan. Once he had learned from his screen of scouting cavalry the direction in which the foe's lines of communication were running, he would often order part of his uncommitted forces to march by a circuitous route to place itself, secretly, in a position near the flank and rear of the enemy army, close to the roads in question. There it would lie concealed for the present.

Meanwhile, the remainder of the reserve—*cuirassiers*, horse artillery and the Imperial Guard—would be brought up behind the French front opposite the threatened enemy flank. These moves would constitute the "second act" of the drama.

The frontal battle would grow in intensity with the intention of drawing into action as many enemy reserves as possible. Once this process was sufficiently advanced, Napoleon would order the concealed corps to make its presence known, as the third phase began. Alarmed by the sudden appearance of a considerable force threatening his line of retreat, the enemy—if he was sufficiently pinned by the actions already raging—would be compelled to find a force to meet the new threat. If Napoleon's timing and calculations were correct (and the matter of timing was of the essence), this could be done only by weakening the sector nearest to the danger. Then, having allowed sufficient time to elapse for these redeployments to take effect, Napoleon would unleash his reserves—ready-massed opposite the weakened sector—pass them through the front and mount a devastating attack with battle-fresh troops, preceded by a hurricane of shot from the massed artillery.

If a breakthrough was achieved, a gap would be made through the enemy's front, and into it would pour the massed squadrons of French light cavalry, sweeping into the enemy's rear, converting defeat into disaster and heading the immediate pursuit of the survivors as the typically ruthless Napoleonic exploitation was put into operation.

It was rare for an engagement to follow these lines exactly, as, obviously, many complications arose, but Napoleon first attempted such an engagement at Castiglione in August 1796, based Friedland upon the scheme in June 1807 and certainly fought Bautzen by this method in 1813. Marengo, too, as fought, held many equivalent features and helped Napoleon to develop his concept. It would be too bold to claim that his battles were always planned along these lines, but the basic method was often present in his mind.

The emperor's interest in minor tactics was limited, and after 1800, as often as not, he left tactical matters to his subordinates. However, we do know his preference for massed batteries, for *l'ordre mixte* of column and line, and his insistence on the proper coordination of all-arm attacks. In Egypt, in 1798, he personally devised a drill for the formation of massive divisional squares of the type employed at the Battle of the Pyramids against the hordes of Mameluke horsemen. He was also convinced of the all-importance of the attack being pressed home with the greatest *élan*, provided that it proceeded from a sound defensive base that could sustain it in case of repulse or failure. He also believed that cannon were the main instruments of firepower, preferring the sabers or bayonets as shock weapons for cavalry and infantry.

The evolution of French tactics and organizations between 1792 and 1815 was partly haphazard and partly deliberate. In the early days of the revolutionary wars, the problem of making effective use of the unskilled *fédérés*—as often as not half starved, underequipped and semimutinous—had encouraged the amalgamation of two unskilled formations with every experienced one. The former mounted mass attacks in crude columns, while the latter provided the light infantry screen and musketry fire support, drawn up in line. This was, of course, an adaptation of Guibert's *ordre mixte*. Under the revolutionary requirements, the old regiments were replaced by three-battalion *demi-brigades*, which combined the functions of shock and fire action. The cavalry of the Revolution was probably the weakest part of the army, being the worst hit by the flight of officers and needing the longest time to recruit and train; at the same time, the artillery was indubitably the most professional and effective arm of the service. The guns silenced their opponents, then supported the French attacks; the cavalry did its best to check the enemy horsemen and to exploit success when it was achieved.

Over the years, the organization of French formations changed considerably. The infantry battalion of the Revolution originally comprised three companies of 330 men apiece; before 1800, however, the number of companies was raised to nine (including one grenadier company), each with between 150 and 200 men. Between 1806 and 1808, a simplification took place, the number of companies being reduced to six (including one of grenadiers and one of *voltiguers*, or light infantry). From 1803 the regiment was reintroduced in place of the *demi-brigade*. The growing popularity of light infantry led to the formations of numerous units. In 1803 there were ninety line and twenty-seven light regiments, and by 1813 there was a total of 243 formations, one-sixth of them light infantry.

The infantry column of attack was often drawn up on a two-company frontage, a formation perhaps fifty to seventy-five men wide and twelve ranks deep. A battalion in line drew up three ranks deep. Combinations of the two made the most of firepower and shock action; bullets and bayonets and adaptations of *l'ordre mixte* were employed up to divisional level. On occasion, for an attack up a defile or other restricted area, attack columns were formed on a single-company frontage. In theory, columns were supposed to deploy into line some 150 yards from the enemy, but in practice they often charged home without pausing to re-form. The light infantry formations were habitually deployed as a screen ahead of the columns, sniping at individual targets. (See also pages 97–100.)

Such commanders as the younger Kellermann, Grouchy, Lasalle and, above all, Murat rapidly transformed the cavalry. Each cavalry *demi-brigade* (later regiment) comprised four squadrons of two *compagnies* (or troops) apiece, each holding up to 116 cavalrymen. There were three categories of cavalry. The "heavies," or *cuirassiers* and *carabiniers*, eventually comprised seventeen regiments of 1,040 troopers apiece and increasingly were retained for service in the Reserve Cavalry, which was used for critical breakthroughs and was organized into divisions. Second, there were up to thirty regiments of dragoons, each with five squadrons and a total of twelve hundred men. Armed with dragoon muskets as well as swords and pistols, they usually fought on horseback; rarely, they were employed on foot. Third, there was the light cavalry—hussars, *chasseurs à cheval*, light horse (later lancers) and the like, the darlings of the ladies—totaling over fifty regiments, many of which contained up to five squadrons, or eighteen hundred sabers, apiece. These dashing horsemen habitually formed the cavalry screen and performed many reconnaissance as well as battle duties. All cavalry were trained to perform a variety of evolutions, including, of course, the charge, a carefully graduated advance that progressively picked up speed as it approached the target. They were also trained to exploit success to the utmost, the need to rally being stressed. (See also pages 93–97.)

The artillery was divided into two main types, horse and foot. Organized into *compagnies* (or batteries) of eight guns and howitzers apiece, horse artillery batteries grew rapidly in number. In 1800 there were eight regiments of foot artillery to six of horse, and the overall number grew a little, though the usual practice was to create additional batteries for already existing regiments rather than to raise new regiments. Brigaded with the *compagnies* were the *pontonniers*, or bridging trains, and battalions of artillery train troops (eight by 1800). In 1805 France possessed a total of over twenty thousand cannon, howitzers and mortars, and by 1813 artillery personnel numbered all of 103,000 men. Artillery tactics were based upon rapid fire (up to five rounds a minute) and the progressive advance to almost point-blank range of the enemy in a series of bounds. From 1806 onward, the heavier guns—twelve-pounders—were often massed in large batteries, and as the quality of the French infantry deteriorated, more guns were added at regimental and divisional levels. Formations of horse artillery and *artillerie volante* (galloper guns), together with a number of twelve-pounders, were invariably kept in army reserve under Napoleon's personal control, for use in special tasks. The most experienced artillery generals—after the emperor himself—included Marmont and Drouot. The guns fired round shot and case or canister, while howitzers fired shells as well as canister and mortars (mostly employed against buildings) fired bombs. There were also, of course, massive fortress guns that never took the field with the armies. (See also pages 100–103.)

Special mention must be made of the Imperial Guard. Originating from the Guards of the Directory and the Guides (or escort) of the Army of Italy, the Consular Guard of 1799 became the Imperial Guard in 1804, when it comprised four thousand grenadiers, two thousand *élite* cavalry and twenty-four guns. By mid-1805 it had grown to over 12,000 men, and by 1812 it numbered all of 60,000; in 1814 no less than 112,500 soldiers could claim some form of membership in the Guard—an immense and much-sought honor that carried privileges of pay and treatment as well as of prestige. The original nucleus became known as the Old Guard. In 1806 the Middle Guard was formed (eventually four regiments strong), and in 1809 the Young Guard came into existence. The first two formations were recruited from the veterans of the army, the Young Guard from the cream of the annual conscript classes. The draining off of the most experienced soldiers and NCOs into the Guard deprived the line formations of their best men, but there is no doubt that the charisma of the Guard was a factor of importance on many a battlefield, second only to that of Napoleon himself. Until 1812, the emperor proved reluctant to use this *élite* force in action, but in the last years it was frequently sent in, especially in 1813 and 1814. The Imperial Guard comprised horse, foot and guns, and thus was, in effect, in its later years, a miniature army. Standards, except possibly in the Young Guard, were maintained from first to last.

Napoleon's use of the power at his disposal can best be illustrated by a typical sequence of events. On most occasions, the French were determined to seize the initiative and attack. First, they would establish the massive "battery of position" and open fire. Its heavy bombardment was designed to shake enemy morale and inflict as much damage as possible on his most exposed formations. Under cover of the fire, swarms of light infantry would advance in open order to within musketry range and snipe at officers or gunners. After this "softening up," a series of heavy cavalry and infantry attacks would be launched. The secret of these was careful timing and co-ordination. As the light infantry drew aside, the massed squadrons of horsemen would thunder past to defeat the enemy cavalry and then, if all was going well, proceed to attack the serried ranks of infantry drawn up beyond. These charges were designed to force the regiments to form squares, rather than to achieve an immediate breakthrough. Although infantry squares were rarely broken by cavalry attack, provided that the men remained cool and steady, they presented good targets for the batteries of French horse artillery that accompanied the cavalry and proceeded to unlimber and go into devastating action at near-point-blank range.

All this frenzied activity was designed to facilitate the main attack, entrusted to the columns of infantry hurrying up from the rear. If the infantry attack was properly timed, the columns and their supporting battalions would be close to the enemy lines before the French cavalry drew off to re-form. Ideally, the French columns would catch the enemy still in square—a formation that, obviously, greatly reduced the amount of firepower that could be brought to bear against the new menace. By this time, the excitement and enthusiasm of the columns had become intense, and after deploying into line to fire a few scattered volleys, they would hurl themselves upon their weary opponents and as often as not rout them.

This was the moment for the reserves to move up and exploit the break-in, with fresh columns and horse artillery batteries forming and widening the walls of the corridor being driven into the enemy line of battle. Into and through this salient would come the massed French light cavalry, reserved for this moment, their sabers rising and falling relentlessly as they fell upon the last islands of enemy resistance, their effect being to convert local defeat into full-scale rout.

Such was one possible tactical battle of a French *corps d'armée*. A whole series of similar blows would be mounted simultaneously against different sectors of the enemy battle line, with variations according to the grand tactical plan; the cumulative effect of such pressure could be overwhelming. Only when the enemy began to use similar formations and tactical concepts did these methods begin to become less effective— as in the Peninsula, where the combination of Wellington's skill in selecting concealed battlegrounds, the general dearth of sufficient cavalry owing to the inhospitable nature of much of the Spanish terrain, his deployment of riflemen on the forward slopes to gain time and the devastating effect of reserved fire by highly disciplined battalions drawn up in protected reverse-slope positions all served to thwart the French onslaughts and turn them back in bloody ruin, one as often as not sealed by a determined bayonet charge. Nevertheless, the methods described brought the French almost a decade of unrivaled success elsewhere.

A complete survey of Napoleon's methods of war must include the nerve center that directed this impressive war machine, La Grande Armée. The direction, administration and coordination of forces that eventually numbered more than half a million men was a daunting task in the days before radio or telegraphy, and the fact that there were many deficiencies of control is less amazing than that the system worked at all. Lazare Carnot, as we have mentioned, had created the nucleus of a rudimentary general-staff organization, in his Bureau Topographique. The ministries of war and marine were situated in Paris, but their activities were taken up mainly with the administration of the conscription laws together with the equipment, supply and movement of men and the overall logistical support of the forces, rather than with matters of policy; for, from first to last, Napoleon kept the tightest personal control over the strategic direction of France's wars, on both land and sea, so that from 1804 his imperial headquarters, or Grand-Quartier-Général, was the supreme authority for the issue of his directives, at least in time of active war.

By 1812, Le Grand-Quartier-Général had expanded from some 250 officers and men to the size of a small army corps. In its heyday it comprised three main sections: the *maison*, Napoleon's personal headquarters; the general headquarters, the responsibility of Marshal Berthier, chief of staff; and the general administrative headquarters, under the *intendant*, for some time the province of Count Daru.

The *maison* was by far the most important; through it Napoleon ruled France as well as directed his campaigns. It was divided into two main, and a number of subsidiary, parts. The true nerve center, the "sanctuary of genius," as it has been called, was the emperor's cabinet, including the Bureau Topographique, or map office. This was small in size, comprising a few dozen key advisers, including civilians, of whom the most important after Berthier (who was *ex officio* a member of both senior sections of the general staff) was the obscure General Bacler d'Albe, with whom Napoleon conducted his twice-daily planning sessions. Second, there was the emperor's personal household—the officers, officials and servants responsible for his personal well-being and service under the general supervision of the marshal of the palace, Duroc, and including a considerable number of general officers serving as *aides de camp*. There were also attendant staffs provided by the key ministries in Paris—the Treasury, the Ministry of Foreign Affairs and the military ministries. In 1812, when the staff was at its largest, some of these institutions were kept well in the rear—the Ministry of Foreign Affairs, for instance, never moving farther forward than Vilna, hard by the Russo-Polish frontier.

The general headquarters was subdivided into several branches and performed much of the routine running of the army. Berthier controlled four major subsections, or *bureaux*. First of these was the chief of staff's own cabinet, roughly equivalent to Napoleon's and particularly concerned with troop movements and all matters of military intelligence. The second *bureau* was responsible for records and personnel, including the maintenance of the daily *cahiers* that detailed the fighting strength of every formation. The third concerned legal matters, including prisoners of war and deserters. The fourth was responsible for headquarters administration, including its quartering,

Order of the day issued by Marshal Berthier as chief of staff, on October 7, 1806 (opposite page). The document concerns the setting up of messenger and postal services at the outset of the campaign against Prussia. Berthier was famed for issuing no-nonsense orders that could not be misunderstood.

GRANDE
ARMEE.

ORDRE DU JOUR.

Au Quartier Général impérial, à Bamberg le 7 Octobre 1806.

D'APRÈS les intentions de l'EMPEREUR, LE PRINCE DE NEUCHATEL, MINISTRE DE LA GUERRE, MAJOR GENERAL, ordonne:

Les maitres des postes aux chevaux, dans toute l'étendue de l'Allemagne, étant dans le cas de rendre des services inportans à l'Armée, sont sous la protection spéciale de SA MAJESTE.

Lorsque les Troupes françaises occuperont un lieu de *poste*, le Commandant enverra sur-le-champ un sous-officier d'infanterie ou de cavalerie en sauve-garde chez le maitre de la poste aux chevaux, afin que sa maison, ses propriétés et ses chevaux soient respectés. Il sera exempt de tout logement militaire.

Le sous-officier en sauve-garde chez lui sera relevé aussitôt qu'il sera possible, par un gendarme.

Les nombre des chevaux de la poste étant insuffisant pour le service, il y sera pourvu par les autorités du pays, qui devront compléter le nombre de 25 chevaux toujours prets pour le service des couriers de SA MAJESTE, de ceux de l'Etat-major et des officiers chargés de missions. Les chevaux supplémentaires seront payés, suisique ceux de la poste, suivant l'usage du pays, par toutes les personnes autorisées à en prendre.

Lorsque des Maréchaux commandans en chef seront établis dans des lieux de poste, les maitres de la poste aux chevaux ne pourront en délivrer sans leur ordre.

Lorsque le Quartier impérial y sera établi ils ne pourront plus en délivrer que sur les ordres du Major-général ou du Grand-écuyer.

M. M. les maréchaux sont invités à tenir la main à l'exécution du présent ordre.

Le Major Général, Prince de Neuchatel et Valengin.

signé: Mal. ALEX. BERTHIER.

(An engraving made in 1805.) Alexandre Berthier, "short, stout and always laughing," was Napoleon's key military subordinate from 1796 to 1815, and a military engineer. His skill at transforming the emperor's often complex orders into clear instructions was unequaled. His mysterious death at Bamberg early in June 1815 deprived his master of irreplaceable services that he would badly need in the "Campaign of the Hundred Days" leading up to Waterloo.

maintenance, movement and its security. The Guard, the artillery and the engineers also ran staff organizations.

The administrative headquarters often functioned well to the rear and contained numbers of departments specializing in munitions, convoys and other aspects of logistical support, including the setting up and administration of the successive *centres d'opérations* that were established in the wake of the main army.

For operational purposes, the emperor was accompanied on inspections or the field of battle by his "little headquarters." This usually comprised Berthier, General Caulaincourt (the grand equerry and master of the horse), the marshal-of-the-day on duty, a couple of *aides de camp*, twice as many orderly officers, one page (entrusted with Napoleon's telescope), his Mameluke bodyguard, Roustam, a groom, an officer-interpreter and a soldier of the escort carrying the map portfolio. Four squadrons of Guard Cavalry habitually formed the escort under command of a general. For normal journeys, Napoleon would ride carefully trained Arab horses, of whom Marengo was the most famous, but for longer distances he would transfer to his *calèche* or his post chaise, each of which was in effect a mobile office.

Equivalent staffs, on a progressively smaller scale, existed at *corps d'armée* and divisional levels. On the whole, the system functioned reasonably well until 1812, when the problems of time and space became almost insurmountable. The staff organization was in some ways top-heavy and inadequate, with curious overlaps of function and design that did nothing to improve its performance. Nevertheless, it was the most sophisticated general-staff system in Europe until the Prussian reforms of the post-1807 period, which eventually developed into the prototype of all modern staffs, with their three main branches: general, adjutant general and quartermaster general.

All in all, the French army became a formidable weapon for Napoleon's limitless ambitions, as, indeed, did the French nation he ruled. Napoleon's was a heroic career that, for good or evil—the balanced view would say both—transformed the continent he dominated for so long. The implications of his achievements were profound, casting their shadow far into succeeding generations and leaving the Napoleonic legend itself to be debated by successive schools of historians either captivated or repelled by the sheer scale of his influence. Napoleon is not to be judged solely as a commander, or as a national leader, or even as a man. He was one of those few whose lives have to be seen as part of history itself, shaping and shaped by the evolution of nations, societies and ideas. If it dazzles the historian in retrospect, we may imagine Napoleon's impact on contemporaries who witnessed at first hand the brilliance of his rise, the finality of his eclipse, the birth and death of the star that guided, as he believed, his future and his destiny.

The Marshalate

The Napoleonic marshalate came into existence on May 18, 1804, as part of the Constitution of the Year XII, which established the Empire. Article 48 empowered the appointment of sixteen active marshals and an indeterminate number of honorific appointments. The dignity—for it was essentially a conferred civil title rather than a military rank as such (*général de division* being the senior army promotion)—brought into existence a group of *grands seigneurs* who came fifth in terms of court rank, subordinate to the emperor and empress, the other members of the imperial family, the designated grand dignitaries of the Empire and the ministers. Among the many privileges they were to enjoy was a cannon salute of eleven guns on certain official occasions.

On May 19 the first list of names was published—eighteen names in all, four of them in the honorific category, named mainly to recognize old revolutionary commanders of great merit and to represent the interests of the army in the Senate. Eventually Napoleon would appoint a total of twenty-five Frenchmen and one Pole to the dignity of "marshal of the Empire." Their selection was not purely based on military valor and attainment. Although all holders of the coveted eagle-spangled blue-and-gold *bâton* had some claim to military distinction, political considerations also played a part in the process. Thus the first eighteen *bâtons* were carefully divided among soldiers who had served on the three main war fronts: Italy, the Rhine and the Pyrenees.

Napoleon's motives in re-creating the dignity (which had been abolished by the Convention in 1793) were complex. On the one hand, he wished to unite a group of influential generals—some already devoted to him, others not—representing a balance among the main factions of the French army and to ensure that the army would accept the newly created Empire. On the other hand, he wished to integrate the military leadership into the new or revived aristocratic hierarchy he intended to establish around his throne. The marshals eventually received high aristocratic titles to add to their military preeminence: almost all became dukes, six were made princes, and two of these became kings (one, Bernadotte, prince of Pontecorvo, founding a dynasty that prospers in Sweden to this day). With the titles went estates and large sums of money in most cases, while the highest decorations of the Legion of Honor and many other honors, French and foreign, were lavished on the deserving as Napoleon defined the term—the loyal, the relations, the favorites (very few) and the talented.

But the price he demanded in return for these honors was high. The marshals were required to go on active service in command of the *corps d'armée* or in senior staff appointments year after year. They were not protected against shot and shell: fully half were wounded one or more times as marshals (Oudinot on no less than eight occasions), and three—Lannes, Bessières and Poniatowski—were killed in action or died of wounds sustained in battle. High rank was not a guarantee of personal survival in the early nineteenth century, as military leadership was carried on very much from the forward edge of the battle area (Napoleon himself, of course, being twice wounded—at Toulon [1793] and Ratisbon [1809]—and narrowly avoiding death at Arcola [1796], in front of Acre [1799] and at Arcis-sur-Aube [1814], besides surviving several assassination attempts). Four more met violent deaths outside of battle: Murat and Ney in front of firing squads, and Brune at the hands of a royalist mob (all in 1815), while in 1835, Mortier, at the age of sixty-seven, became the victim of an "infernal machine" intended for Louis-Philippe. Berthier's demise in 1815 remains a mystery; he may have been a fifth.

Even when not on campaign, Napoleon kept his marshals busy with diplomatic,

The execution of Marshal Ney, Prince of the Moskowa, on December 8, 1815, in the Luxembourg Gardens, Paris. (By Dubourg, after Goubaud.) If the opportunities offered to Napoleon's key subordinates were vast, the potential penalties were daunting. Marshal Ney was executed six months after Waterloo for having changed sides once too often. He personally gave the order to fire.

Marshal Louis Davout (1770–1823). (Colored lithograph.) Together with Massena and Suchet, "the Iron Marshal" was Napoleon's ablest subordinate, and the youngest man to be made a marshal (in May 1804). His conduct of the Battle of Auerstädt and his defense of Hamburg in 1813–14 were superb. He also had his shortcomings, as he demonstrated during the retreat from Moscow, but on Saint Helena Napoleon described him as "one of the purest glories of France."

administrative and court duties, which gave them little time to enjoy their privileges. He also fanned their rivalries and dislikes—even hatreds—believing in the benefits of "divide and rule." He intended them to be instruments of his imperial will both on campaign and in battle, and did little to encourage the development of individual talents or independent command skills by way of formal training. Three—Massena, Davout and Suchet—were truly notable commanders in their own right, and would have made names for themselves regardless of any connection with Napoleon; but many of the remainder were far from outstanding commanders at the strategic or operational level, although all were good tacticians and brave individuals able to inspire their troops.

All was well, therefore, while they remained beneath their master's eye. But when the exigencies of service separated them from the emperor (as in 1812, when Napoleon was fighting in Russia and other French troops were fighting in Spain), problems would often arise. Untrained in independent campaigning, incapable of fighting in a properly integrated command team (as no marshal would acknowledge any other as his superior), the marshals in Spain and elsewhere often allowed their personal feuds to overcome their sense of duty when Napoleon was not present to keep them in line and up to the mark; the results were defeats, disappointments and failures. War-weariness became increasingly noticeable after the disasters of 1812 and had not been unknown among the marshals in earlier years. Only those who were incapacitatingly wounded or had the fortune to incur Napoleon's wrath and were in consequence left unemployed were able to secure any real rest or time to live with their families and enjoy their privileges. In the end, the system let the emperor down badly. At Fontainebleau in April 1814, a group of marshals, led by Ney, mutinied and enforced Napoleon's first abdication. During the Bourbon restoration, most of the marhsals made their peace with the new regime and several served Louis XVIII in high positions. In 1815, when Napoleon returned from exile on Elba for the "Hundred Days," only a handful of his former marshals rallied to the *tricolor*; others continued to be loyal to the Bourbons or made themselves conspicuous by their absence from Paris, ignoring summonses from Davout (Napoleon's minister of war) or finding excuses for not complying with his orders on behalf of the emperor.

Of course, Napoleon was, from first to last, a supreme opportunist himself, and it is small wonder that his key commanders copied him in this respect, and that when the moment of supreme testing came, they looked to their individual interests. That said, the marshalate formed a fascinating and colorful group. They came from every stratum of French society, including the ranks (both commissioned and noncommissioned) of the pre-1789 Royal Army. Their ages also covered a wide span, averaging forty-four in 1804. Their characters were equally different: glory seekers, feuders, barely disguised (if disguised at all) looters on the grand scale, they left their mark on the early nineteenth century. Some were cultivated men; others the very reverse. But few military careers, whether considered individually or collectively, have ever rivaled the drama, the opportunities proffered or the penalties incurred of those of the twenty-six senior officers called to carry the *bâton* of a marshal of the Empire.

THE MARSHALS

(in alphabetical order)

Name	Dates	Apptd. marshal	Title
Augereau	(1757–1816)	1804	duke of Castiglione
Bernadotte	(1763–1844)	1804	prince of Pontecorvo (later crown prince and king of Sweden)
Berthier	(1753–1815)	1804	prince of Neuchâtel (and later of Wagram)
Bessières	(1768–1813)	1804	duke of Istria
Brune	(1763–1815)	1804	no title
Davout	(1770–1823)	1804	duke of Auerstädt (later prince of Eckmühl)
Gouvion-Saint-Cyr	(1764–1830)	1812	count (later marquis)
Grouchy	(1766–1847)	1815	hereditary marquis
Jourdan	(1762–1833)	1804	count (by the Bourbons)
Kellermann	(1735–1820)	1804 (hon.)	duke of Valmy
Lannes	(1769–1809)	1804	duke of Montebello
Lefebvre	(1755–1820)	1804	duke of Danzig
Macdonald	(1765–1840)	1809	duke of Tarentum
Marmont	(1774–1852)	1809	duke of Ragusa

Massena	(1758–1817)	1804	duke of Rivoli (later prince of Essling)
Moncey	(1754–1842)	1804 (hon.)	duke of Conegliano
Mortier	(1768–1835)	1804	duke of Treviso
Murat	(1767–1815)	1804	grand duke of Clèves (later king of Naples)
Ney	(1769–1815)	1804	duke of Elchingen (later prince of the Moskowa)
Oudinot	(1767–1847)	1809	duke of Reggio
Pérignon	(1754–1818)	1804 (hon.)	count (later marquis)
Poniatowski	(1763–1813)	1813	hereditary Polish prince
Sérurier	(1742–1819)	1804 (hon.)	count
Soult	(1769–1851)	1804	duke of Dalmatia
Suchet	(1770–1826)	1811	duke of Albufera
Victor	(1764–1841)	1807	duke of Belluno

The Cavalry

"Cavalry is useful before, during and after the battle," Napoleon once declared, indicating the universality of the roles of the mounted arm. Scouting, covering, fighting and pursuing—these were the traditional tasks of horsemen in time of war. Speed, shock, good order and carefully maintained formations, together with the correct employment of reserves, were the chief secrets of successful mounted action, but among these the emperor rated discipline as the most important.

In 1800 the French army comprised eighty-five mounted regiments of varied quality. The best were the thirty-eight regiments of light cavalry, full of keen volunteers; most of the twenty dragoon regiments were understrength, but the worst were the twenty-seven regiments of "battle cavalry," who had lost many officers through emigration and purges at the time of the Revolution. Mounted regiments were often employed in small formations attached to infantry divisions, but this practice the first consul hastened to change. The concept of the Reserve Cavalry began to develop. Each *corps d'armée* retained its division of light cavalry and dragoons, but the heavies were drawn off into organic divisions, together with the balance of the light and dragoons.

In La Grande Armée every type of cavalry was placed in one of three categories, each with specific tasks. First came the heavy cavalry, of which there were two main varieties. The backbone of the heavies came to be the famous *cuirassiers*: large men wearing horsehair-crested metal helmets and breast- and back-plates, riding powerful horses, wielding long straight swords and further armed with pistols and (later) musketoons or carbines. There were eventually seventeen regiments of cuirassiers, one of them a Dutch formation. At full establishment each was divided into four squadrons of two *compagnies*, or troops, apiece, and comprised 1,040 troopers. They were formed into autonomous divisions and invariably made up a major part of the Reserve Cavalry, together with the second variety of heavy cavalry: the two regiments of *carabiniers à cheval*, which were virtually indistinguishable from the *cuirassiers* from 1809, when they adopted brass-coated helmets and body armor. Additionally, the Imperial Guard included an elite heavy cavalry formation of its own—the Horse Grenadiers, part of the Old Guard, who bore the nickname "les Grosses Bottes" ("the Big Boots"). These troopers never wore armor but sported tall bearskins, and under Colonel Lepic they were to achieve wonders.

The French heavy cavalry received extra pay and were highly regarded throughout Europe. Their role was primarily in battle, using their formidable size and weight to ride down the opposition and to create and exploit gaps in the enemy's line of battle. In later years it proved difficult to find sufficiently good replacements and remounts, but their reputation remained intact until Waterloo.

The cavalry of the line comprised between twenty and thirty regiments of dragoons. A major problem was a shortage of horses, and until 1806 there were dismounted as well as mounted dragoon regiments; indeed, in 1804 there were two divisions of the former. All eighteenth-century dragoons were officially able to fight mounted or dismounted and carried dragoon muskets and bayonets as well as pistols and swords; but in the early nineteenth century they were normally regarded as cavalry rather than mounted infantry, except in Spain. There were generally twelve hundred dragoons to a regiment in five squadrons, but after the severe losses of horses in Russia from 1812 they generally had four, two mounted and two dismounted. Most wore brass helmets. The Old Guard cavalry had a Regiment of Dragoons from 1806.

French cuirassiers *(heavy cavalry). (Part of a painting by Meissonier.) These steel-helmeted and breast- and back-plated cavalry rode large horses and wielded long straight swords. They were justly feared by their opponents, forming part of Napoleon's Reserve Cavalry.*

"Vive l'Empereur." (By Detaille.) Hussars (wielding curved
sabres here) together with dragoons were the cavalry "maids of
all work" in Napoleon's armies.
They formed the cavalry screen
ahead of the corps d'armée,
fought in battle as needed and
led the pursuit of a defeated foe
or covered the retreat of the
French forces after a reverse.

Their functions were varied. They formed parts of cavalry screens ahead and on the flanks of the army. They were expected to protect lines of communication and to execute raids and other special missions. During the Peninsular War their importance as line-of-battle troops was enhanced by the absence of most *cuirassiers* elsewhere. Consequently, they were frequently called upon to fight Wellington's cavalry in open battle as well as to pursue guerrillas. All in all, Grouchy was one of the ablest commanders of dragoon divisions, as he demonstrated at Eylau, Friedland and in Russia in 1812.

Third, there was the light cavalry. These adventurous troopers wore the most extravagant uniforms, regarded themselves as "the darlings of the ladies," and developed their own mystique. There were several types. By 1811 there were thirty-one regiments of *chasseurs à cheval*, between ten and fifteen regiments of hussars (the most sumptuously dressed of all) and eventually nine regiments of lancers (or *chevau-légers-lanciers*), which were raised from a number of sources, including transferred squadrons (and some whole regiments) of *chasseurs* and dragoons. The light cavalry expanded when the French were called upon to fight Russian armies, which were strong in light horse and Cossacks. Hussars and *chasseurs* carried similar weaponry—sabers, carbines and pistols—and were often brigaded together to form regiments of between twelve hundred and eighteen hundred men serving in between four and eight squadrons. Light horsemen also (from 1809) carried the eight-foot lance. As might be expected, the light horsemen were strongly represented in the cavalry of the Imperial Guard. There was an Old Guard Régiment de Chasseurs à Cheval from 1804; the Company (later, Squadron) of Mamelukes first raised in Egypt in 1799, also attached to the Old Guard, like the First (1807) and Second (1810) Régiments de Chevaux-lanciers, known respectively as the Polish Blue and Dutch Red Lancers of the Guard; and three

Polish Light Horse of the Imperial Guard, 1808. (By Detaille.) This crack unit made the charges at Somosierra that opened the pass leading to Madrid, suffering terrible losses in the process. They were later equipped with lances (useful for attacking troops in square or in flight), and became known as the Polish (Blue) Lancers of the Guard.

regiments of Eclaireurs raised in 1814, four more of Gardes d'Honneur (from 1813) and the Légion de Gendarmerie d'Elite, going back to 1804.

Light cavalry duties were particularly arduous and included playing many roles in reconnaissance and pursuit. The Imperial Guard light cavalry usually provided the emperor's personal escort on campaign; Napoleon's favorite garb was the green undress uniform of a colonel of *chasseurs à cheval*. The most celebrated commanders of light cavalry included Colbert, Lasalle and Lefebvre-Desnoüettes.

Such, in barest outline, was *l'arme blanche* of La Grande Armée. There were also numerous provisional and allied regiments of all types raised for short periods of time. The mounted arm was transformed from a near-laughingstock in the Armies of the

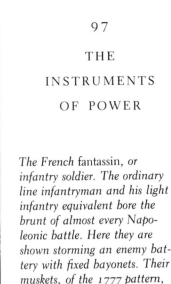

The French fantassin, or infantry soldier. The ordinary line infantryman and his light infantry equivalent bore the brunt of almost every Napoleonic battle. Here they are shown storming an enemy battery with fixed bayonets. Their muskets, of the 1777 pattern, fired twenty-four balls to the pound to a range of some 250 meters, but were accurate only at ranges of under 100 meters.

Revolution into a most formidable weapon, which perhaps saw its greatest days from late 1806 to 1812, when the horse studs of Prussia were available to supply the deficiencies in French horseflesh. The pursuit after Jena-Auerstädt was a masterpiece of light cavalry operation, and the heavy cavalry arguably saw its finest day at the Battle of Eylau in February 1807.

The Infantry

The foot soldier is the backbone of every army, and that of Napoleon was no exception. The infantry arm was organized in battalions, three of which formed a regiment from 1803, when the *demi-brigades* of the revolutionary period were given back the far older title. Two or more regiments formed a brigade, and two or more brigades made up an infantry division, which frequently also had a battery of eight-pounder cannon attached to it under command.

The main distinction within the infantry was between formations of line and light troops. By 1803 the mass of battalions had been organized into 90 line regiments and 27 light regiments. Ten years later 127 new line regiments (many of them provisional or allied formations) had been called into existence. The internal organization of a battalion varied at different periods. Until after Austerlitz, the standard three-battalion line regiment comprised a total of twenty-seven companies, or one company of grenadiers and eight of fusiliers per battalion. Each was commanded by a *chef de batallion* (major) aided by an *adjudant major* (lieutenant) and an *adjudant sous-officier* (senior warrant officer). A company was commanded by a captain or a lieutenant, and was subdivided into two *pélotons* (platoons), each with a subaltern, a sergeant and a number of corporals. The grenadier company was made up of the best soldiers with a minimum of two years' meritorious service; the minimum height was five feet five inches. They wore grenade badges and bearskins, and enjoyed extra pay and other privileges. On numerous occasions a whole series of grenadier companies were brigaded into special temporary formations for extraordinary missions—for instance, Oudinot's Grenadiers at Austerlitz—and during such periods were detached from their parent formations.

Regimental headquarters was headed by the colonel, assisted by a major, an *adjudant major* and a number of warrant officers, a quartermaster, a paymaster and an "eagle bearer" with two aides (the equivalent to British "color-sergeants" or American "senior sergeants"). There were also a drum major, bandmaster and seven musicians; a surgeon with varying numbers of assistants; and a wagon master. Four skilled craftsmen—two armorers, a tailor and a shoemaker—were also attached to headquarters, together with a regimental provost staff. An up-to-strength regiment on paper comprised 3,400 infantrymen and a company totaling 140 officers and men, not including the regimental headquarters staff.

Line regiments wore blue coats with brass buttons, white breeches and black gaiters. Crossbelts supported a *giberne* (cartridge box) holding twenty-four rounds of powder and ball, and a short sword and bayonet. A shako or forage cap was the normal headgear. A pack carried a soldier's essentials, including a rolled blanket and greatcoat. A broad gold or red stripe or stripes on the sleeve indicated noncommissioned rank, while brass shako plates bearing regimental numbers, repeated on the cartridge box, revealed formation membership. *Fantassins* carried the Charleville "1777" flintlock musket: a muzzle-loading smoothbore .70-caliber firearm, with an effective range of 250 yards or less, prone to misfire and at best capable of firing four rounds in three minutes under fighting conditions. Officers wore gorgettes upon the chest and gold epaulettes to designate rank. They carried swords and pistols; colonels and majors were normally mounted.

Light infantry were equipped in much the same manner, except that their buttons and embellishments were of pewter and their jacket collars were red (officers' lace being silver). The equivalent of grenadiers were called *carabiniers* and sported bearskins and epaulettes. *Infanterie légère* units were organized similarly to the line units, carried the same musket and trained under the same regulations. However, they had a reputation for greater dash and vigor, and were accordingly often used for perilous duties in advance guards, specializing in skirmishing in deployed order. One such regiment was attached to each infantry division.

In early 1804 the emperor instituted an innovation throughout the army by which one company per light infantry regiment was to be called a *voltiguer* ("leaper") company, made up of nimble soldiers. The practice was extended to the line next year, and from 1808 these companies were awarded the post of left of the line, second only in prestige to the grenadiers or *carabiniers* who formed on the extreme right.

Between 1806 and 1808 a gradual change in organization reduced a line battalion

Foot grenadier of the Old Guard. (By Detaille.) The grenadiers were the élite infantry of the army. Entry into their ranks was deemed an honor reserved only to soldiers of proven valor and experience. Members of the Old Guard enjoyed privileges of pay, rations and quarters. From 1813 many were commissioned into line regiments to inspire the new conscripts.

to six larger companies apiece: one of grenadiers, one of *voltiguers*, and four of fusiliers. The same change was made in the light infantry, who besides a company each of *carabiniers* and *voltiguers* had four of *chasseurs*.

Over the years other types of infantry formations appeared, including *légions* of foreign attached troops, cohorts of embodied National Guardsmen and the numerous provisional regiments already mentioned.

Regimental artillery was provisionally discontinued by Napoleon following the Peace of Amiens in the belief that the six-pounders were too burdensome to accompany infantry in the field, seriously curbing the troops' mobility. However, because of the progressive deterioration in the overall standard of his infantry as casualties mounted and veterans were replaced by ever larger numbers of raw recruits or foreign troops, Napoleon was induced to restore the former arrangement. From 1809 to 1810 a company of artillery comprising four four-pounders was provisionally attached to each infantry regiment, and from 1811 the practice was confirmed. Only after the losses of horses and *matériel* sustained in Russia in 1812 was it again discontinued.

The *élite* infantry formed the basic element of the Imperial Guard. Built upon the earlier Guards of the Directory and of the Consulate, the Old Guard came to comprise regiments of foot grenadiers and *chasseurs* as well as selected cavalry and artillery formations. At Marengo the Consular Guard numbered only 2,089 all ranks, but by the time of the coronation in 1804 there were 5,000 grenadiers besides 2,000 cavalry and twenty-four guns. By mid-1805 the foot component had risen to 8,000, and the size continued to increase. In 1806 Napoleon created what became the Middle Guard—two regiments of fusiliers and as many of flankers (raised from gamekeepers and forest wardens, crack shots all). Then, three years later, the emperor added the Young Guard—recruited mainly from the pick of each year's class of conscripts— who were placed in regiments of Imperial Guard light infantry, *tirailleurs* and *volti- guers*.

To serve in the Imperial Guard in whatever capacity was deemed a great honor. Except in the Young Guard, the minimum qualification was five years' service and two campaigns. The selection and transfer of suitable recruits was a continuous process. High pay and numerous privileges, including special rations, were the advantages of belonging to Napoleon's "favored children." Although the Young Guard was much used in action from the first, the emperor proved chary in sending the Old Guard "*au feu*"—much to its chagrin and discontent. This changed from the time of the retreat from Moscow, the Old Guard being much to the fore in the battles of the last years of the Empire. Some regarded the siphoning off of the most talented soldiers into an elite organization as wasteful and even demoralizing; however, the Imperial Guard also served as a training institution for junior officers. When appointed to a commission, a former guardsman carried with him into his new unit the high standards learned in the ranks of the Guard, so there were reciprocal advantages in the system, particularly in the later years.

The Artillery

"It is with guns that war is made," stated Napoleon. "Great battles are won by artillery." Since the future emperor commenced his career as a gunner, there is little wonder that he paid great attention to this arm of the French forces, setting up a special headquarters for it in 1800 and militarizing the drivers of the artillery train at much the same time. Further improvements and reforms were continually being called for during the years of the Empire. Some were attained, others not; but with a distinguished body of senior gunners—Marmont, Lauriston, Drouot and Eblé prominent among them—the French artillery formed a redoubtable part of the army.

In the Consulate period there were eight regiments of "foot" artillery, six of "horse," two battalions of *pontonniers* and eight more of train troops. In 1813 there were nine regiments of artillery *à pied*, each comprising twenty-seven companies (or batteries) of guns (in earlier years they had held only twenty companies). Additionally, in 1800 there were six regiments of horse artillery (*artillerie à cheval*), and this number was retained throughout the Consulate although the number of companies had risen to eight apiece by 1814. Whereas artillerymen of horse formations were mounted, foot artillerymen marched alongside their pieces and were intended to keep up with walking cavalry. *Pontonniers*, as their title implies, repaired or set up bridges. After the losses sustained in Russia in 1812, a third battalion was created (an earlier third formation

(Photograph by the author.) Nicknamed "the Emperor's Beautiful Daughters," twelve-pounder guns were the real killers of the Napoleonic battlefield. With a range of up to eighteen hundred meters, they were formidable weapons, requiring a crew of fifteen men to fire, load and move.

had been absorbed into the second in 1801). Once again varying numbers of companies were assigned to each. There were also units of skilled artificers and armorers, and fortresses were partially manned by companies of veterans. The *train d'artillerie* battalions had five, then six companies each, and additional battalions were added as the years passed. Thus in 1812, with the Russian campaign in view, a dozen were raised, to be responsible for ammunition resupply and for the movement of all heavy artillery stores, not least the guns themselves. The basic artillery uniform was dark blue with red linings and facings of various types according to branch. The train troops wore gray uniforms piped in blue. By 1813 the overall artillery arm comprised 103,000 men. Eight years earlier, the total number of pieces available (including fortress pieces) had comprised 4,506 large, 7,366 medium and light, 8,320 howitzers and 1,746 mortars. Many of these were kept in depots or fortresses. The largest number taken into the field with a single army seems to have been the 1,393 that crossed the Niemen in June 1812.

The French artillery and engineers had been the least affected by the purges and emigrations of officers during the Revolution. Therefore, less rebuilding was in some ways required, although improvements were always being studied and sometimes implemented. A good gun crew could theoretically fire up to five rounds a minute, although two and a half seems to have been the average. Thus a company of six cannon, using prepackaged rounds containing ball and powder, could fire some fifteen shots in one minute. The larger the gun, the slower the rate of fire: thus the "Emperor's beautiful daughters," as the army nicknamed the twelve-pounders, fired only one round in sixty seconds.

The largest reform of the artillery was that masterminded by Marmont and carried out during the Peace of Amiens, leading to the so-called System of the Year XIII. The numbers of guns were considerably increased, the administration simplified and the types and calibers of cannon regulated. The Gribeauval System of the 1770s was based on twelve-pounders, eight- and four-pounders and six-inch howitzers, and was continued during the Revolution. Among the changes effected by Marmont was the

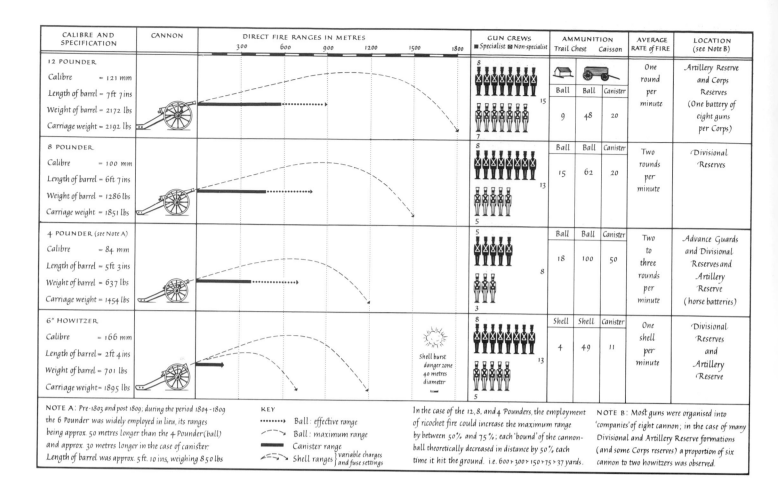

CALIBRE AND SPECIFICATION	CANNON	DIRECT FIRE RANGES IN METRES	GUN CREWS ■ Specialist ⊠ Non-specialist	AMMUNITION Trail Chest — Ball	AMMUNITION Caisson — Ball	AMMUNITION Caisson — Canister	AVERAGE RATE of FIRE	LOCATION (see Note B)
12 POUNDER Calibre = 121 mm; Length of barrel = 7ft 7ins; Weight of barrel = 2172 lbs; Carriage weight = 2192 lbs		300 600 900 1200 1500 1800	8 specialist / 7 non-specialist (15)	9	48	20	One round per minute	Artillery Reserve and Corps Reserves (One battery of eight guns per Corps)
8 POUNDER Calibre = 100 mm; Length of barrel = 6ft 7ins; Weight of barrel = 1286 lbs; Carriage weight = 1851 lbs			8 / 5 (13)	15	62	20	Two rounds per minute	Divisional Reserves
4 POUNDER (see Note A) Calibre = 84 mm; Length of barrel = 5ft 3ins; Weight of barrel = 637 lbs; Carriage weight = 1454 lbs			5 / 3 (8)	18	100	50	Two to three rounds per minute	Advance Guards and Divisional Reserves and Artillery Reserve (horse batteries)
6″ HOWITZER Calibre = 166 mm; Length of barrel = 2ft 4ins; Weight of barrel = 701 lbs; Carriage weight = 1895 lbs		Shell burst danger zone 40 metres diameter	8 / 5 (13)	Shell 4	Shell 49	Canister 11	One shell per minute	Divisional Reserves and Artillery Reserve

NOTE A: Pre-1803 and post 1809; during the period 1804-1809 the 6 Pounder was widely employed in lieu, its ranges being approx. 50 metres longer than the 4 Pounder (ball) and approx. 30 metres longer in the case of canister. Length of barrel was approx. 5ft. 10 ins, weighing 850 lbs.

KEY
- ·········· Ball: effective range
- ‒ ‒ ‒ Ball: maximum range
- ▬▬▬ Canister range
- ‒‒‒ Shell ranges } variable charges and fuse settings

In the case of the 12, 8, and 4 Pounders, the employment of ricochet fire could increase the maximum range by between 50% and 75%; each 'bound' of the cannon-ball theoretically decreased in distance by 50%, each time it hit the ground. i.e. 600 > 300 > 150 > 75 > 37 yards.

NOTE B: Most guns were organised into 'companies' of eight cannon; in the case of many Divisional and Artillery Reserve formations (and some Corps reserves) a proportion of six cannon to two howitzers was observed.

replacement of the four-pounder, "regimental" guns with the larger six-pounders; until 1809 the use of regimental artillery was discontinued, as the new pieces were rather too bulky for attachment to infantry regiments. Also, a number of the eight-pounder divisional guns were replaced by death-dealing twelve-pounders to improve range and hitting power on the battlefield. A five-and-a-half-inch howitzer was introduced in preference to the six-inch variety. It became standard practice from 1804 for twelve-pounders to be attached to army corps (one or two batteries each) and to the Artillery Reserve, while the eight- and six-pounders were used for advance guards and divisional tasks. Every company officially comprised eight pieces, six of the designated caliber and (to provide a broader capability) a pair of howitzers.

From 1809, once again recourse was made to regimental artillery—a development reflecting the deterioration in infantry recruit standards. By 1813 Napoleon was trying to provide five guns for every thousand men of all categories. The nearest he came to this figure was probably at the Battle of Leipzig in 1813, when he achieved three per thousand.

The basic statistics of the main French artillery pieces can be observed in the accompanying diagram. The French employed four types of artillery ammunition. Solid round shot, the range of which could be increased considerably by utilizing ricochet (bouncing) fire, was the most commonly fired. Canister shot, an antipersonnel weapon used at short range, consisted of tin cans filled with musket balls. Explosive shells (hollow round shot packed with explosive and detonated by a lit fuse) were used

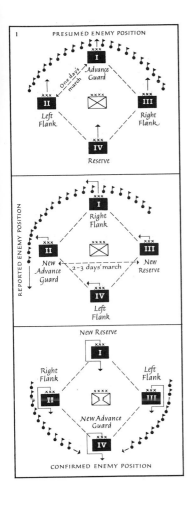

(By Ramon.) The Imperial Guard had its own artillery, including light six-pounder guns (with a range of 1,250 meters) in batteries (or "companies") of horse artillery who were supposed to be able to keep up with cavalry formations in action. A complete horse artillery unit (six guns and two six-inch howitzers) needed well over a hundred horses to draw it and its ammunition and stores.

by howitzers and mortars, often for destroying buildings or achieving air bursts over formed bodies of enemy troops. And the French (particularly coastal batteries) occasionally made use of red-hot shot when they wished to set fire to targets such as wooden ships.

Artillery was expected to play three roles on the battlefield. First, heavy fire at the outset was intended to shake enemy morale. Second, massed fire against the selected point of attack was often entrusted to the Artillery Reserve, in preparation for the major cavalry and infantry onslaught. Third, horse artillery provided cavalry attacks with close support, engaging squares at short range, and was particularly useful in the pursuit.

Artillery tactics varied, but Napoleon came increasingly to rely upon massed batteries of up to a hundred guns, as at Eylau (1807), Wagram (on the second day, July 1809), Borodino (1812) and Waterloo (1815). The French were noted for bold handling of their pieces, moving forward by bounds to shorten the range if the situation favored doing so. The classic example was *général de brigade* Sénarmont's aggressive advance at Friedland, closing the range from sixteen hundred yards to just sixty as his men moved toward the Russian infantry—but at a cost of half his gunners.

Such, then, was Napoleonic artillery. Of course, the Imperial Guard had its batteries of both "foot" and "horse," each cannon having two caissons of ammunition apiece as compared to the usual one caisson. The Guard Artillery often formed a vital part of the Army Artillery Reserve.

Constructive Achievements

Although Napoleon's name will always be associated in the popular mind with the great campaigns he waged and battles he fought, his most lasting achievements were in the realms of law and administration. Many of the reforms he wrought and innovations he instituted remain enshrined in French and European life to the present day. This positive aspect of his life's work contrasts markedly with his more destructive activities as a soldier and deserves attention.

In his earlier years Napoleon was an idealist and given to experimenting in matters of government and administration. As a general of the Republic he believed it his duty to reorder conquered areas according to republican principles on the French model. Thus in 1796 he created the Cispadene and Transpadene republics in north Italy, merging them on June 27, 1797, into the Cisalpine Republic. Similarly, Genoa became the Ligurian Republic, designed, like its neighbor Lombardy, along French lines. En route for the Levant in 1798, Napoleon occupied Malta and in one week banished the Knights of Saint John and reordered every aspect of its life. It was not on a mere whim that the expedition to Egypt was accompanied by five hundred *savants* drawn from all the professions: once Cairo had been occupied, Napoleon lost little time in setting up L'Institut d'Egypte and set in motion a wide range of ambitious (though in this case only transient) political, economic and cultural reforms.

His most important constitutional work was, inevitably, conducted in France itself, partly in order to consolidate and secure his personal power.

By the end of 1799, the Constitution of the Year VIII had established a council of state, a senate, a tribunate and a legislative assembly. As first consul, aware of widespread war-weariness, he used the Marengo and Hohenlinden campaigns of 1800 to bring about peace with Austria, and the Peace of Amiens with Great Britain in 1802 earned France at least a respite from warfare. Once Napoleon became consul for life, the Tribunate (which had opposed his elevation) was greatly restricted in its powers, and he began to create a hierarchical social order, establishing a consular court and inducing forty thousand *émigrés* to return by declaring an amnesty in April 1803. The Empire, proclaimed in May 1804, lasted less than eleven years, but during that time a new nobility, greatly extended between 1806 and 1808, sprang up around the throne.

Napoleon's greatest constructive work lay in the daunting task of remodeling French law. The celebrated Code Napoléon consisted of several parts. First, the Civil Code (Napoleon having attended fifty-seven seven-hour sessions to supervise the work of Cambacérès's committee of experts) was promulgated in March 1804 and established the citizen's right to equality before the law, religious toleration, the inviolability of property and the superior place of the father in the family; once and for all it swept away the relics of feudal power and rationalized the fourteen hundred decrees passed since 1789. In 1807 the Commercial Code reordered every aspect of industrial and agricultural life, brought about full employment, more stable prices and a favorable balance of trade. In 1808 came the Criminal Code, setting up a superior system of circuit judges but rejecting the concept of juries; two years later it was followed by the

The Imperial Family. A contemporary depiction of Napoleon, his brothers Joseph, Louis and Jérôme, his son-in-law, Joachim Murat, and his stepson Eugène Beauharnais. Joseph, Louis and Jérôme became kings of Spain, Holland and Westphalia respectively, while Eugène was made viceroy of Italy. Only Lucien Bonaparte kept a comparatively low profile, and is not depicted here.

FAMILLE IMPÉRIALE
de Napoléon 1er

revised Penal Code. Taken together this represented a huge and lasting achievement, much of which spread through Germany, Italy and Holland, and substantial parts of which remain in force today. But the place of women in society or law remained subservient.

Meanwhile, beginning in 1801, a committee of the Council of State was investigating the educational system, aiming to "create a loyal and informed citizen . . . a citizen first, a soldier second." Every *commune* was to have a primary school, each department a state secondary school and every large town was to have its *lycée*. Higher education was also established, and from 1808 L'Université de France was to supervise all education, with stress to be laid upon mathematics, science and history.

Long before this, Napoleon had taken a great risk and "restored the ancient altars" to France. The concordat with Rome (signed in 1801 but first published in 1803) infuriated staunch republicans but pleased the great majority of Frenchmen. After protracted negotiations with the papacy, Napoleon retained power over the appointment of bishops, while the Organic Articles of the Clergy assured the loyalty of all priests to the state. Indeed, Napoleon was to make full use of the pulpit for the dissemination of secular information.

Equally important was the care Napoleon lavished—as both consul and emperor—on the machinery of state, which was comprehensively overhauled. To restore law and order, in 1802 he instituted a new nationwide police force, responsible to Paris. The next year, special traveling tribunals were set up. Local government was rigidly centralized. From February 1800 each department was headed by a prefect, with a *sous-préfet* in each district. Every *commune* had a mayor, and each level had a local Council of Notables. Napoleon exercised complete control over the appointment of important officials at all levels. He made increasing use of highly intelligent young men as state auditors, giving them great responsibility at an early age in many administrative fields. As in the army, he encouraged proven talent to the full.

Of fundamental importance was Napoleon's financial reorganization of France. Aided by Gaudin, Mollieu and Barbe-Marbois, he set about recalling the worthless *assignats* issued by the revolutionary governments and instituted a far superior tax assessment and collection system. From 1800 eight officials per department were charged with fulfilling these duties. That same year the Bank of France became the sole issuer of paper money and controller of the national debt (paying 6 percent interest on loans). Napoleon personally supervised all ministerial budgets with a severe eye, and the institution of the Public Audit Office in 1807 greatly reduced embezzlement. The sale of state lands boosted revenue, and a form of income tax realized 660 million francs a year. There were numerous indirect taxes—on wine, salt, coaches, tobacco and playing cards, for instance—but there were no new taxes until the *droits réunies* were imposed as war costs soared. The overall effect was to rally the French economy: the value of government stocks rose sevenfold between 1799 and 1807 as Napoleon strove to transform France into a prosperous power base. In later years the extra taxes were only slightly more popular than the hated conscription of men to fill the ranks of the army. But it is quite clear that Napoleon achieved a lasting transformation of the French economy despite the ravages of ultimately unsuccessful wars. The proof lies in the fact that by 1818 the post-Waterloo Bourbon government was able to repay the huge war indemnity imposed by the victorious Allies.

Of course, there were darker sides to Napoleon's achievement. France was a police state—with all the apparatus of informers, spies, purges and state terror—but to a lesser extent than under the preceding, more extreme, republican governments. The press was rigidly censored: in January 1801 all but thirteen of Paris's seventy-three newspapers were closed; by 1811 there were only four still publishing. Opposition was bought over or ruthlessly suppressed. Constitutional checks on the emperor's power were ignored, bypassed or simply removed. Government by state decree, *senatus consultum*, increasingly became the norm.

Nevertheless, the Napoleonic reconstruction of France was an amazing achievement by any standards. Napoleon worked harder than any of his assistants. "I work in my study, at the table, at the opera, in bed. I have recognized the limitations of my legs and eyes, but not of my capacity for work." As a wag remarked, "God made Bonaparte, and then he rested." To which the royalist comte de Narbonne added cynically, "God should have rested a little earlier." Of course, in the later years Napoleon experienced a growing sense of both delusion and disillusion, but to the end he kept his hands firmly on the reins of power.

FIVE

DECLINE

In the space of a few years, Napoleon had destroyed successively the armies of Russia, Prussia and Austria; but Great Britain remained, hostile and implacable across the Channel, protected by the supremacy of the Royal Navy. Napoleon had long abandoned the idea of invasion and had turned instead to a new tactic—the Continental System, by which France would subdue Britain through blockade.

The system had come into being shortly after Jena, and consisted of an embargo on British trade with the European territories dominated by France. With each successive victory, the embargo was written into the peace treaties; it was extended, moreover, to European neutrals, who were told that trading with Britain would be regarded as a hostile act. As a scheme, it was a good one; as a practical proposition, it proved both ineffective and, indeed, rebounded on its inventor. For Britain, after all, traded not only with Europe but with a far-flung empire unchallengeable while she held command of the seas. She demonstrated her power by forbidding seaborne trade with France in war materials and, in August 1807, took possession of the Danish fleet to prevent its falling into French hands. The blockade against England was difficult to enforce and was bitterly resented by the European powers. Even Napoleon's own brother, Louis of Holland, defied the ruling and in 1810 was forced to abdicate because of it. Above all, the administration of the system forced Napoleon—who gained purely nominal advantages—into a number of decisions that seriously affected his European grand strategy.

But for the moment Napoleon had every reason to be confident and now set his sights on Portugal. Britain's oldest ally refused to subscribe to the Continental System, and if she fell to France the Royal Navy would be deprived of the use of the Tagus, and Portuguese ports—at home and in Brazil—would be closed to British trade. Accordingly, within a month of leaving Tilsit, Napoleon laid plans to overthrow Portugal's regency government.

On August 2, 1807, the Corps d'Observation de la Gironde was formed under General Junot and by October 16 a second force was in readiness under Dupont.

The GIANT COMMERCE overwhelming the Pigmy Blockade!!

1807

Commercial war. (By Wood-
ward.) The British response to
Napoleon's "Continental Blockade" was the Orders in Council
of early 1807, declaring an economic blockade of France. This
cartoon purports to show how
many items of British manufac-
ture were vital to the
Continent.

Merciless propaganda pressure was applied, and Spain was secretly induced to aid the forthcoming invasion with both facilities and troops. Early in November Junot stood poised at the head of twenty-five thousand men, not far from the Portuguese frontier, and French demands on Portugal became ever more strident.

On November 16 Junot was ordered to advance. The crossing of the mountains along the frontier proved difficult, but two weeks later Junot managed to reach Lisbon, against feeble opposition, fulfilling to the letter Napoleon's order. However, he arrived at the head of only two thousand troops, the rest having fallen exhausted from the ranks, to find that the regent had evacuated the capital, having removed a great deal of treasure and the Portuguese fleet.

Napoleon and Godoy, the *de facto* manager of the Spanish government, set about partitioning Portugal, but the invaders were widely detested, and popular revolts soon broke out. Moreover, Franco-Spanish relations were far from easy, for Napoleon now had firsthand information on Spain's disregard of the Continental System. Holding Godoy, a sometime private soldier in the Royal Guards and now lover to the Spanish queen, in total contempt, Napoleon secretly began to prepare for a French takeover of power in Spain. With key bases such as Valladolid, Burgos and Vitoria already partly in French hands, Napoleon expected to accomplish this without too much difficulty; three French corps were already in position, and on February 16, 1808, Murat was appointed the emperor's lieutenant in Spain. By the end of the month, subterfuge and minimal force had secured the French such key fortresses as Pamplona and Barcelona, and all was nearly ready.

Playing upon the known divisions within the Spanish royal family, Napoleon engineered a crisis. Threats against Charles IV's life (supposedly made by his son, Ferdinand) had induced the king to flee his capital, but a local rising trapped him at Aranjuez. Responding to Charles's urgent entreaties for French aid, Napoleon ordered Murat to occupy Madrid. Then, in the guise of mediator, he summoned the various parties to Bayonne in France in late April. There he showed his hand: Charles was compelled to abdicate in favor of Napoleon as "caretaker," and his son was similarly bullied into renouncing his rights.

This barefaced takeover was crowned on May 10 by the proclamation of Joseph Bonaparte as king of Spain, the vacant Neapolitan throne being awarded to Murat. But not surprisingly, Spanish hostility soon became apparent. As early as April 1 a minor rising occurred in Madrid, but those of May 2 were far more serious. Spaniards' loyalty to their Bourbon rulers proved unexpectedly strong, and by the end of the month a wave of terror had struck as Spanish collaborators and several Frenchmen were murdered throughout the country. By June 10 all the provinces were openly arming, and the French found themselves with a truly national war on their hands. Admittedly, liberal elements among the Spanish aristocracy and *bourgeoisie* welcomed the change in power as the only means of freeing the state from corruption, the Inquisition and outdatedness; but the mass of the people were strongly opposed. On the twenty-ninth, Murat, seriously ill, left for France.

To pacify the country, Napoleon ordered "flying columns" of fast-moving troops. At this stage there were 120,000 French troops already in Spain, and at first progress seemed to be good. Bessières defeated part of the Spanish royal army at Rio Seco on July 14. Dupont, moving into Andalusia, occupied Córdoba, but then had to fall back to Bailén, where, on July 20, he surrendered three divisions to General Castaños. This news caused a great sensation in Spain and throughout Europe. The capitulation also unfortunately coincided with Joseph's first entry into his capital, hardly a happy omen for the new reign; by August 6 the new king had abandoned Madrid and fallen back with most of his forces behind the River Ebro.

A new complication arose. Spanish appeals for British aid brought Sir Arthur Wellesley and fourteen thousand men to Portugal. On August 21 this force decisively defeated Junot at Vimeiro and at a convention at Cintra Junot agreed to abandon Portugal. These setbacks led Napoleon to make two key decisions. The first was to summon experienced troops from the Elbe. The second was to take command in Spain in person. On September 7 L'Armée d'Espagne was formally designated. But before he could leave Spain, Napoleon had to secure himself in central Europe, especially as he was about to transfer one hundred thousand veteran troops to Spain, almost a third of his forces in Germany. Accordingly, on September 27 he met Tsar Alexander for two weeks of talks at Erfurt. The atmosphere was notably different from that at Tilsit. In return for vague promises to keep watch on Austria, which Napoleon feared might take the opportunity to strike in his absence, the tsar extracted the right to occupy Moldavia and Wallachia in the Balkans and also French acknowledgment of Russian gains in Finland. With this one-sided agreement Napoleon had to be content, and only time would show that his faith in Alexander was misplaced. The "spirit of Tilsit" was already a dead letter, and Alexander, rather than Napoleon, had dominated the congress.

The central *junta* of Spain could call upon some two hundred thousand troops, many of indifferent quality, besides numbers of partisans. Their military leaders were unreliable, except possibly Blake and Palafox, but at the same time, the growing British army, thirty thousand strong and now commanded by Sir John Moore, was preparing to send twenty thousand men to cooperate with the Spanish authorities.

Yet Spanish plans were muddled and uncertain. In contrast, by early November the emperor had 200,000 men massed behind the Ebro. Of these, over 160,000 were available for the great offensive. Napoleon's plan envisaged an advance over the Ebro followed by two flank attacks, each of them making a double outward wheel, through Logroño and Burgos respectively to encircle Blake to the northwest and Palafox and Castaños to the east. With those armies eliminated, the road to Madrid would lie open.

The campaign proper opened on November 7, though Lefebvre had attacked Blake against orders on October 30 near Durango, giving him the chance to fall back before the trap could be sprung. But the first stages were successful enough. Burgos was eventually seized by Soult on November 10, following the dismissal of Bessières for tardiness, and next day Napoleon was able to resume the execution of the master plan. Victor, chastened by a minor setback to part of his force, was soon in hot pursuit of Blake, and Ney swung east to trap Castaños.

The problems posed by supply and the difficult terrain thwarted the French in their pursuit of complete success, but by the twenty-third they had three minor victories to their credit, while Napoleon had 45,000 experienced troops massing around Aranda ready to head the dash for Madrid. Five days later, 130,000 men were on the move toward the capital. Napoleon selected the Somosierra Pass for his crossing of the last of the mountains and on the thirtieth forced his way through the 9,000 Spaniards trying to block the road, but only after causing heavy casualties to the Polish Light Horse by his insistence on premature and unsupported attacks. Before dusk on December 4, Madrid was in French hands.

Napoleon now believed that the conquest of Spain was all but achieved. As he regrouped his forces around Madrid before launching them southward against the weak Spanish forces that still remained, only one uncertainty nagged him. What had happened to General Moore, of whose presence in Spain he had first heard in mid-November?

In fact, Moore was closer than the emperor knew. After learning of the initial defeats of Blake and Castaños, the British general had considered an immediate retreat toward Lisbon but had then decided to march to the aid of Blake's successor, General La Romana. He had in support five thousand recent reinforcements under General Baird, and, on December 11, Moore advanced with a total of twenty-five thousand men from Salamanca. He struck at once for Sahagun in the hope of surprising Soult's II Corps in a scattered situation, though Soult reacted to this threat in time. But when news of the advance reached Madrid on December 19 the effect was electric. All Napoleon's hatred for Britain burst forth, and he immediately canceled his orders for an advance into the south of Spain, substituting an all-out attempt to trap and destroy Moore. On the twenty-first, he hounded his men over the ice-bound Guadarrama Pass, ordering Soult to pin Moore until the main army could attack his flank and rear.

However, Moore was not going to be so obliging. As soon as he learned of Napoleon's move from Madrid, he ordered a headlong retreat over the mountains toward

The passage of the frozen Guadarrama Pass. (By Gelée, after Taunay.) In a desperate attempt to trap Sir John Moore's British army, Napoleon hounded his men over the icy pass west of Madrid on December 21.

Corunna, requesting the Royal Navy to make preparations for the evacuation of the army there. A race developed through bitter weather, but Moore managed always to keep ahead of his pursuers, turning from time to time to engage their advance guard. Both armies suffered great distress during this period, but on December 31 Napoleon conceded that the British were likely to reach Corunna. He promptly handed over the pursuit to Soult and began to divert superfluous formations back toward Madrid, where Joseph, surrounded by a hostile population, was desperate for troops. The emperor was therefore not present at the Battle of Corunna on January 16, 1809, where Moore, at the cost of his own life, repulsed Soult and won time for the evacuation of the remainder of his army.

It was never Napoleon's way to be associated personally with failure. He also had other reasons for turning away, for alarming news of plots in Paris came hard on the heels of intelligence reports that Austria was secretly mobilizing on the Danube. So it was that on January 6 Napoleon headed for Valladolid on what would prove to be the first stage of his return to France. Thus he left the Spanish theater without completing the conquest he had set out to achieve. Moore's army might have been forced into a desperate retreat and evacuation from the mainland, but its commander had effectively ruined the French plan for the subjugation of southern Spain and Portugal; before many months were out, the British army had returned under Wellesley (later to become duke of Wellington), ready to make an already difficult situation for the French an impossible one. For, although the regular Spanish forces were scattered, the will of the Spanish people was far from broken, and the guerrilla struggle, backed by the British army's presence, would make the "Spanish ulcer" incurable for the French.

The emperor himself was never to return to Spain, though Wellington was to record the view that "if Boney had been here, we'd have been beat." So, in the years that followed, the Peninsular War placed an increasing strain on French resources as they were being stretched in Continental campaigns. A succession of French marshals failed to bring victory, and Joseph was never more than a nominal ruler of a disaffected people, holding on uneasily, and far from enthusiastically, with the aid of French troops sorely needed elsewhere.

Meanwhile, far away in Vienna, the "War party" led by the Austrian empress Ludovica was growing in influence. Francis II and all sections of his court were equally keen to seek revenge for Austerlitz, the only point at issue being the question of timing. Those advocating immediate action argued that Napoleon's involvement with Spain and the absence of his key subordinates made the moment favorable. The reasoning was persuasive, and on February 8, 1809, the decision was made. The declaration of war came two months later.

Since the humiliation at Austerlitz, the Austrian army had been transformed into a national army. The first-line strength had been raised to 350,000, supplemented by a *Landwehr* that would eventually total 240,000. Archduke Charles had copied the *corps d'armée* system, revised the drill book, reorganized the cavalry and increased the artillery to comprise 760 field guns. But the senior commanders, except for Charles, remained rather stolid and uninspiring, and the staff system continued to be defective. The Austrian plan for 1809 was to send only a holding force into north Italy and to use the VIII Corps for a mighty blow south of the Danube to destroy the French forces in the Ulm-Augsburg area; first, however, they would capture Ratisbon, the French army's vital link with forces in the Nuremburg-Bamberg area.

Napoleon, back in Paris, was taking urgent measures to strengthen his army in Germany, which, thanks to Spain and the many garrison detachments needed there, could field barely 80,000 of its nominal 120,000 troops. A hundred and ten thousand men, due for conscription in 1810, were mobilized a year early, and France's allies were abruptly told to produce another 100,000, for the emperor required an army of 260,000 in Germany and 150,000 in Italy. Divisions were redesignated as corps, new officers were commissioned from the ranks and by late March the 174,000 men available in Germany were renamed La Grande Armée de l'Allemagne. By that time, taking all sectors outside Spain, Napoleon could deploy some 275,000 men against the Austrian Hapsburgs. This number fell far short of his target, and the quality of the troops was not particularly high, but he hoped to improve the situation before it came to open war. It was little wonder that he felt bitter over the tsar's failure even to attempt to implement the Erfurt agreement.

Moreover, Austria was determined to strike the first blow. On April 9, without formal declaration of war, the Austrian forces began to move, and within a day had invaded Bavaria. Berthier, in command of the French army in Napoleon's absence, was taken largely by surprise, and in bewilderment and in direct contravention of a paragraph in the emperor's orders decided to concentrate Davout, Oudinot and Lefebvre at Ratisbon—right in the path of the advancing enemy. This made the French forces vulnerable to being split in two, around Augsburg and Ratisbon, and to risk being defeated in detail. "In this position of affairs, I greately desire the arrival of your Majesty," wrote Berthier. His Majesty was fortunately on his way. Leaving Paris on the thirteenth, Napoleon reached Donauwörth on the seventeenth. He at once took steps to reconcentrate the whole army behind the River Ilm and near Ingolstädt, even if it meant abandoning Ratisbon.

A confused five days of fighting came to a climax at the double battle of Abensberg-Eckmühl on April 20–22. On the twentieth, Napoleon broke through the Austrian center, forcing Archduke John, commanding the isolated Austrian left wing, to retreat hurriedly for Landshut on the River Isar; only Massena's slowness on the road saved him from catastrophic defeat. Two days later, leaving a force under Bessières to pursue the enemy left beyond Landshut, Napoleon advanced the rest of his forces against the Austrian right-wing corps (which Davout had successfully pinned and contained), and defeated them at Eckmühl. The Austrian army, not the French, had been split and defeated. However, for once the French pursuit was not pressed, enabling Archduke Charles to withdraw the bulk of his forces to the north bank of the Danube through Ratisbon. But the road to Vienna now lay open before Napoleon. The situation had been transformed.

For their part, the French needed a brief chance to rest and reorganize; it was also considered necessary to regain Ratisbon. With this accomplished on the twenty-third, the emperor marched on the Austrian capital, leaving the experienced Davout to press Charles north of the Danube and sending Lefebvre to watch the approaches to the Tyrol. The advance gained fresh urgency from news of a French setback at Sacile in north Italy. The advance on Vienna would ease pressure on the French defeated in Italy, as the Austrians would be recalled through the Alps to help guard the Austrian capital. On May 13, Vienna opened its gates to the French conqueror, while a disillusioned Beethoven removed the dedication to Napoleon from his Third Symphony.

By now the French battle strength at Vienna, despite reinforcements from Spain and Saxony, was only 82,000. No less than 94,000 troops (excluding Eugène Beauharnais's 57,000 in north Italy) were engaged in secondary duties south of the Danube, containing or besieging Austrian detachments, guarding the extensive communications and coping with a rash of local risings; even Davout's corps had been reallocated to these duties. Archduke Charles, however, in great secrecy had massed 115,000 men quite close to Vienna. Napoleon was unaware of this, but he knew that part of the Archduke John's force was marching hotfoot from Italy, which made it all the more important for the French to defeat Charles, once he was located.

The first requirement was to secure a bridgehead on the Danube's northern bank.

The site selected was opposite Löbau Island, four miles below Vienna, and the French sappers at once began to construct a bridge to the island, while a feint was mounted at Nussdorf above Vienna. The work began on May 13. But as French intelligence had failed to discover, Charles was moving closer to the Danube, determined to contain any French crossing.

The crossing began late on May 20, Massena's IV Corps leading; Löbau had been occupied without opposition the previous day, and a further bridge was thrown from the island onto the Muhlau salient. Then problems arose. The Austrians upstream sent down a series of floating mills, and the first of these smashed through the vital main bridge; not until morning could the flow of troops be resumed. Still there was no sign of the Austrian army. Charles, however, knew every French move, and at 10:00 A.M. on the twenty-first ordered five columns to attack along a six-mile front at Aspern, Essling and Gross-Enzersdorf. Shortly after 1:00 P.M., the battle opened, to the amazement of the French.

Caught straddled over the river, with the rearward bridge being put out of action repeatedly, the French army was not in an enviable position. Before the day was out, the French had managed to pass a total of 31,400 men into the action, but the foe was three times as strong. Thanks to superb fighting, in which both Massena and Lannes played a major part, and to overcaution on the part of the Austrians, the French managed to cling to the villages on the north bank. The French heavy cavalry also shared in this achievement, narrowly averting the danger of annihilation until nightfall brought a welcome pause.

The capture of Ratisbon, April 23, 1809. (By Martinet.) The second Danube campaign got off to a bad start under Berthier's command until Napoleon's arrival. The emperor quickly regained the initiative in a week of heavy fighting, and then stormed Ratisbon on the Danube. To the great consternation of his men, Napoleon was slightly wounded in the right heel by a spent round. He was soon back in command.

Napoleon at Aspern. (Contemporary print.) Despite herculean fighting, the French were contained by Archduke Charles and eventually forced to abandon the battle. On the insistence of the Imperial Guard, Napoleon withdrew to Löbau Island, from which he took a more distant view of the latter stages of his army's withdrawal. This was his first true defeat in battle.

Once both bridges were in operation again, the French were able to build up their strength to sixty-two thousand men and 144 guns by dawn. They were still massively outnumbered, but Napoleon was determined to fight. At 7:00 A.M. Lannes and Oudinot attacked the center of the Austrian line. The Austrians recoiled, until Charles himself rallied the line. The French began to run short of ammunition, and Bessières's attempts to keep the initiative with a series of cavalry charges failed. Worst of all, the upstream bridge had parted again, which meant that Davout's corps could not cross to build the French army, now seventy-three thousand strong, to the strength needed to win the day.

By midday the bridge was open again, but only briefly, before a new gap was torn. Napoleon now took the hard decision to call off the battle and withdraw his weary men onto Löbau Island. Given the renewed pressure by the Austrians, withdrawal was not easy to achieve, and the Young Guard (newly raised in 1809) had to be employed to win a breathing space. At the insistence of both his officers and his men, the Imperial Guard threatening to down arms if he stayed near the fighting, Napoleon handed over command of the withdrawal to Lannes. By 3:30 A.M. on the twenty-third, the last troops were on Löbau, and the forward bridge was dismantled.

There is no disguising that Aspern-Essling ended in a French defeat. With a loss of twenty-two thousand men, the French may have inflicted twenty-three thousand casualties on the Austrians, but they had been repulsed from the north bank. Napoleon had committed grave errors. To cross the river, relying on a single bridge and with no accurate knowledge of the foe's positions, had been to court disaster. Poor reconnaissance, lack of surprise, nonexistent measures for protecting the bridge . . . it was an ill-planned operation; against the sound plan of Archduke Charles, the gamble had failed to come off. For a day he moved like a sleepwalker.

Napoleon, however, could still learn from his mistakes. While the Austrians did nothing to exploit their success, the emperor at once started devising plans. Six weeks of preparation followed. Löbau Island was converted into a fortress, with 129 mounted guns. Two sturdy bridges—with upstream breakwaters and stockades to ward off floating missiles—linked Löbau with the south bank by late June; gunboat flotillas were also stationed on the river. The army's artillery was built up to a total of 500 pieces, and massive reinforcements were summoned to the area, including Eugène and Macdonald from the south, Marmont from Graz and Davout from Pressburg. By July 1, 160,000 troops were close to Vienna, and more were drawing near. As for the Austrians, Charles did little besides strengthen his fortifications facing Löbau; his hopes of a general German rising against the French proved illusory, and he was anxious about belated Russian maneuvers in Galicia.

In early July Napoleon moved on to Löbau, and the Muhlau salient was reoccupied to distract the Austrians' attention. Napoleon's plan called for a massive crossing to the east, rather than to the north, off Löbau Island across extemporized bridges, followed by a mighty wheel to take the line of villages in flank and rear. Aware that something

The second bridge to Löbau Island. (By Gros, after De Laborde.) In the Battle of Aspern-Essling (May 21–22, 1809) success for the French depended upon two fragile bridges linking Löbau Island with the south bank of the Danube. They were repeatedly broken by floating mills sent down-current by the Austrians near Vienna, seriously compromising the French buildup of forces on the northern bank.

was in the wind, Charles consulted with his generals about the best measures to adopt. They eventually decided to man the villages only lightly, drawing up the main army along the northern edge of the Marchfeld Plain with the center near the village of Deutsch-Wagram and the left behind the Russbach stream. By this time, Austrian strength had grown to almost 146,000.

During the stormy night of July 4, the French plan was put into operation, just as the last formations were hurried onto Löbau Island. Eight pontoon bridges were suddenly swung from the east side of the island, and troops led by Massena's IV Corps began to pour onto the north bank of the Danube. The crossing went like clockwork, with minimal confusion. All bridges held, and the local enemy troops were overwhelmed, though the main Austrian forces were not encountered at first.

The capture of Gross-Enzersdorf by midmorning enabled a new bridge to be built and provided the French army with a useful pivot for deploying during the main battle. In midafternoon the French, at Napoleon's order, set about enlarging their bridgehead; Aspern and Essling were both captured.

Hoping to snatch a quick victory that evening, Napoleon ordered his right and center to attack the enemy positioned behind the Russbach. Unfortunately, some of Eugène's troops were routed and Oudinot was checked; these setbacks meant that the battle would have to be renewed the following day. Archduke Charles, cheered by the evening's events, was soon planning an attempt to surprise and roll up the French left wing, from the direction of the Bissamberg, and thus cut off the French from Löbau.

The Battle of Wagram. (By an unknown artist.) Six weeks after Aspern-Essling, Napoleon recrossed the Danube, this time after taking major precautions to safeguard his bridges. Archduke Charles was surprised by the scale of the operation, but it took two days of hard fighting to defeat the Austrians. This folk-art painting shows the charge of the chasseurs à cheval *and Polish Light Horse of the Imperial Guard near Gerasdorf on July 6.*

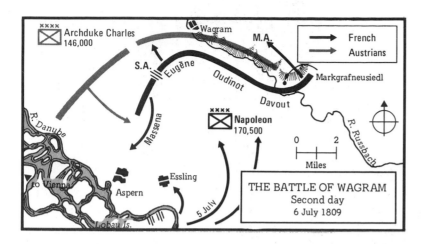

THE BATTLE OF WAGRAM
Second day
6 July 1809

Napoleon, too, was issuing his orders. Massena on the left was to be on the defensive; the center was to distract the Austrians with local attacks; the main move was to be by Davout on the right, with the Army of Italy ready to launch the breakthrough attempt in the center when the moment came.

The Austrians got in the first blow on the sixth, by a secondary attack against Davout. No sooner had this been checked, and Davout told to implement the main plan, than news came that Bernadotte's Saxons had been routed near Aderklaa. Napoleon forthwith dismissed the marshal from his command. Then, at about 8:00 A.M., came the main Austrian onslaught against one of Massena's divisions. Some thirty-seven thousand men came out of the mist, and soon Massena's eight thousand were in full retreat. Fortunately, Eugène extemporized a linking line with Macdonald's troops and corps artillery. Then Napoleon arrived to take charge. He cunningly moved Massena's remaining troops southward behind the firing line, brought the left back to the level of Löbau Island so that its massed guns could be brought to bear, and filled the gap thus caused in his center by deploying the artillery reserve in a vast battery of 122 guns.

These measures served to stabilize the situation on his left. The day, however, was not yet won. Shortly after midday, Davout's slow but steady attack pressed back the Austrian left through Markgrafneusiedl. At this moment, the French battle line was shaped like an immense Z. The time had come for the *coup de grâce*, and Eugène's Army of Italy swept forward. It failed to break through, but Archduke Charles had seen enough. Despairing of his brother Archduke John's appearance from Pressburg, he ordered a general retreat, but it was not until the seventh that Napoleon realized all was over. Against their own thirty-two thousand casualties, the French had inflicted forty thousand on the Austrians.

There was no immediate pursuit, but the Austrians were demoralized, and after four days of maneuvers, an armistice was signed. On October 14, after several months of wrangling, the Peace of Schönbrunn was signed. By the terms, three million Austrian subjects were involved in boundary adjustments; a huge indemnity and a restricted army were the price of failure. Napoleon had again been the victor, but by only a narrow margin.

Austria's defeat in the Wagram campaign seemed to have reestablished Napoleon's authority in Europe more conclusively and dazzlingly than ever. But appearances were

Princess Marie-Louise of Austria (1791–1847). The daughter of the Austrian emperor Francis II, and great-niece of the ill-fated Marie-Antoinette, she was chosen by Napoleon as his second wife. Marshal Berthier carried out a marriage by proxy on March 11, 1810, and later that month Marie-Louise arrived in France to meet her husband for the first time.

deceptive, and his very success held within it the seeds of ultimate failure. For, in the last resort, it was impossible for one nation to subdue an entire continent. The fervor of revolution, and the revolutionary ideals Napoleon claimed to represent, indeed gave his armies a spirit and cohesion unmatched by those of the antiquated regimes he had confronted. Yet the disasters he inflicted did not eliminate those regimes; rather, they forced them to have to rethink, to modernize and to become potentially ever more formidable. Moreover, Napoleon's victories were not followed by the reforms hoped for by his liberal admirers. Liberals and nationalists in Germany and elsewhere, who had once prayed for his success, now looked to his downfall as the only way to relieve Europe of military oppression. Plots against his life became more frequent, not only from right-wing extremists but now from left-wing patriots. Increasingly he was opposed by Europe's peoples as well as by their governments. For himself, Napoleon had set a course from which there was no going back. The Continent would not accept his hegemony by agreement; it took one campaign after another to achieve stability by force against ever more potent enemies, who were prepared to forget their own dissensions in the face of the threat Napoleon posed. Moreover, at this stage in his career, the emperor was no longer the man he had once been. Some physical deterioration had begun. His mental powers were not quite so pronounced and he was beginning to suffer that fate of all conquerors: a dangerous belief in his own infallibility.

It was at this critical juncture that Napoleon made a change in his personal life. He had long been alarmed by Josephine's failure to produce an heir, and now the possibility of assassination made him determined to safeguard the dynasty at the expense of his wife. Accordingly, despite Josephine's frantic remonstrations and his own genuine fondness for her, she was divorced; and, in February 1810, he was betrothed to Marie-Louise, daughter of the Austrian emperor.

The marriage brought personal happiness and, on March 20, 1811, the longed-for son, who was christened Francis Charles Joseph and promptly proclaimed king of Rome. But the marriage also symbolized a growing rift with Russia, whose government

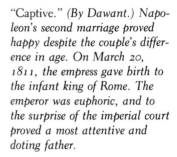

"Captive." (By Dawant.) Napoleon's second marriage proved happy despite the couple's difference in age. On March 20, 1811, the empress gave birth to the infant king of Rome. The emperor was euphoric, and to the surprise of the imperial court proved a most attentive and doting father.

had been negotiating for a marital alliance with the emperor. The collapse of these negotiations did not cause, but certainly underlined, the breakdown of the spirit of Tilsit.

The breach with Russia had been complex and gradual. The aftermath of Erfurt was one source of strain, but it was soon eclipsed by others. From the tsar's viewpoint, there were several bones of contention. The Continental System was unpopular in high court circles, and the presence of French troops east of the River Oder was deeply resented, for Russia had always regarded Poland as its front yard. Third, Russian statesmen challenged Napoleon's determination to restrict Russian expansion in the Balkan region at the expense of the Turks. Finally, of course, the tsar could only regard Napoleon's abrupt marriage to an Austrian princess as a deliberate affront to the Romanov family honor.

Napoleon, too, had his grievances. He could not tolerate Russia's barefaced flouting

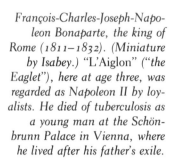

François-Charles-Joseph-Napoleon Bonaparte, the king of Rome (1811–1832). (Miniature by Isabey.) "L'Aiglon" ("the Eaglet"), here at age three, was regarded as Napoleon II by loyalists. He died of tuberculosis as a young man at the Schönbrunn Palace in Vienna, where he lived after his father's exile.

of his economic sanctions against Britain. Russian intrusions into the affairs of the grand duchy of Warsaw and continued probes toward Constantinople appeared to reveal dark secret ambitions totally contrary to French interests. The Russian minister of war, Barclay de Tolly, was also known to be hurrying through a modernization of the Russian army along French lines, another portent of trouble.

By late 1811 both sides were preparing for war. Russian engineers fortified the Dvina-Dnieper river lines, while Napoleon built up depots in Prussia and Poland and began creating a vast army in eastern Europe, bullying a dozen countries into providing contingents. Uniquely, he also organized twenty-six transport battalions with which to supply them, for he was aware that underdeveloped western Russia—forest and plain dominated—would present grave logistical problems.

By May 1812 the French had massed 650,000 troops. That this threat alone did not bring the tsar to seek a *rapprochement* indicated that the Russians would offer a determined opposition. Nevertheless, Napoleon prophesied a quick, victorious campaign of some five weeks' duration. At this stage, he had no intention of marching to Moscow to dictate a victor's peace. A two-week conference with his confederates, both willing and unwilling, including the emperor Francis and the king of Prussia, was held at Dresden in an attempt to bring Alexander to his senses. However, in the diplomatic offensive preceding the outbreak of war, the tsar indubitably came off best. Sweden professed friendly neutrality; accommodations were made on the Finnish and Moldavian fronts, thus releasing Russian armies; and in July Great Britain would promise money and the presence of a fleet in the Baltic. On the other hand, pending the transfer of forces from the peripheral areas, Russia could field only some 220,000 men in the west by mid-June, in two armies under the command of Barclay de Tolly and Bagration. A third army under Tormassov was being formed far to the south.

As Alexander would not negotiate, Napoleon was ready to strike. La Grande Armée de Russie was organized into a central group of three armies, commanded by Napoleon, Eugène and Jérôme, echeloned back to Warsaw, with semiautonomous corps on each distant flank. Behind these 449,000 troops, two lines of reserve formations stretched back into central Germany. However, owing to the operations in Spain, which were tying down over 200,000 French troops, less than half Napoleon's vast array was composed of French nationals. Thus its reliability was uncertain, in both military and political terms; and problems of command, language, supply and control would prove daunting when added to those of distance, climate and terrain. Still envisaging a quick victory, Napoleon selected the region north of the Pripet Marshes for his offensive; nearer to his main bases at Danzig and Königsberg, it posed a double threat (toward Moscow and Saint Petersburg) and would permit a closer supervision of unreliable Prussia. From there, he planned to cross the River Niemen near Kovno with his main force, supported by Eugène's army, in order to break through Barclay's extended forces and destroy them piecemeal by use of envelopment attacks. Meanwhile, Jérôme's army was to lure Bagration toward Warsaw, then pin him at the River Narew or the River Bug while part of the northern French forces, having dealt with Barclay, swept into his rear. The flanking corps, commanded by Macdonald and the Austrian Schwarzenberg, were to keep abreast of the major formations, pressing up the Baltic coastline toward Riga or deep into Volhynia. As for the Russians, their strategy seemed to envisage a withdrawal toward the fortified river lines before they made a determined stand to hold the "river gap" between the rivers Dvina and Dnieper while Bagration attacked the French flank from the south.

On June 24, after closing up to the Niemen and establishing a number of bridges, La Grande Armée poured forward into Russian Poland. From the first, however, its advance was hampered by the unaccustomed reliance on slow-moving transport and food columns. As a result, and also because of the Russians' elusiveness, a succession of separate attempts failed to trap the enemy into a decisive engagement. The first, the maneuver of Vilna, June 24– July 8, saw Murat's successful capture of Barclay's former headquarters, but Napoleon's corps were unable to move up in support of their right flank. Farther south, Jérôme proved wholly incapable of either luring or pinning Bagration, who set out almost at once for the northeast hoping to join Barclay. As a result, when Davout led a rapid lunge southward from Vilna, he struck empty air. Stung by Napoleon's criticisms, Jérôme promptly abandoned his command and left the front for Westphalia.

After a brief pause to reorganize his scattered formations, and to bring his chaotic rear areas into some form of order, Napoleon transferred his full attention to the northern sector, making a second attempt to trap Barclay on the Dvina near the fortified positions of Dünaburg and Drissa, while Davout, in temporary command of Jérôme's army, pursued Bagration with orders to prevent, at all costs, a linking of the Russian forces. The operations between July 16 and 26 again failed to force a battle, but the Russians were compelled to abandon their defensive river-line barrier. Up to this time, the Russian retreat was probably deliberate, but now the only strategy open to them was dictated by the need to survive and the hope that they could join their two armies together. In fact, Bagration's 48,000 men were steadily marching to join Barclay's 110,000, despite repeated efforts of the French to interpose a force between them. Napoleon's chances of defeating a divided foe in detail were fast diminishing, and he had already been drawn farther into Russia than he had originally anticipated.

Another pause followed, but then, between August 12 and 16, the French advanced once more, this time toward Smolensk. The blazing heat of summer was taking its toll of men and horses alike, and far away in Volhynia the newly formed Russian Third Army was in action against both Reynier's VII Corps and Schwarzenberg. Severe fighting was also reported by Oudinot around Pulotsk to the north. By this time, the French front already measured five hundred miles, and problems of control were fast becoming insuperable. Even worse, on August 4 Barclay and Bagration had at last linked up to the west of Smolensk, though the two generals were soon in bitter disagreement.

Seeking to retrieve the situation, Napoleon hurled his main forces into the "river gap." With Murat drawing the Russians westward toward Inkovo on August 8, the bulk of the army crossed the Dnieper in a surprise move and attempted to sweep on to Smolensk, there to sever the Russian line of retreat to the east. Thanks to the stalwart fighting by a single Russian corps south of the Dnieper, however, the French advance was slowed, giving Barclay and Bagration time to recognize their danger and, on the fifteenth, to order a pell-mell retreat to Smolensk and forestall the French. For three days, August 17–19, a serious battle raged around Smolensk's southern outskirts, but the result was an indecisive French victory. At a cost of ten thousand casualties, the French inflicted perhaps twelve thousand on their enemy, but, thanks to General Junot's failure to cut the vital Smolensk-Moscow highway near Lubino to the east of the city, the Russians were again able to retreat in fighting order. Yet another attempt to force a decisive battle had come to nothing.

So far, great inroads had been made into Russian territory; but there were no signs of a weakening Russian resolve, and already the French rear was under spasmodic attack by Cossacks and partisans. The emperor now faced the most critical decision of the campaign. Should he press on or hold his position for the winter before mounting a new effort in 1813?

In the end, Napoleon's instinct as a gambler forced him on, even though his front now extended 700 miles from flank to flank, and the battle power of his central army group had dwindled to only 156,000 men. Moscow still lay 280 miles ahead, but rather than lose it, Napoleon argued, the Russians would surely accept a decisive battle. So the advance was resumed from August 28. The fatal decision had been made.

By this time, the tsar had become increasingly critical of his commanders' conduct of the campaign, and from August 20 the highest command was entrusted to Kutusov, now a veteran of sixty-seven, with direct orders to fight for Moscow, the capital and holy city of Russia. The general selected a position some seventy miles west of Moscow and prepared for battle near the township of Borodino. On September 5 the leading elements of the French arrived from the west and captured the outlying Schivardino Redoubt.

The sixth passed in probes and reconnaissances, as both sides completed their preparations. Rejecting Davout's plea for an outflanking sweep to the south, Napoleon settled for a massive bombardment: a clearing action against Borodino on the left, a tactical outflanking attack on the far right near Utitsa and a main attack against the center of the Russian position, which was guarded by the *flèches* earthworks and the imposing Raevski Redoubt. Kutusov, for his part, placed almost half of his 120,800 men and 680 cannon behind the Kalatsha River on his right, in the belief that Napoleon would try to outflank that wing.

On the seventh, the battle began as the 133,000 French, aided by 585 cannon, began to advance. On the left, Eugène rapidly cleared Borodino, but on the right, Poniatowski was soon held up in the woodland around Utitsa. In the center, a massive battle of attrition raged as three French corps were sent progressively into action. The fortunes of war swung to and fro over the critical fieldworks, but nowhere could the French establish a true mastery.

Napoleon, unwell, played mainly a negative role in the day's events. When the Raevski Redoubt at last passed into French hands and the chance of victory seemed real, he repeatedly refused to send in his last reserve—namely, the Imperial Guard. The Russians were therefore given the chance to withdraw to a neighboring ridge, where they again turned defiantly. By dusk, a lull born of common exhaustion settled over the terrible scene, which held thirty thousand French and perhaps forty-four thousand Russian casualties. The French expected the battle to be renewed the next day, but Kutusov, against the advice of his generals, determined to withdraw overnight with his ninety thousand battle-worthy survivors. (For a fuller description of this great battle, see pages 129–34.)

The burning of Moscow. (By Artaria.) The French occupied Moscow on September 14, 1812, and found it almost deserted. The next day fires broke out in several districts, lit deliberately on the orders of Count Rostopchin, the city governor. An immense conflagration destroyed two-thirds of the Russian holy capital, only the area around the Kremlin surviving unharmed. Since much food and drink was left in the cellars, Napoleon did not order the evacuation of the city until October 19.

*Strategic overstretch. This car-
toon by an unknown artist
summarizes Napoleon's strategic
dilemma in 1812. Over two
thousand miles separated Moscow from Madrid, and it was
impossible for Napoleon to mas-
termind simultaneously the Peninsular War and the Russian
campaign. In the end he came a
cropper, suffering disasters on
both fronts and ultimately for-
feiting his military reputation
and empire, represented here by
the tumbling hat, orb and scep-
ter. The cartoon is entitled
"From Top to Bottom . . . or
Causes and Effects."*

The prize for this incomplete French victory was Moscow, occupied on September
14. But Napoleon found the city almost deserted, and a day later a great fire laid two-
thirds of Moscow in smoldering ruins. Alexander still refused to countenance French
peace proposals, and over a period of weeks it gradually became apparent to Napoleon
that he had entirely misinterpreted both the tsar's character and his people's indomitable
will to resist. His situation grew steadily more critical. With only ninety-five thousand
operational troops left, the French were soon outnumbered even by Kutusov, now
reinforced to 110,000. Worse, fresh Russian armies were approaching—Steinheil and
Wittgenstein from Finland, and Tshitsagov from Moldavia—and the strategic initiative
was passing to Napoleon's opponents. The emperor was also aware of the depredations
being carried out against his overextended communications by Russian irregulars and
the steady approach of winter. Then, on October 18, Murat's cavalry was severely
shaken by a Russian surprise attack southeast of Moscow. By then Napoleon had
already decided to retreat. So it was that on the one hundred and twentieth day of the
campaign, the French left Moscow, weighed down by loot from the capital.

The tide had turned.

Napoleon's first plan was to retire to Smolensk through the prosperous and un-
ravaged countryside around Kaluga to the south. But between October 23 and 25, a
sharp brush with part of Kutusov's army at Malo-Jaroslavetz, during which the emperor
was almost taken captive, persuaded him to swing his march back to the original line
of advance. The fifty-mile-long French column found its retreat over the already twice-
ravaged countryside; though the men were continually harrassed by Cossacks and
partisans, Kutusov held off, moving parallel and to the south of the column. Soon
French supply arrangements broke down, and the cohesion of the once Grande Armée
began to crack. Smolensk and its considerable depots were reached on and after
November 9, but the famished and undisciplined soldiers wantonly destroyed most of
the stores. By this time, the first snows and frosts had been encountered, and Russian

attacks were increasing, one of which separated Ney and the rear guard from the main army.

Napoleon could not linger at Smolensk. He was already aware that he was engaged in a race against time, for new Russian armies were converging from the north and south, driving in the overextended French flanks into a narrowing corridor. The danger was that these forces would get ahead of the French and sever their line of retreat toward Poland. On the twelfth, therefore, the head of the French column left Smolensk, and five days later Napoleon launched the Imperial Guard in a telling attack against a Russian force at Krasnoe. This determined Kutusov not to press for a major engagement. Notwithstanding, the French situation was becoming increasingly desperate. On the eighteenth alarming news arrived that Tshitsagov had captured the crucial French depots at Minsk. Then the French troops' spirits were raised by the near-miraculous reappearance of Ney, whom Napoleon promptly dubbed "the bravest of the brave." His valiant fighting and epic march enabled him to save nine hundred men of his corps. By this juncture, there were barely forty thousand French soldiers combat-worthy, with a rabble of perhaps twice as many stragglers clinging to the rear of the column.

On November 22 dire news arrived from the town of Borisov, revealing that Tshitsagov, at the head of thirty-four thousand men, had indeed won the race to the River Beresina and destroyed the vital bridges ahead of the French. Napoleon ordered that his state papers be destroyed and prepared for the worst. An unseasonable thaw had turned the Beresina into a torrent, and there appeared to be little chance of his army surviving as Wittgenstein, thirty thousand strong, closed in from the north,

Crossing the Beresina: the second day. (By Victor Adam.) The retreat from Moscow started off well, but once Napoleon decided to fall back along his original line of advance, problems multiplied. By sheer skill—and the self-sacrifice of General Eblé and his bridge builders—the emperor managed to avoid the Russian trap by crossing the Beresina in a five-day operation. But once the battle was over his army had lost a further twenty-five thousand casualties and possibly fifty thousand non-combatants.

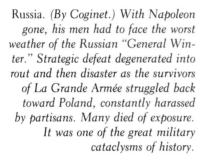

Russia. (By Coginet.) With Napoleon gone, his men had to face the worst weather of the Russian "General Winter." Strategic defeat degenerated into rout and then disaster as the survivors of La Grande Armée struggled back toward Poland, constantly harassed by partisans. Many died of exposure. It was one of the great military cataclysms of history.

pushing Victor's and Oudinot's depleted corps before him, and Kutusov warily moved up from the rear with sixty-five thousand more. It seemed that the trap must close about Napoleon.

A combination of luck and brilliant generalship saved Napoleon and his eagles. With great skill, he succeeded in fooling Tshitsagov, and thanks to the selfless exertions of his pontoon train, two bridges were built across the Beresina near Studienka at a fortunately discovered ford. Between November 25 and 29, the French poured over the river while desperate fighting raged along both banks. Nevertheless, the Russians had lost their opportunity, and possibly forty thousand French survivors escaped the trap before the bridges were destroyed; some fifty thousand dead or captured, many of them noncombatants, had been the price.

The road to Vilna and Poland now lay open before the emaciated French forces. Napoleon left the army to its despair on December 5, returning to Paris to quash rumors of his death, rumors that had already resulted in one near-successful conspiracy, and to start building new armies. Commanded by a disgruntled Murat, the survivors staggered on toward Poland, while terrible weather conditions added further to the loss of life. The king of Naples soon departed in his turn for his sunny kingdom, and it was left to Eugène to supervise the last stages of the retreat. The Russians were now content to leave the French to the weather and made no further serious attempts to engage. So it was, therefore, that the new year of 1813 saw some ninety-four thousand

French and Allied survivors come out of Russia; by this time, the four hundred thousand men of the original central army group had been reduced to twenty-five thousand.

The legend of French invincibility now lay utterly shattered. But the Russians had lost at least 125,000 soldiers and perhaps a million civilians since June 1812. However, the soil of Holy Russia was clear of the invader, and preparations for the liberation of Germany were soon being put in hand.

The Battle of Borodino
September 7, 1812

The village of Borodino stands on the banks of the River Kalatsha some seventy miles west of Moscow. It was the scene of one of the goriest major engagements of the Napoleonic Wars, as Napoleon, at the head of 133,000 troops (fewer than half of them French) and 585 cannon, confronted the recently appointed Prince Golenischev-Kutusov commanding the Russian First and Second Armies, a total of 120,800 men and 680 guns.

The main battle area was bounded by the old and new post roads linking Moscow and Smolensk. The countryside is undulating, with steep ravined streams and interspersed villages and woodland. The Russian right wing lay east of Borodino behind the fordable but obstructive Kalatsha. It was entrusted to General Barclay de Tolly's First Army, comprising three infantry corps, with three cavalry corps in support. Borodino, garrisoned by part of the Russian Imperial Guard, was both the hinge and the advanced post of the position, linked by a bridge to Gorki, where Kutusov established his headquarters. The Russian center and left, commanded at the outset by Prince Bagration's three infantry and single cavalry corps, stretched for two miles from the Raevski Redoubt—a twenty-gun artillery position overlooking Borodino and the

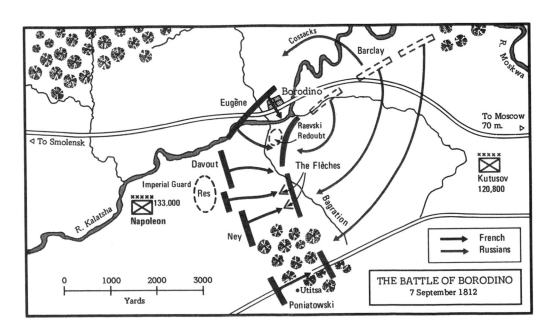

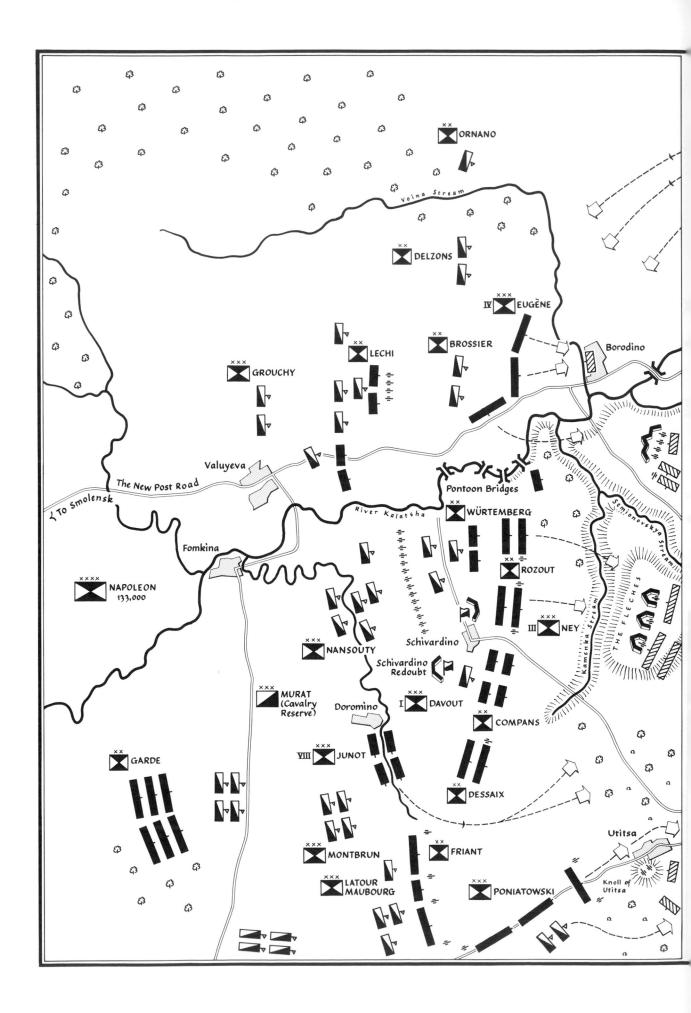

ORNANO

Voina Stream

DELZONS

IV ××× EUGÈNE

Borodino

BROSSIER

LECHI

××× GROUCHY

Pontoon Bridges

Valuyeva

The New Post Road

River Kalatsha

×× WÜRTEMBERG

Semionovskya Stream

To Smolensk

Fomkina

×× ROZOUT

THE FLECHES

Kamenka Stream

×××× NAPOLEON
133,000

Schivardino

III ×× NEY

Schivardino
Redoubt

××× NANSOUTY

I ××× DAVOUT

Doromino

××× MURAT
(Cavalry
Reserve)

×× COMPANS

×× GARDE

VIII ××× JUNOT

×× DESSAIX

Utitsa

××× MONTBRUN

×× FRIANT

Knoll of
Utitsa

××× LATOUR
MAUBOURG

××× PONIATOWSKI

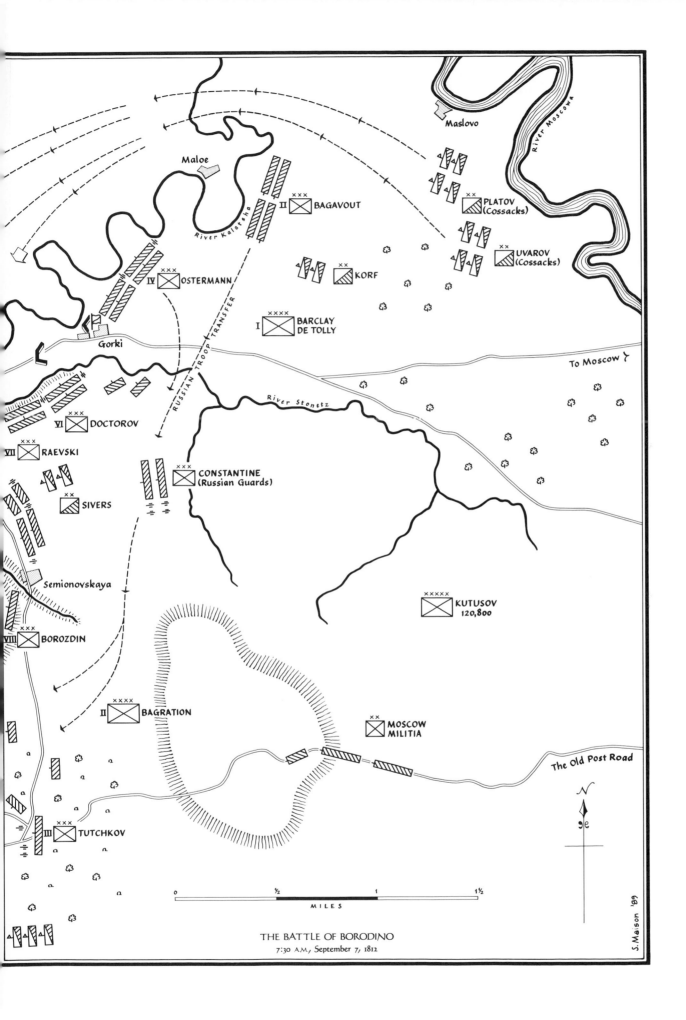

Maslovo

Maloe

II BAGAVOUT

PLATOV
(Cossacks)

River Kalotsha

IV OSTERMANN

KORF

UVAROV
(Cossacks)

I BARCLAY
DE TOLLY

RUSSIAN TROOP TRANSFER

Gorki

To Moscow

River Stonetz

VI DOCTOROV

VII RAEVSKI

CONSTANTINE
(Russian Guards)

SIVERS

KUTUSOV
120,800

Semionovskaya

VIII BOROZDIN

II BAGRATION

MOSCOW
MILITIA

The Old Post Road

III TUTCHKOV

N

0   ½   1   1½
MILES

THE BATTLE OF BORODINO
7:30 A.M., September 7, 1812

S. Maison '89

Kalatsha—past the ruined village of Semionovskaya with its three earthworks, or *flèches*, to a pronounced knoll beyond the village of Utitsa on the Old Post Road. Some three thousand yards to the west stood the redoubt of Schivardino, held as an advanced post by General Gorchakov. Kutusov deployed 17,000 regular cavalry, 7,000 Cossacks, 72,000 infantry, 10,000 Moscow militia and 14,500 gunners holding an initial convex five-mile front.

The French approached early on September 5 in three columns. A stiff action cleared Gorchakov out of Schivardino, where Napoleon set up his headquarters on the sixth, by which time his whole army was in position. Eugène's IV Corps was placed opposite Borodino beyond the Kalatsha, while Poniatowski's V Corps drew up on the extreme right opposite Utitsa. In the center were deployed Ney's III Corps and Davout's I, supported by Junot's VIII, Friant's division of I Corps held in reserve, Murat's Reserve Cavalry and the Imperial Guard. The French had an overall numerical superiority of some 12,000 men but considerably fewer guns. The men and horses of the French were all tired.

The sixth passed in unreal calm as Kutusov improved his fortifications and Napoleon considered his plan of battle. Davout suggested that he should be sent off overnight to envelop the Russian left flank. "Ah, you are always for turning the enemy," Napoleon riposted. "It is too dangerous a maneuver." His numerical superiority was too slight for such a move. He also ruled out an attack on the Russian right: the Kalatsha posed too many difficulties. Consequently the battle must be an attritional frontal onslaught against Kutusov's center and left, after a preliminary bombardment by 120 guns and an initial probe by Eugène against Borodino. His staff noted that the emperor was far from fit (he had a heavy cold and a recurrent bladder complaint), but his dejection was somewhat lightened by the arrival of a portrait of the infant king of Rome.

By the misty but dry dawn on the seventh the French were posted. By a miscalculation the guns were placed too far back and had to be resited farther forward. At 6:00 A.M. the guns at last opened fire. At first all seemed to be going well for the French. Eugène cleared Borodino and while Poniatowski closed up on Utitsa on the right, Davout made ground in the center. However, when the French IV Corps pushed a division over the Kalatsha toward the Raevski Redoubt it was routed with loss, while Russian light infantry in the woods of Utitsa checked the V Corps. The major French thrust lines did not go unnoticed by Kutusov, who began to transfer troops from his disengaged far right to reinforce his hard-pressed center and left.

The struggle for the *flèches* rose to a new peak as at 8:00 A.M. Ney and Friant joined Davout in a renewed assault against generals Raevski and Borozdin, but the Russians were reinforced in time by Baggavout from the right wing. The battle swung to and fro, but the Russians held their ground as French losses mounted, Davout being among the wounded, although he refused to leave the field. All the while Napoleon remained at Schivardino, querulously querying all pleas for aid, above all refusing to send forward the Imperial Guard. "I do not want it destroyed."

The pressure was increased as Junot's VIII Corps and much of the Reserve Cavalry were fed into the battle. A new attack by Eugène took temporary possession of the key Raevski Redoubt but was driven out. Russian artillery took a heavy toll of Junot's Westphalian troops at the same time as General Morand's attempt against the Raevski Redoubt was repulsed with loss. Poniatowki was also giving up a little ground on the right, and Napoleon had to redeploy Friant from reserve again to stabilize the line. The forces on the flanks had made little progress since their early successes, and the attritional nature of the battle in the center was clearly established. All French reserves, except only the Guard, had been committed. Could the pressure be maintained?

At 10:00 A.M. a renewed attack on Semionovskaya by elements of three French corps began to make a little ground at a cost heavy in casualties. A huge cavalry battle swayed back and forth, and then the Russians opened up with massed cannon. "A formidable array of guns spat forth death," recalled Caulaincourt. "The Great [Raevski] Redoubt belched out a veritable hell on our center." Marshal Ney was wounded, but the Russians also received a grievous loss when Prince Bagration was mortally wounded. News of this casualty so dispirited the Russian infantry that they at last abandoned the *flèches* near Semionovskaya, and a jubilant Murat hurled his cavalry after them, hoping to convert their retreat into a total rout. But once they had reached the Psarevo Plateau a few hundred paces to the rear, the Russians turned about, re-formed their lines and refused to cede another yard.

Nevertheless, it seemed as if the battle was on the point of being won, if only Napoleon would release the Guard. Repeated requests for him to do so met with an unwavering response. In earlier years, the emperor would have been much farther forward, continuously assessing the state of the battle and inspiring his troops to renewed efforts. On this occasion he played almost a negative role. Napoleon's highly untypical attitude earned Kutusov a respite, during which he reordered his buckling line. Soon after midday Tolstoi's fresh corps came up from the quiescent right flank. At this moment, the Russian commander in chief chose to launch a telling counterstroke. Noting how weakly Eugène was occupying Borodino village, Kutusov ordered generals Platov and Uvarov to take seven thousand Cossacks and five thousand regular cavalry over the Kalatsha and assault the French in the village's vicinity. This move took the French and Italian troops in the area completely by surprise, and they were soon sending urgent pleas for assistance.

This disturbing news compelled Napoleon to postpone a new all-out attack on the Raevski Redoubt while parts of Eugène's corps and Grouchy's cavalry recrossed the river to meet the unforeseen attack. A long struggle ensued, but eventually the Russian horsemen withdrew. Thus, by 2:00 P.M. the postponed attack against the redoubt was once again ready to be launched. While all of two hundred French guns blasted the position, Eugène's three tiring divisions renewed a frontal attack as the Second Cavalry Corps (commanded by General Caulaincourt, brother of Napoleon's master of the horse) prepared to assault the daunting position from the rear. Once again all hell was let loose as the French infantry advanced in columns, but so preoccupied with their approach were General Raevski's defenders that the French cavalry were able to sweep around the earthworks and break in from the rear, led by Caulaincourt at the head of the Fifth Cuirassiers. The general was shot down at once, but his men triumphed; by 3:00 P.M. four Russian regiments had died to a man and the redoubt was at last in French hands—this time for good.

Stunned anew by this disaster, the Russian line grudgingly began to give ground. Eugène tried to organize a pursuit with every available horseman, but Barclay de Tolly used all his remaining cavalry to check the French advance five hundred yards beyond the redoubt. Now it was the viceroy of Italy's turn to beseech Napoleon to release the

The death of General Auguste Caulaincourt at Borodino. (By Habermann.) The climax of the engagement at Borodino, one of the bloodiest battles in recorded history, was the storming of the Raevski Redoubt from the rear by Auguste Caulaincourt. Borodino won Napoleon Moscow, but it did not win the war.

Guard: he met with no more success than his predecessors. "I will not demolish my Guard. I am 800 miles from France and I will not risk my last reserve." As a result the Russian cavalry was able to cover the orderly withdrawal of their weary infantry.

Kutusov was not yet prepared to admit defeat. Doctorov and the Russian Imperial Guard Corps were ordered to prepare a counterattack toward the French center. Noting this, Napoleon authorized the use of the Artillery Reserve. These eighty guns were rushed forward at the critical moment, and their concentrated fire was so effective that the Russian attack never materialized—which was probably as well, given the French troops' exhaustion.

Meanwhile, on the far right, Poniatowski was making a new effort against the Utitsa Knoll—this time, successfully—and at 5:00 P.M. it passed into his control. Incredibly there was still plenty of fight left in the Russians. They fell back, but in good order, and only to the next ridge, the arrival of part of the Moscow Militia serving to strengthen their resolve.

In fact, a new attack was beyond either contestant. The firing slowly died away, and some care could at last be devoted to the many wounded; a huge number, however, could not be helped. To gain a bare mile of ground the French had suffered well over thirty thousand casualties, including forty-seven generals, thirty-two staff officers, eighty-six *aides de camp* and three dozen colonels of regiments. It is estimated that the Russians lost forty-four thousand killed and wounded. Overnight they withdrew.

SIX

DEFEAT

Terrible as the disasters of 1812 were, few could have foreseen that in the following year Napoleon's empire would disintegrate. For the emperor, time was running out. In February 1813, Prussia signed an alliance with Russia, and it remained only for Austria to take the field once more and all Europe would be in arms against him. Napoleon could scarcely believe that Austria, now tied dynastically to France, would mobilize against him; but Metternich, the foreign minister, was prepared to consider a settlement only if France abandoned her German conquests and suppressed the grand duchy of Warsaw and the Confederation of the Rhine. Napoleon responded: "Your Sovereigns born on the throne can let themselves be beaten twenty times and return to their capitals. I cannot do this because I am an important soldier. My domination will not survive the day when I cease to be strong and therefore feared."

In the end, Napoleon's inability to reverse the course he had set himself would mean his destruction. For the moment, his immediate task was to repair the damage of the Russian campaign and prepare to face his Russian and Prussian enemies in the field. A hundred and thirty-seven thousand conscripts were completing their initial training. To these he added eighty thousand men from the National Guard, called up a portion of the conscript class of 1814 and a further hundred thousand from the classes of 1808 and 1809–10, transferred twelve thousand from the navy and three thousand from the *gendarmerie*, demanded twenty thousand from the French municipalities and thirty thousand from Italy. France became one vast workshop, as superhuman efforts were called for to clothe and equip these new forces. The gravest problem was the shortage of horses, and hence the deficiency of cavalry, although the quality of the new levies in general left much to be desired. Yet somehow, despite the continued drain of the Spanish front, where Wellington was rapidly establishing the upper hand, another half million men were found for the battles to be fought in Germany.

Napoleon had ordered Eugène to fall back to the River Elbe near Magdeburg, there to cover the formation of the new French army near Mainz as Kutusov advanced over the Oder with a first wave of 120,000 men, spread over a broad front. By mid-April Napoleon had assembled 226,000 men and 457 guns. His first plan envisaged a savage advance through Prussia to relieve besieged Danzig, but his strength was not yet sufficient, especially as the Confederation of the Rhine was restive and Dresden was threatened. Accordingly, on April 15, he decided to advance from Erfurt on Leipzig in the hope of snatching a quick victory and compelling the Allies to retire back over the Elbe while he continued to Berlin. But from the start, the French were hampered by insufficient information of the foe's exact whereabouts; their shortage of cavalry gravely affected their operational efficiency throughout 1813.

By April 25 the emperor was at Erfurt, and while the Army of the Elbe under Eugène advanced through Merseburg to distract the foe, the Army of the Main swept toward Lützen. There, on May 2, the emperor won the Battle of Lützen against General Wittgenstein. Because of their weak reconnaissance, the French had not anticipated the action, but Napoleon jumped at the chance, and thanks to the superb mobility of his corps was able to increase his fighting force in the area from an initial 45,000 to 110,000, which was more than enough to defeat the 75,000 Prussians and Russians. The enemy, however, was able to retire on Bautzen relatively unharassed, for once again the shortage of French cavalry precluded an all-out pursuit. Nevertheless, the emperor ordered a general advance on Bautzen, where Wittgenstein had taken up a strong position behind the River Spree. Typically, Napoleon decided to attack as soon as possible. Rapidly reorganizing the two French armies into a single force, on May 20 Napoleon mounted a frontal attack while Ney swept down from the north in a classical envelopment. The Allies were defeated, though the French failed to mount an effective pursuit; the plan had been excellent but the execution faulty; the result was, therefore, inconclusive.

Both sides needed a breathing space and on June 2 agreed to an armistice. The negotiations that followed were neither successful nor wholly sincere but served to win time while armies were strengthened. By the end of the summer, when fighting was renewed, it was evident that the French had been outmaneuvered. Austria had at last joined the Allies, as had Bernadotte, the crown prince of Sweden and Napoleon's former marshal. The Allies now had an overall preponderance of manpower, perhaps eight hundred thousand to the emperor's total of seven hundred thousand, the great bulk of whom were inexperienced conscripts.

Napoleon decided to make Dresden his defensive center of operation, massing his stores there and deploying his forces between the Oder and the Elbe to make the most of his central position. By mid-August he had some 300,000 troops in the region. Opposing him was an army of 120,000 under Bernadotte, near Berlin; Blücher's Army of Silesia, 95,000 strong, around Breslau; and Schwarzenberg's 240,000 Austrians centered on Kulm to the south.

The Allies' new strategy was to avoid battle with the emperor himself, concentrating on his subordinates. Time and time again, Napoleon was forced to adjust his plans as new crises arose. On August 24, instead of attacking Blücher as he had intended to do, he decided to sweep against the rear of Schwarzenberg's Army of Bohemia through Pirna. Shortly after, he learned that Saint-Cyr, at Dresden, was on the point of losing the vital bases to Schwarzenberg. This could not be countenanced; he dropped his Pirna plan in favor of a desperate rush to bolster Saint-Cyr. The result was the

Battle of Dresden on August 26–27. Too late, the Allies realized that they were facing Napoleon in person. By the twenty-seventh Napoleon had assembled 120,000 men to face Schwarzenberg's 170,000, and with a mighty attack the French destroyed the Allied left wing. After losing 38,000 casualties to France's 10,000, Schwarzenberg ordered a retreat. Once again, however, Napoleon could not pursue effectively, and as a result the Allies were able to wipe out a force of 20,000 French isolated at Kulm, on the twenty-ninth. The previous day, Marshal Macdonald had been severely mauled by Blücher at the River Katzbach, and details of Oudinot's defeat at Grossbeeren also arrived. Thus the French success at Dresden was largely offset by three disasters elsewhere. The omens were not propitious for the French, and the confidence and determination of the Allies increased.

Napoleon tried to organize a great drive on Berlin, but in vain. Sporadic attacks on his marshals' troops kept him on the move from one battle to another. The Allied strategy was paying off: Napoleon was afforded no chance to launch a major blow; he was being played like a bull in the arena, and his overmarched troops were dropping with fatigue. Meanwhile, French influence in Germany was steadily eroding, only Saxony remaining fully loyal to Napoleon. These developments forced the emperor to abandon all thought of operations east of the Elbe.

The Allies, scenting the kill, decided to concentrate all moves toward Leipzig so as to place the French links with the Rhine in jeopardy. By early October the ring was closing, and the French were driven back step by step toward Leipzig. Still obsessed with the need to conserve Dresden, Napoleon divided his forces—a fatal step, as events were to prove. With 150,000 men, the emperor advanced north to try to envelop Blücher and Bernadotte on the River Mulde. But the Allies now knew how to counter this well-tried Napoleonic maneuver and refused to be flustered. On October 12 Napoleon realized that his bluff had been called and retired toward Leipzig, where Murat and Marmont were giving ground before Schwarzenberg. By the fourteenth Napoleon had assembled almost 200,000 men to face Schwarzenberg's 203,000, Blücher's converging 54,000 and Bernadotte's more distant 85,000. The climactic "Battle of the Nations" was about to begin.

Early on the sixteenth, the enemy was present in strength only to the south, so Napoleon left weak forces to the north and east of the city and strained every nerve to win a victory over Schwarzenberg. But the Army of Bohemia survived the ordeal unbroken, thanks largely to the distraction caused by the arrival of Blücher from the north and the defection of some Württemberg troops. Napoleon's failure to win on the first day was fatal; Allied predominance would steadily mount thereafter, to a total of three hundred thousand men and fifteen hundred guns. Napoleon would be outnumbered three to two in terms of both troops and artillery. The odds were growing long.

The seventeenth passed relatively quietly, as the Allies planned six concentric attacks for the eighteenth, with the main effort from the east. Napoleon, for his part, planned to reduce his perimeter and prepared for a retreat over the rivers Elster and Lippe, to the west of the city. On the third day of the battle, however, the French line proved capable of holding all attacks, though some Saxon troops defected. The overall situation was not favorable, so by dusk, Napoleon was issuing orders for a general retreat. He had lost the battle.

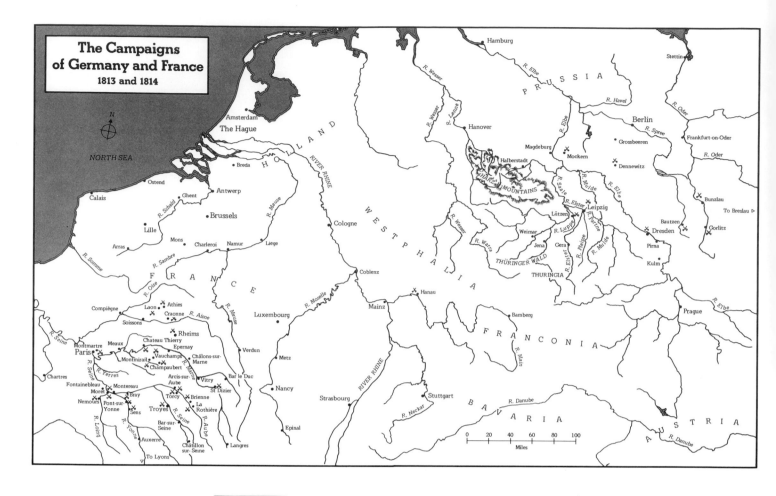

The Campaigns of Germany and France
1813 and 1814

NORTH SEA

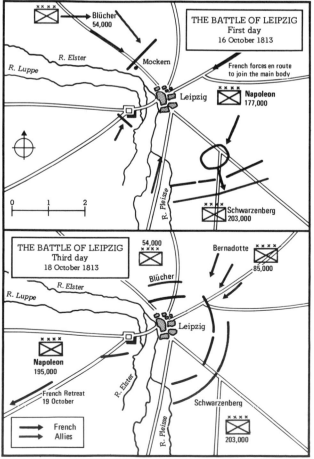

THE BATTLE OF LEIPZIG
First day
16 October 1813

Blücher
54,000

R. Elster

R. Luppe

Mockern

French forces en route
to join the main body

Leipzig

Napoleon
177,000

R. Pleisse

Schwarzenberg
203,000

0   1   2

THE BATTLE OF LEIPZIG
Third day
18 October 1813

R. Elster

R. Luppe

54,000

Blücher

Bernadotte

85,000

Leipzig

Napoleon
195,000

French Retreat
19 October

R. Elster

R. Pleisse

Schwarzenberg

203,000

French →
Allies →

View of the Grimma suburb of
Leipzig, 1813 (opposite page, top).
(By James Atkinson.) "The Battle
of the Nations" raged for three
days, and by its close Napoleon
had effectively lost control of Germany and sacrificed another half
million soldiers. Among the many
thousands slain was the Polish
prince Poniatowski, newly appointed a marshal, who drowned
trying to swim the River Elster with
severe wounds.

The victors meet after the terrible engagement (opposite page,
bottom). Prince Schwarzenberg
(mounted) salutes the three Allied
monarchs present: (left to right)
Tsar Alexander I, the Emperor
Francis I of Austria (the title he assumed after losing the crown of the
Holy Roman Empire) and Frederick William III of Prussia. The
remaining Allied commanders,
Crown Prince Bernadotte of Sweden (the former Napoleonic marshal), who in fact took only a
minimal part in the battle, and
General Blücher of Prussia, are not
shown.

The withdrawal continued all night and into the nineteenth. Unfortunately, the main bridge was demolished prematurely, and the French rear guard was forced to surrender. The French had lost, overall, thirty-eight thousand casualties and now thirty thousand prisoners. The Allies lost at least fifty-four thousand killed and wounded, but they had completed the liberation of Germany. Napoleon was about to be driven back west of the Rhine forever.

For the second consecutive year, Napoleon had lost casualties in excess of four hundred thousand men, and the successful retreat to the Rhine—which included a small victory at Hanau against his new Bavarian foes on October 30—could not disguise this huge setback. Napoleon had fought with skill, but his methods were predictable, and his opponents had by now absorbed the lessons of thirteen years of Napoleonic warfare. Above all, both Napoleon and France were tiring; they had lost the initiative. It only remained for the Allies to penetrate the Empire's last stronghold, France itself.

Napoleon's defense of France is often regarded as his supreme moment. However true this may be of its technical aspects, and however much one may admire his *Götterdämmerung* performance, Napoleon must stand charged with pressing matters beyond the logical limit. In 1814, neither the people nor his commanders were wholly behind him. Delusion and egocentricity had made sad inroads on one of the greatest intellects of all time: Napoleon refused to accept the hopelessness of his position.

Somehow, between November 1813 and January 1814, the emperor scraped together another army. Over one hundred thousand men were tied down in besieged fortresses beyond the Rhine, and Wellington was pinning as many more in the south of France. By conscripting pensioners and mere boys, *les Marie-Louises*, a force of almost 120,000 was found for the eastern frontiers, which were now threatened by at least 350,000 Allies fresh from their liberation of Germany. Allied dissensions won the French a little time, but in the new year of 1814 General Bülow advanced into Holland; Blücher crossed the Rhine between Coblenz and Mainz; while Schwarzenberg, two hundred thousand strong, headed for the Langres Plateau. At the rear, Bernadotte and Bennigsen set about containing Marshal Davout's well-led but isolated forces around Hamburg.

Meanwhile, defections continued. In early January Murat, king of Naples and Napoleon's own brother-in-law, came to an agreement with the Allies. Next, the king of Denmark deserted him. Paris itself was full of plotters seeking to ensure their future. But Napoleon would not give up. As the Allies pushed back the cordon of barely seventy thousand troops who were defending the frontiers, he hastened his preparations for a campaign based upon the strategy of the central position and designed to safeguard the heart of what remained to him—Paris.

Selecting the Army of Silesia for his first effort, Napoleon failed to surprise Blücher at Saint-Dizier. Pressing on, he fought a disappointing action at Brienne on January 29, only narrowly avoiding capture, and was defeated at La Rothière three days later. In all, this represented a parlous opening for the French campaign, and Napoleon fell back on Troyes.

Fortunately, the Allies were bickering over permissible peace terms. As Napoleon set out to strike at the Army of Bohemia, he learned that Blücher was again advancing on Paris along the Marne approach. The emperor raced northward to repulse the Army of Silesia, and in a series of staggering blows caught and defeated the overextended Prussians and Russians in three battles in five days—Champaubert on February 10, Montmirail on the eleventh and Vauchamps on the fourteenth. These marvels Napoleon accomplished with only thirty thousand men, inflicting twenty thousand casualties on an opponent who began with fifty thousand men. Fortunately for Blücher, the arrival of General Winzingerode with a Russian corps of thirty thousand, fresh from the conquest of Belgium, saved the Army of Bohemia from complete eclipse and enabled it to return to the offensive quickly. But there was no denying Napoleon's enduring martial skill, and the morale of his tiny army soared.

Napoleon was now determined to mete out similar treatment to Schwarzenberg, currently near Montereau and Nogent on the upper Seine. Paris, now very close to the southern front, gave itself over to a fit of panic. But Schwarzenberg could not maintain his impetus; attacked in the rear by infuriated French peasantry, worried about a French force near Lyons threatening his flank and, above all, apprehensive when he learned that Napoleon was heading south from the Marne, the Austrian hesitated. He had good reason. Within three days of disengaging from Blücher, Napoleon was near the Seine, and Schwarzenberg was fortunate to suffer only a serious repulse at Montereau on February 17. The Allies fell back in disarray for Troyes. Hopeful of success, Napoleon rejected another offer of peace terms. It was a month of great French achievement, in which Napoleon had fully exploited the Allies' basic error of operating in two disunited armies. On the other hand, Napoleon was living on borrowed time.

The Allies made one last peace offer to Napoleon in early March, to no avail. Blücher was already advancing on Paris once more, pushing Marmont and Mortier before him. Napoleon secretly moved north, and after a delay for bridge building crossed the Marne at La Ferté. Blücher had by then cautiously pulled back, and after crossing the Aisne was heading for Laon, in order to join his reinforcements, which would bring his strength up to more than eighty-five thousand. Napoleon was still determined to close with this army, despite alarmist reports from Macdonald in the south that Schwarzenberg was again moving forward and had retaken Troyes on March 4. The result was a considerable action at Craonne on March 7 in which Ney and Mortier induced Blücher to withdraw his whole army to Laon. There, on the ninth and tenth, a second, confused battle was fought, in which Marmont's VI Corps courted destruction but were able to escape because of the stalwart holding of the key Festieux defile by 125 soldiers of the Old Guard. After suffering six thousand casualties, Napoleon was able to withdraw his remaining forty-two thousand men. He had, nevertheless, been defeated and gave orders for the fortifications of Paris to be readied. However, on March 13 Napoleon swept a force into Rheims behind Blücher, causing the Prussian to retire again toward Laon. Schwarzenberg at once halted his advance over the Seine, and Napoleon seized the opportunity afforded by this hesitation to transfer his exhausted troops southward. In the nick of time, the Allies drew back toward Troyes once again.

Although he intended to strike toward Saint-Dizier, Napoleon was also anxious to frighten off the Army of Bohemia. Accordingly, he headed for Arcis-sur-Aube, and there he engaged a substantial part of Schwarzenberg's eighty thousand Allies with

Napoleon's farewell at Fontainebleau. (By Horace Vernet.) Following the mutiny of several marshals, Napoleon found himself forced to abdicate. On April 20, 1814, he made his farewells in the Court of the White Horse at the palace of Fontainebleau, not far from occupied Paris, while the Allied commissioners (far right) looked on. It was a highly emotional moment. The emperor then departed for the island of Elba off the Italian coast, being heard to murmur that he would "return before the violets bloom again."

only twenty-one thousand men on March 20–21. In the end, the emperor was again forced to break off the battle and retire over the Aube, heading for Sompuis to join Macdonald and Kellermann. Still believing that the game could be won, he headed for Saint-Dizier, thus severing Allied communications on the twenty-third. Napoleon was confident that this well-tried maneuver would bring the enemy back and thus away from Paris, where the populace was in a state of great alarm. For four days he waited, but there was still no sign of the enemy's reacting as he had hoped.

Napoleon gradually realized that his bluff had been called. The Allies continued to press on for Paris, ignoring his presence in the rear, and by the thirty-first Mortier and Marmont were fighting on the Heights of Montmartre. Napoleon, bowing to the advice of his staff, headed for Paris. When he reached Fontainebleau on the thirty-first, he learned that Marmont had signed an armistice and that the Allies were swarming into Paris. The imperial family only just managed to slip away in time.

At Fontainebleau, a disappointed emperor still talked of continuing the struggle, but on April 2 the marshals, led by Ney, rebelled. "The army will not march," said Ney. Two days later, Napoleon was persuaded to abdicate, first in favor of the king of Rome, then, on April 6, unconditionally. On April 12, as the Allies decided what to do with him, Napoleon unsuccessfully tried to take poison. On the sixteenth the Allies announced that the emperor would be ceded the tiny island of Elba, granted an allowance and allowed to keep a guard of six hundred soldiers. His family were

Napoleon's residence on Elba. (Photograph by Grapholito, Turin.) The fallen emperor was in fact allowed to be ruler of Elba. His house in Portoferraio was called "the Windmills." He was visited there by his mother, at least one of his sisters and his loyal Polish mistress, Marie Waleskwa—but not by his wife or son. He spent the first months of exile refashioning every aspect of Elban life. Exhausting all possibilities, he soon became bored—and restless.

The Spring of 1815. The restored Bourbon monarchy of Louis XVIII was soon unpopular. This cartoon shows Bonapartists tending their buzzing beehive (the bee was one of Napoleon's imperial symbols, denoting "industry") while Bourbonists attempt to water their wilting lilies (the symbol of the House of Bourbon). Meanwhile, an eagle (Napoleon) prepares to fly as his military supporters play This Year, Next Year . . . with a bunch of violets. The propaganda war was clearly still in operation.

not, however, to join him. On April 20 Napoleon reviewed the Old Guard for the last time and bade them farewell. Eight days later he boarded HMS *Undaunted* at Saint-Raphaël and sailed for exile. On the thirtieth the Bourbon king Louis XVIII, restored by the Allies to the French throne, signed the Treaty of Paris, which restricted France to her frontiers of 1792. The long Napoleonic Wars were at last over—or so it seemed.

The island of Elba contained Napoleon for less than ten months. His friends in France kept him closely informed of developments, and he was soon aware that the Bourbons

The Imperial Stride. (Cartoon, 1815.) Napoleon—clutching a drawn sword and an olive branch in one hand and a standard in the other—makes nothing of the distance between Elba and France, while King Louis XVIII (right, wearing a candle snuffer) and his courtiers issue meaningless orders as onlookers.
"Let us pack our cases," says the figure at the left. Napoleon sailed from Elba on February 26, and landed with a thousand men near Cannes at 5:00 P.M. on March 1, 1815.

The Gates of Grenoble placed at Napoleon's feet (opposite page, top). On March 7 Napoleon reached Grenoble, the first major French town he had entered since he came ashore. The population greeted him with joy, which he acknowledged from the balcony of the Trois Dauphins hotel. This welcome was critical: "Before Grenoble I was an adventurer; after Grenoble I was a prince."

were becoming highly unpopular with both the demobilized troops and the population as a whole, the peasantry in particular suspecting that the reactionaries desired to overthrow the Revolution's land settlement. By February 1815 he had made up his mind to risk one last grand gamble. On Wednesday, March 1, he landed near Cannes accompanied by a thousand followers and four guns.

As the news was rushed to Paris and Vienna, where the Allied statesmen were meeting in congress to try to reorder post-Napoleonic Europe, the emperor set out for Grenoble. Louis XVIII sent troops to intercept him, but all deserted to their former leader, including Marshal Ney, who had taken service under the Bourbons. Napoleon's advance on Paris became a triumphal progress and on March 19 the Bourbons fled for Belgium. The next day, Napoleon reentered the capital to the acclaim of the people.

The Allies at Vienna declared Napoleon an outlaw on March 27, and at once the Seventh Coalition was formed. England and Prussia agreed to put a force of 150,000 men into the field, and Austria and Russia promised another 400,000 by early July. Not being recognized as de facto ruler of France, as he'd hoped, Napoleon announced mobilization on April 8, but reimposed the unpopular conscription only three weeks later. The 200,000 men taken over from the Bourbons were soon joined by 75,000 loyal veterans and a further 15,000 volunteers; an additional 150,000 conscripts might have materialized within six months, but he could not afford to wait so long, for the Allies were already on the move, determined to invade France in great strength at three widely separated points in July.

Napoleon's options were two. Either he could wait with his forces near Paris and refight a campaign based on the rivers as in 1814 or he could launch a blow against the only enemies already in the field—namely, Wellington and Blücher, with their

The Allies' Oven, or the Corsican Ready to Be Cooked. A colored engraving of the newly formed Seventh Coalition: Russians, on the left, encourage Blücher to cook Napoleon's goose; while the emperor of Austria (with a weathercock in his hat) opens the oven door, the prince regent stokes the fire with eagle standards (an allusion to the British role of paymaster) and the king of Prussia (right) hurries up with frontier claims of pastry. Napoleon exclaims, "To the death!"

joint 209,000 men in the Netherlands region. He chose the latter course, not wishing to subject the French population to a repetition of 1814 and hopeful that a quick victory would break the Allied resolve. At the least it could bring down Lord Liverpool's British government.

In great secrecy, the French began to move 125,000 men toward the northeastern frontiers while French agents spied out the Allied dispositions. Napoleon planned first to fool Wellington with demonstrations toward the coast as if to threaten the duke's communications with the Channel ports, then drive a wedge between the two enemy armies and defeat them in detail, thereafter occupying Brussels. To command his army, Napoleon chose the repentant Ney, a great hero to the rank and file; Grouchy, a competent cavalry commander; and Soult as chief of staff. Berthier had recently died under mysterious circumstances at Bamberg; Murat's offer of aid had been rejected; and the able Davout had been appointed governor of Paris and minister of war, a key political post. Many better senior officers were no longer available, overlooked or (arguably) misemployed. From June 7 all the frontiers of France were sealed for security. The previous day, the five French corps, the Imperial Guard and the Reserve Cavalry had begun to move from their scattered locations toward the designated area of concentration around Beaumont, not far from the Belgian frontier.

On the fourteenth Napoleon reached Beaumont. The next day, the French Armée du Nord advanced to the Sambre in three columns—the left under Ney, the right under Grouchy and the central reserve under Napoleon in person—and crossed into Belgium. The Allies were taken almost wholly by surprise, and Wellington's first reaction was to order his army to move west of Brussels toward Mons in the belief that Napoleon would attempt to envelop his right flank. Blücher, who had realized that something was afoot the previous day, ordered his army to concentrate forward around Fleurus, directly in the path of the French right wing. The Allies thus obligingly drew apart rather than together.

The immediate aim of the French was to master the road running through Quatre Bras down to Sombreffe, which was practically the only Allied line of lateral communication. Which enemy they would fight first would depend on circumstances. By late on the fifteenth Ney was within sight of Quatre Bras when the appearance of a small Allied force, whose commander had intelligently disregarded Wellington's order to move west, convinced him that Wellington was hidden nearby with his main army. He halted. On the other flank, Grouchy had fought against an advanced Prussian corps for most of the day and pressed it back to Fleurus. This was the situation by nightfall.

It was while attending the duchess of Richmond's ball at Brussels that night that Wellington realized he had been mistaken. At once he issued new orders summoning his army toward Quatre Bras, but he was aware that he would be fortunate to assemble enough men to fend off Ney if the marshal attacked early enough in sufficient force. The Allied Reserve, General Picton's Fifth Division, was, however, still at Brussels. Blücher meanwhile continued to order his four corps to mass near Fleurus on the morrow. Realizing that this was the case, Napoleon decided to try conclusions with the Prussian first. Ney was to capture and hold Quatre Bras while the emperor joined Grouchy to defeat Blücher. Thereafter, Napoleon would swing his reserve to reinforce Ney for a decisive trial of strength with Wellington. The omens appeared propitious.

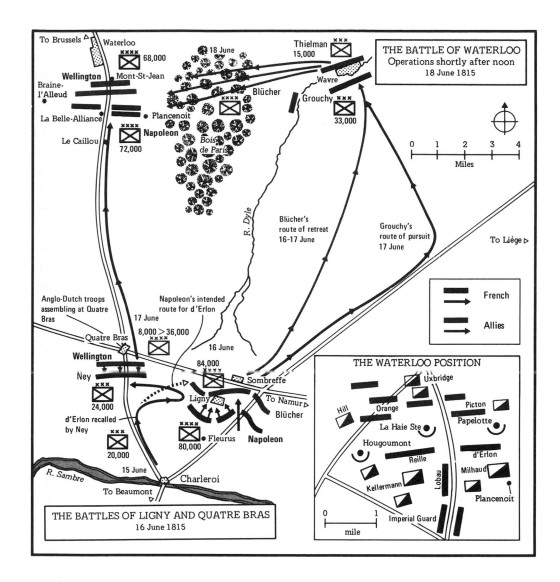

THE BATTLE OF WATERLOO
Operations shortly after noon
18 June 1815

THE WATERLOO POSITION

THE BATTLES OF LIGNY AND QUATRE BRAS
16 June 1815

The sixteenth therefore saw two battles about seven miles apart. By 2:30 P.M. the emperor and Grouchy were in action against Blücher's eighty-four thousand men at Ligny. Ney had attacked at Quatre Bras only half an hour earlier—very belatedly, considering his proximity to the skeleton forces facing him—the delay enabling Wellington to reinforce the position to eight thousand men and sixteen guns, with many more on the way. It would be a race against time, but six hours had been gained thanks to Ney's inactivity throughout the morning.

Blücher was soon under heavy pressure, but Napoleon needed Ney's reserve (commanded by d'Erlon) to clinch the battle by appearing on the Prussian right flank. Orders were accordingly sent, but through a series of confusions Ney countermanded General d'Erlon's move, and the I Corps consequently took part in neither battle on the sixteenth—though its presence at either would have been decisive. This muddle reduced the scale of the defeat that had been inflicted on the Prussians by nightfall and also enabled Wellington to achieve parity, then superiority, over Ney at Quatre Bras. Still, Napoleon had defeated one adversary and checked the other, and he expected to see Wellington destroyed the next day. A fatal error, however, was his belief that the Prussians were retreating toward Namur and Liège along their communications. In fact, by better luck than judgment, they were retreating north toward Wavre and thus were keeping in contact with Wellington. Blücher, who had been unhorsed in the battle, was saved by an aide and restored to his army later that night. His determination to sustain his ally Wellington would be of great importance to the outcome of this campaign, for his chief of staff, General Gneisenau, preferred to head for the Rhine at once.

On the seventeenth, the emperor, who was far from well, failed to order a full pursuit of the Prussians until after midday. This serious oversight was compounded by Ney, who again wasted the whole morning. Now, instead of being pinned to Quatre Bras, Wellington was able to thin out his forces progressively and retire toward the ridge of Mont-Saint-Jean. He had received assurances by this time that Blücher would aid him the next day. Although Ney was hounded into action, to find himself facing only a rear guard, and Napoleon raced his reserves across country to try to intercept the retreat, the emperor failed to catch Wellington, for heavy rain hindered the French more than it hampered the Allies, who were using the main road from Charleroi to Brussels. By evening, therefore, Wellington had reached his intended position at Mont-Saint-Jean (he had selected it as a possible battleground some time earlier). The French, after assuring themselves that Wellington was in fact present in force, turned in for the night in the pouring rain, two miles to the south. The scene was set for the Battle of Waterloo.

Wellington's position was strong. His force was posted in the main behind a three-mile ridge, bisected by the highway; to the front, three strongpoints had been occupied: La Haie Sainte in the center, Hougoumont Château to the right, Papelotte on the left. A substantial force was left to the west of the battlefield near Braine-l'Alleud in case the French attempted a characteristic outflanking movement. On the battlefield itself, he deployed sixty-eight thousand British and Allied troops and 156 guns, with

The road back from Quatre Bras to Brussels. (By Crofts.) Wellington acknowledges the salute of the North British Dragoons (the Scots Greys) as he leads back a column of British infantry and French prisoners toward Mont Saint-Jean on June 17, 1815.

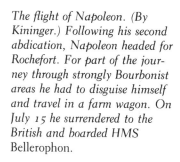

The flight of Napoleon. (By Kininger.) Following his second abdication, Napoleon headed for Rochefort. For part of the journey through strongly Bourbonist areas he had to disguise himself and travel in a farm wagon. On July 15 he surrendered to the British and boarded HMS Bellerophon.

greater strength on his right, for he expected the Prussians to reinforce his left. His strategy would be to cling on grimly to his positions until Blücher could move forces from Wavre to his aid. Napoleon did not take this possibility seriously, though Grouchy had reported the Prussians to be at Wavre late on the seventeenth.

A day later the Battle of Waterloo was lost (see pages 151–59). The French army disintegrated into a horde of fugitives, but the Old Guard added further luster to its name by its steady retreat, covering the flight of the rest. For a time, the emperor stayed with one of the retiring squares but later transferred to his coach, then to his horse, and eventually reached safety. The next morning (the nineteenth), Grouchy was also retreating in good order, but Wellington and Blücher, who had met near La Belle–Alliance the previous evening, had won a devastating victory. This was all the more amazing considering that many of Wellington's troops were not of first-line quality (most of his Peninsular veterans were over the Atlantic in Canada and the United States taking part in a separate war, and many of the Dutch and Belgian formations making up his army were of questionable quality), while Napoleon's army had been made up almost wholly of veterans. However, the choice of questionable senior commanders, an army filled with doubts about comrades' loyalty and the loss of irreplaceable time on the morning of the eighteenth had contributed to Napoleon's last defeat. The price was thirty-three thousand casualties and 220 guns lost, or sixty thousand since the fifteenth; the Allies, on the other hand, had lost twenty-two thousand men at Waterloo, including Prussians, or fifty-five thousand since the short campaign began. But whereas the Allies, with Austrians and Russians moving to their aid, could absorb these losses, France could not. Napoleon's gamble had undeniably failed.

Napoleon still spoke of retrieving the situation, but his credibility was gone. Not

Longwood. (Photograph by Jarrold.) Napoleon's last home was a simple planter's house. In it, his minuscule court tried to function. From it, Napoleon waged a ceaseless propaganda war against Hudson Lowe.

The British government would only refer to Napoleon as "General Bonaparte." The distinguished exile had many rows with the British governor, the oafish Sir Hudson Lowe (left). In this French drawing Lowe says: "Yes, General, this is truly a little island for so great a man as you!" Napoleon replies: "Fortunately, it is exactly the opposite for you, Sir Lowe!"

even his ministers would support him, and on June 22 he was persuaded to abdicate for the second, and final, time. There was still some fighting outside Paris, but Napoleon's meteoric career was over. On July 3 he left for Rochefort, planning to escape to the United States, but the Royal Navy was blockading the port. On the fifteenth he agreed to board HMS *Bellerophon*, hoping that the British prince regent would afford him sanctuary in England. But it was not to be. Without setting foot in the land of his mortal foe, he was shipped to exile on the rocky South Atlantic isle of Saint Helena.

The conditions of his virtual imprisonment were embittered by the callous severity of the governor, Sir Hudson Lowe. The former emperor soon despaired of the Allies' allowing his family to join him; Marie-Louise had returned to Austria, and his four-year-old son, the new duke of Reichstadt, was kept at Vienna (until his premature death in 1832). Napoleon spent the weary years, attended by a small staff, in contemplation and dictating his memoirs. Eventually his health deteriorated, and on May 5, 1821, Napoleon Bonaparte died. So ended one of the most eventful and dramatic lives in human history.

The Battle of Waterloo, June 18, 1815

"A whole is the sum of its parts," according to Euclid, and any study of the famous Battle of Waterloo, fought out south of Brussels on Sunday, June 18, 1815, needs to take into account the events of the preceding three days and the events on three other (but closely linked) battlefields. For Waterloo is really the story of two double battles separated by two days: Quatre Bras and Ligny, fought on June 16, and Waterloo and Wavre, contested on the eighteenth. The overall outcome sealed the reputation of the first duke of Wellington and Field Marshal Blücher, and ended the amazing career of Napoleon Bonaparte, arguably the greatest commander of all time. It inaugurated a period of almost forty years of peace between the "great powers" of Europe (a record only surpassed in our own generation, since 1945) and brought Great Britain, and to a lesser extent, Prussia, to positions of international preeminence.

Nightfall of June 17 found both armies concentrated, divided by barely a mile, while the rain lashed down to compound the misery of most of the troops. Napoleon visited his outposts in the early hours to reassure himself that Wellington was not slipping away in the dark, then slept for a few hours at Le Caillou. At his headquarters in the posting inn at Waterloo village, the duke was reassured by Blücher that come daylight he would march from Wavre, seven miles to the east, with at least two corps to reinforce his allies holding the two-and-a-half-mile ridge of Mont-Saint-Jean. This was enough for Wellington: he would stand and fight with his back to the Forest of Soignies. The night passed slowly for both armies.

With the dawn came brighter weather, but the ground was muddy. Napoleon, doubtless scorning the "sepoy general" whom he had never before met in action, postponed the opening of the battle until after 11:00 A.M. to allow the ground to dry out and thus facilitate the siting of the 246 French guns. It was not until ten o'clock that he thought of sending a message to Grouchy, with two corps near Wavre, ordering

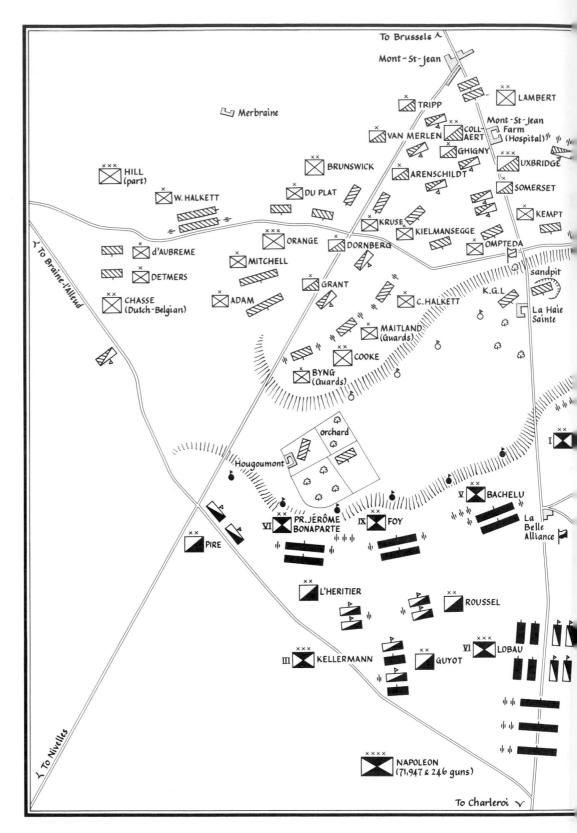

To Brussels ∧

Mont-St-Jean

LAMBERT

Merbraine

TRIPP

VAN MERLEN

COLL-
AERT

Mont-St-
Jean
Farm
(Hospital)

GHIGNY

UXBRIDGE

BRUNSWICK

ARENSCHILDT

SOMERSET

HILL
(part)

DU PLAT

W. HALKETT

KEMPT

KRUSE

KIELMANSEGGE

ORANGE

d'AUBREME

DORNBERG

OMPTEDA

sandpit

MITCHELL

DETMERS

GRANT

C. HALKETT

K.G.L

La Haie
Sainte

CHASSE
(Dutch-Belgian)

ADAM

MAITLAND
(Guards)

COOKE

BYNG
(Guards)

orchard

Hougoumont

I

BACHELU

V

La
Belle
Alliance

PR. JÉRÔME
BONAPARTE

FOY

IX

VI

PIRE

L'HERITIER

ROUSSEL

LOBAU

VI

KELLERMANN

III

GUYOT

NAPOLEON
(71,947 & 246 guns)

To Charleroi ∨

To Braine-l'Alleud

To Nivelles

him to draw closer to the main army's position. These delays would cost him dearly
before the day was out. Unhurriedly the Armée du Nord took up its battle positions.
A corps drew up on each side of the Brussels-to-Charleroi highroad: Reille's three
divisions to the left and d'Erlon's four to the right, in front of which seventy guns of
the Grand Battery were sited; on each flank was placed a force of light cavalry. In the
second line, again divided by the road, massed the cavalry of Kellermann and Milhaud,

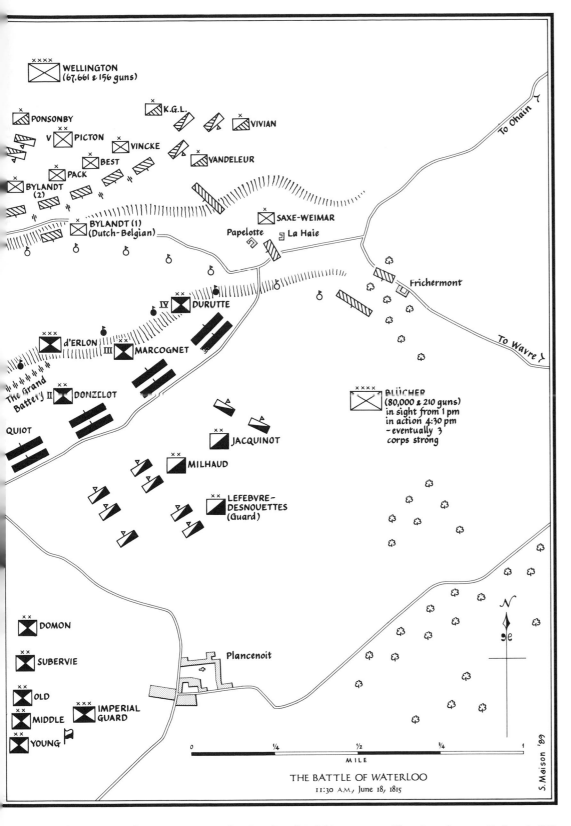

WELLINGTON
(67.661 & 156 guns)

PONSONBY

K.G.L.

VIVIAN

V PICTON

VINCKE

VANDELEUR

BEST

PACK

BYLANDT
(2)

SAXE-WEIMAR

BYLANDT (1)
(Dutch-Belgian)

Papelotte

La Haie

Frichermont

IV DURUTTE

d'ERLON

III MARCOGNET

To Ohain

To Wavre

The Grand
Battery

II DONZELOT

BLÜCHER
(80,000 & 210 guns)
in sight from 1 pm
in action 4:30 pm
–eventually 3
corps strong

QUIOT

JACQUINOT

MILHAUD

LEFEBVRE–
DESNOUETTES
(Guard)

DOMON

SUBERVIE

OLD

Plancenoit

IMPERIAL
GUARD

MIDDLE

YOUNG

N

0   ¼   ½   ¾   1
MILE

THE BATTLE OF WATERLOO
11:30 A.M., June 18, 1815

S. Maison '89

to the west and east respectively. In the third line, centrally placed, was Löbau's VI
Corps, more cavalry and reserve artillery; and last, in rear of all, the Imperial Guard.
Napoleon established two command posts, one at Rossomme, the other near La Belle–
Alliance alongside the highroad and just behind I Corps' leftmost division. His plan,
when at last it was issued, was straightforward. After a preliminary bombardment of
Wellington's position, d'Erlon would advance to seize the center of Mont-Saint-Jean

ridge, assisted by a diversionary attack by Reille's II Corps against Hougoumont; the cavalry would then pour through the central gap. Napoleon spoke confidently of sleeping that night in Brussels. With seventy-two thousand men at his disposal and a marked superiority in guns, the emperor foresaw little difficulty in defeating the ragbag of formations facing him, some of whom—the Dutch and Belgians—had been his allies until the previous year. This was to underestimate badly both Wellington and Blücher.

Wellington's plan of battle hinged upon awaiting reinforcement by the Prussians. Facing south, most of his troops were drawn up on reverse slopes out of sight of the French; but one Belgo-Dutch brigade was left forward, while swarms of light infantry were pushed ahead to dominate no-man's-land, maintain contact with the garrisons of the forward posts of Hougoumont, La Haie Sainte and Papelotte, and protect the Allied artillerymen manning their pieces along the ridge's crest. Anticipating Blücher's arrival from the east, Wellington placed more troops on his right, on the side toward Braine-l'Alleud. The two corps under Lord Hill and the prince of Orange that constituted his major formations were integrated with one another, thus interleaving British, German and Belgo-Dutch infantry, with the bulk of the light cavalry brigades in central support and the heavy cavalry under Lord Uxbridge on both sides of the main road. Barely a third of the duke's army was British, and only one division of these (Picton's Fifth) could be considered veterans, for the bulk of the formidable Peninsular army was still over the Atlantic.

The morning hours passed by, and still Napoleon waited. Near Wavre and Limale, Marshal Grouchy began to deploy his two corps, but already, unbeknown to him, two Prussian corps, followed by a third, were heading into the Bois de Paris and toward Mont-Saint-Jean, leaving only one, under Thielmann, to face the French right wing. Napoleon's order of recall would not reach Grouchy for several hours.

Shortly after 11:00 A.M. the French massed battery opened fire. At the same time, Prince Jérôme Bonaparte led his division of Reille's corps into the woods facing Hougoumont Château. Both events achieved far less than Napoleon had hoped. Many cannonballs lodged in the mud short of Wellington's concealed formations, and only Bylandt's exposed brigade took heavy punishment. As for Jérôme's attack, although it cleared the Allied skirmishers from the adjoining woodland, it completely failed to enter the château or its walled garden. The garrison of British Guardsmen repulsed all attacks, and in fury Jérôme drew another division to support his vain attack. For his part, Wellington only sent light reinforcements into Hougoumont from the ridge behind. Thus the intended French distraction ended by tying down the greater part of Reille's II Corps for the rest of the battle. Only once did the French penetrate into the courtyard, and were promptly expelled; although the main building was ignited by howitzer fire at 3:30 P.M., as late as nine o'clock that evening fighting was still continuing around Hougoumont.

An equally disappointing result awaited Napoleon's main attack. At 1:30 P.M., d'Erlon's advance attack was launched against Wellington's left center. Owing to a muddled order, two of his four divisions adopted an outdated massed formation, and these presented the British gunners with a perfect target. Although the better-deployed divisions on d'Erlon's flanks made some ground, neither was able to capture either La

Haie Sainte (stalwartly held by Major Baring with one battalion of the King's German Legion) or Papelotte on Wellington's extreme left flank. Even worse, when d'Erlon's battered central divisions at last reached the crest, they found themselves facing Picton's veterans. Although Picton himself was shot down, his men held firm and repulsed the French, whose retreat rapidly became a rout as Anglesey launched both his heavy cavalry brigades into action, the Household Brigade crashing into d'Erlon's left flank while the Union Brigade—including, contrary to their orders, the Second North British Dragoons (Scots Greys)—charged through their center. Two French eagle standards were captured as the French infantry reeled back.

Unfortunately the Scots Greys and other cavalry failed to rein in, continuing their charge over the valley to attack the French Grand Battery. Although they reached the guns, they were promptly counterattacked in flank by Jacquinot's lancers and severely mauled. This setback cost Wellington almost half his heavy cavalry, but the undoubted defeat of the I Corps had earned the Allies invaluable time—and every hour that passed was allowing Blücher to draw closer.

Napoleon had known since shortly after 1:00 P.M. that Prussians were approaching his right flank near the village of Plancenoit but still thought he had time to crush Wellington. To meet the new threat he deployed Löbau's VI Corps at right angles to

The fight for Hougoumont, June 18, 1815. (By Dighton.) The defense of this château to the right front of Wellington's position was critical throughout the battle. Although set on fire by French artillery, it never passed into French possession despite the fact that Prince Jérôme Bonaparte flung almost two divisions into the struggle.

his front in order to meet the newcomers, thus forming a new flank. By 4:30 P.M. the fight for Plancenoit was engaged. Löbau proved incapable of withstanding Bülow's corps, and Napoleon found himself forced to commit first the Young Guard, then part of the Old, as the battle for Plancenoit swung first this way and then that. By late afternoon almost all the French reserves had been sucked into the battle. And there was still no sign of Grouchy.

Meanwhile, there had been dramatic developments in Wellington's center. The gallant Major Baring fought off one attack after another, many of them led by Marshal Ney in person, and La Haie Sainte remained untaken. During one such forward foray, Ney noticed signs of what he took to be a general withdrawal by Wellington's center (which in fact had fallen back a hundred paces to avoid French artillery fire). The marshal immediately ordered Milhaud's massed squadrons to cross the battlefield from right to left in order to mount a heavy charge against Wellington's right center on the ridge behind Hougoumont and La Haie Sainte. In his haste, however, he neglected to order up horse artillery and infantry in support. Furthermore, the frontage of the attack was restricted by the Allied army's two advanced strongholds, while the muddy nature of the ground restricted the speed of advance to at best a fast trot rather than a full charge. The right center of Wellington's line transformed itself into twenty infantry squares, around which fifteen successive cavalry attacks beat in vain. The gunners manned their pieces until almost the last moment before running to take cover within the nearest square; some chose to lie beneath their cannon trails and limbers until the peril passed them by. Then, as the French recoiled to re-form for another attack, the guns were immediately remanned to pour a death-dealing fire into their retreating backs. *Cuirassiers*, lancers, dragoons—none could break the fire-fringed

Charge of the North British Dragoons. (By Lady Butler.) The famous charge of the Scots Greys helped repulse the major attack by d'Erlon's I Corps at about 2:00 P.M. Crying "Scotland forever!" they smashed into Donzelot's and Marcognet's aghast divisions and routed them, but then charged on to attack the French Great Battery, where many were killed in a well-timed countercharge by Jacquinot's lancers.

squares, although conditions within them became appalling: clouds of powder smoke and sweltering heat and thirst were added to the groans and cries of dying men and horses. The French cavalry had not even taken the repeated opportunities to spike the Allied guns while they were temporarily in their power.

Napoleon, who to this point had been content to leave control of the battle to Marshal Ney, was not pleased by what his telescope revealed. "He is compromising us as he did at Jena!" exclaimed the emperor. By 4:00 P.M. it was clear that Milhaud had shot his bolt; but to extricate his surviving horsemen would require the commitment of Kellermann's cavalry corps and another half hour of heavy losses to the mounted arm. So Wellington's battered but intact line survived another major onslaught—and more Prussians were emerging from the slippery mud-bound tracks of the Bois de Paris.

Over at Wavre, Marshal Grouchy was only just beginning to go into action at Limale against the single Prussian corps, that of General Thielmann, which Blücher had left to guard his rear. Earlier in the day General Gérard had begged Grouchy "to march on the sound of the cannon" to the west, but Grouchy had insisted on obeying Napoleon's last-received order—that of the previous night. Since the morning order of recall did not reach him until late in the afternoon, it arrived far too late for Grouchy to march from before Wavre to Mont-Saint-Jean.

But all was not well for the Allies. French cannon fire had caused horrendous casualties, and Wellington's army had also suffered considerably from the onsets of the enemy infantry and cavalry. Bylandt's brigade had needed to be withdrawn as early as 1:30 P.M., and one Hanoverian unit (the Cumberland Hussars) had fled in mid-afternoon, spreading panic all the way to Brussels. And now, at about 6:00 P.M., the great crisis suddenly arrived in the center. Ney at last became master of La Haie Sainte, launching a properly coordinated attack at a moment when Baring was out of am-munition. Ney next rushed up a battery of guns to within two hundred yards of the Allied center, sited it athwart the highroad and opened a devastating fire at several already shaken formations. Wellington brought up Vivian and Vandeleur's light cavalry brigades from behind Papelotte on his extreme left and created a flimsy line behind his wavering infantrymen. "Give me night or give me Blücher," he exclaimed. It was in fact Ziethen's corps that began to make a timely arrival on the left wing.

Marshal Ney scented victory. His chief of staff was sent off at a gallop to entreat the emperor to send up the Guard to clinch the success. "Troops? What does he expect me to do—make some?" was Napoleon's response. The fact was that almost all the Imperial Guard was deployed toward Plancenoit, where Bülow's Prussians had been reinforced by Pirch's corps some time before. Not until approximately 7:30 P.M. did Napoleon manage to collect some eleven battalions, mostly of the Middle Guard. He led them forward as far as La Belle–Alliance in person before being persuaded to hand them over to Ney, who had by now had three horses killed beneath him and was almost speechless with rage and exhaustion.

A new lull descended on the scene, broken only by the thunder of the Imperial Guard's drums. Noting the dark-uniformed masses of Ziethen's infantry flooding over the horizon, Napoleon ordered his aides to ride up and down the weary French lines and announce that the newcomers were in fact Grouchy's divisions, arriving on the

enemy's flank and rear in the time-honored fashion. For a moment French morale revived—but only for a moment. By now the Imperial Guardsmen, most feared veterans in Europe, were breasting the forward slope of Mont-Saint-Jean in four columns. They had veered away from the highroad to the left and were accordingly approaching the section where the British Guards Brigade lay waiting for them amid the high corn. "Now Maitland! Now's your time!" ordered Wellington, and as the surprised Imperial Guardsmen attempted to deploy, the scarlet lines rose from the ground almost before their feet, and telling volleys tore into their ranks. All four columns received similar treatment, and some British battalions swung forward to bring flanking fire to bear. The Guard hesitated, and then began to retire downhill. "La Garde recule!" The incredible news flashed through the French army. Then Grouchy's supposed reinforcements began to open fire—into the French positions. "Treason!" The French began to waver, and sensing his moment Wellington waved his hat three times and his whole line surged forward with a deep-throated roar as the bayonet points came down. La Haie Sainte was retaken, and as Blücher's cavalry swept onto the field from the east, the cry went up among the French troops, *"Sauve qui peut!"* Soon a horde of fugitives was rushing back toward Genappe. Napoleon sought shelter in a square formed by the Old Guard in an attempt to cover their comrades' flight; the emperor was then persuaded to leave and head for Charleroi. The square continued to defy the Allies. Offered the chance to surrender, General Cambronne uttered the

The last stand of the Old Guard. (By Hippolyte Bellangé.) Two squares formed by the Old Guard stood firm in an attempt to cover the flight of their compatriots. Summoned to surrender, General Cambronne (left of the eagle standard) is reputed by legend to have cried: "the Guard dies but never surrenders!" In fact, he yelled the one-word expletive "Merde!" The Battle of Waterloo was over, and with it Napoleon's astonishing career.

one immortal word *"Merde!"* Allied artillery thereupon pulverized the square into atoms. The Battle of Waterloo was essentially over.

As Prussian cavalry thundered forward in pursuit of L'Armée du Nord, at 9:00 P.M. Wellington had a historic meeting with Blücher near the farm of La Belle–Alliance. *"Quelle affaire!"* the aged Prussian commander in chief remarked; ". . . which was about all the French he had," Wellington dryly commented. To win the battle had cost the Allies 22,000 casualties among their 138,000 men present (including the 70,000 or so Prussians who had joined in the later parts of the action). To lose it had cost Napoleon 43,500 men. Over by Wavre each side had lost 2,500 men as Grouchy, early on the nineteenth, began to disengage from Thielmann and retire south. But Napoleon had lost more than just his men and one battle: he had finally forfeited his reputation.

SEVEN

NAPOLEON'S LEGACY

Napoleon has inspired many and conflicting assessments in the years since his death in 1821. To his admirers—and they are many—he is "the man of destiny," "the tragic martyr of Saint Helena" or "Papa Violette" (a reference to his comment as he left Fontainebleau for exile in April 1814 that he would return before the violets bloomed again).

Many important men have commented upon his attainments in glowing terms. To the German Goethe, he was "always enlightened by reason, always clear and decisive, and gifted at every moment with enough energy to translate into action whatever he recognized as being advantageous or necessary. His life was the stride of a demigod from battle to battle and from victory to victory . . . it could . . . be said that he was in a permanent state of enlightenment, which is why his fate was more brilliant than the world has ever seen or is likely to see after him."

French commentators have mainly been commendatory, sometimes carrying their plaudits to the verge of idolatory. The nineteenth-century writer Alfred de Musset, more balanced than some, could not in the last resort resist the emperor's allure. "Never had there been so many sleepless nights as in the time of that man; never had there been seen . . . such a nation of desolate mothers; never was there such a silence about those who spoke of death. And yet there was never such joy, such life, such fanfares of war, in all hearts. Never was there such pure sunlight as that which dried all this blood. God made the sun for this man, they said, and they called it 'the Sun of Austerlitz.' But he made this sunlight himself with his ever-thundering cannons which dispelled all clouds but those which succeed the day of battle."

A more balanced view, still far from uncritical, was that of the great French historian Alexis de Tocqueville: "Napoleon himself—that singular, incomplete, but truly marvelous being, whom one cannot contemplate attentively without treating oneself to one of the most curious, one of the strangest spectacles that can be found in the universe.

"I should like to show how much, in his prodigious enterprise, he actually owed to his genius, and with what opportunities the condition of the country and temper of the times presented him. . . . Starting with his interior administration, I want to contemplate the spectacle of his almost divine intelligence grossly laboring at the compression of human freedom; that perfect and scientific organization of force, such as only the greatest genius living in the most enlightened and civilized age could conceive of; and under the weight of that admirable machine, society flattened, stifled, and increasingly sterile, intellectual activity slowing down, human mind languishing, souls shrinking, great men ceasing to appear, and a limitless, flat horizon against which nothing can be seen, no matter in which direction one's eyes may turn, save the colossal figure of the emperor himself."

Even Karl Marx had to acknowledge Napoleon's role in establishing nineteenth-century bourgeois society. "Napoleon created inside France the conditions that made it possible for free competition to develop, for the redistributed land to be exploited, and for the newly liberated productive energy of the nation to be put to use; beyond the borders of France, he swept away the feudal institutions. . . ."

There have also been numerous detractors, horrified by the tyranny and death that accompanied Napoleon's achievements, particularly in the later years. "The beast incarnate," "a talented thug," or, in Thomas Carlyle's phrase, "the Sheep-Worrier of Europe," who became deluded by his own propaganda image—these are among the terms of opprobrium frequently to be found. The South American liberator Simon Bolívar feared, after Waterloo, that Napoleon might arrive in the New World. "If South America is struck by the thunderbolt of Bonaparte's arrival," he wrote, "misfortune will ever be ours if our country accords him a friendly reception. His thirst for conquest is insatiable; he has mowed down the flower of European youth . . . in order to carry out his ambitious projects. The same designs will bring him to the New World."

Thomas Jefferson, the great American statesman, sympathized with Napoleon's fate on Saint Helena but was no admirer. Commenting on the book about the emperor written by Dr. O'Meara (one of Napoleon's medical advisers during his last years), Jefferson wrote: "The book proves also that nature had denied him the moral sense, the first excellence of well-organized man. If he could seriously and repeatedly affirm that he had raised himself to power without ever having committed a crime, it proves that he wanted totally the sense of right and wrong. If he could consider the millions of human lives which he had destroyed or caused to be destroyed, the desolations of countries . . . the destitutions of lawful rulers of the world without the consent of their constituents, to place his brothers and sisters on their thrones, the cutting up of established societies of men . . . and all the numberless train of his other enormities; the man, I say, who could consider all these as no crimes must have been a moral monster, against whom every hand should have been lifted to slay him."

Another contemporary critic, the well-known and influential Madame de Staël, whose salon had been closed on Napoleon's order, wrote: "His victories created him a prince; it took his love of etiquette, his need of flattery, his titles, his decorations, his courtiers to make the upstart reappear in him. Yet no matter how senseless his policy of conquest may have been, it may be said that once his soul had sunk so low as to see no more greatness except in despotism, he became incapable of managing without perpetual war: for what would a despot be without military glory in a country such as France? Was it possible to oppress the nation . . . without at least giving it the fatal compensation of oppressing other nations in turn? The greatest evil plaguing mankind is absolute power."

"Absolute power," as Lord Acton was to remark, "tends to corrupt absolutely." Napoleon referred to this possibility only twice. Once in 1810, when a meal had lasted longer than the stipulated twenty minutes, he leapt to his feet with the humorous remark "Power is beginning to corrupt!" The second reference comes in the 483d maxim, culled from his writings and utterances: "In the long term, too much power ends by depraving even the most honest man."

Napoleon indubitably had many weaknesses, but total corruption was not among them. Nor was he, as the great Russian novelist Tolstoi contended, "a man of no convictions, no habits, no traditions, no name, not even a Frenchman, by the strangest freaks of chance, [who], as it seems, rises above the seething parties of France, and without attaching himself to any of them, advances to a prominent position. . . . The brilliant personal qualities of the soldiers of the Italian army, the disinclination to fight of his opponents, and his childish insolence and conceit, gain him military glory. Innumerable so-called *chance* circumstances attend him everywhere. . . . *Chance,* millions of *chances,* give him power." To Tolstoi there were no great men. All were mere leaves, whirled to and fro at the whim of the winds of Fate.

No, Napoleon controlled his destiny far more than Tolstoi would have us believe. It is true that his earlier idealism changed as the years passed, and that he became a dictator, even a tyrant. Ludwig van Beethoven had his reasons when he tore up the dedication to his Third Symphony. Perhaps Talleyrand, no great admirer of Napoleon's, was near the mark when he observed in conversation with Lord Holland in 1822: "His career is the most outstanding that has occurred for one thousand years. . . . He was certainly a great, an extraordinary man, nearly as extraordinary in his qualities as in his career; at least so upon reflection, I, who have seen him near and much, am disposed to consider him."

In the course of this book, much has been said about Napoleon's brand of generalship, and some of his personal characteristics have been described and assessed. More remains to be said, however, concerning his powers of personality if an overall view is to be obtained of this dynamic man. As he once declared, "The base must equal the height . . . intellect and character in equal proportion"; and, "The mind is the sail; character the ballast." Above all, he was the epitome of charismatic leadership—that rare ability to inspire subordinates, whether military or civil, by creating a pervasive atmosphere compounded of three elements: first, the communication of a strong personal conviction of his capabilities, determination and powers of judgment; second, the demonstration of the power to command a respect bordering on fear or love, or a combination of the two, engendering an intense desire to please; and third, the ability to give an impression of panache and boundless drive.

Napoleon indubitably possessed the power to inspire total acceptance of, and confidence in, his intentions and abilities, and was able in consequence to wring the utmost effort, devotion and zeal out of the vast majority of his subordinates, to the total or near exclusion of all other considerations, promoting a feeling of membership of an exclusive elite. As General Sir Archibald Wavell described it in a lecture at

Cambridge on the eve of the Second World War: "To learn that Napoleon won the campaign of 1796 by manoeuvre on interior lines or some such phrase is of little value. If you can discover how a young, unknown man inspired a ragged, mutinous, half-starved army, and made it fight; how he gave it energy and momentum to march and fight as it did; how he dominated and controlled generals older and more experienced than himself—then you will have learnt something. Napoleon did not gain the position he did so much by a study of rules and strategy, as by a profound knowledge of human nature in war."

At the outset of his career as an army commander Napoleon did not, after all, have very much obviously in his favor—least of all his physical appearance. "More like a mathematician than a general" was the opinion of Lasalle. "Owing to his thinness, his features were almost ugly in their sharpness; his walk was unsteady, his clothes neglected, his appearance produced on the whole an unfavorable impression, and was in no way imposing," wrote Count Yorck von Wartenburg. Yet within minutes of first meeting his cynical and hostile divisional commanders in 1796, he had imposed his mastery. First he made them smile as he enthusiastically showed off his wife's miniature; then, "a moment later he put on his general's hat and seemed to have grown two feet. He questioned us on the position of our divisions, on the spirit and effective forces of each corps; prescribed the course we were to follow; announced that he would hold an inspection on the morrow, and on the following day attack the enemy." So recalled Massena of their first meeting. Another present, the rough-diamond general Augereau put it even more concisely: "This little bugger of a general has actually scared me."

Napoleon's gift for charismatic leadership was an important part of his ability to inspire confidence in his men. Nor was he slow to make the most of his achievements for propaganda purposes. His conduct at Arcola is a case in point.

One physical feature was, however, compelling. Wartenburg continued: "In spite of his apparent bodily weakness he was tough and sinewy, and from under his deep forehead there flashed, despite his sallow face, the eyes of genius, deep-seated, large and of a grayish-blue color, and before their glance and the words of authority that issued from his thin, pale lips, all bowed low."

First impressions can be deceptive; they can also be extremely important. Clearly Napoleon knew how to impress his key subordinates, and his recipe of familiarity followed by severity was one he would repeat continually over the years.

If Napoleon had a great impact on his commanders, it may be imagined how he was capable of inspiring the rank and file. Always theatrical, he used both stick and carrot to get his way. He believed in seeing and being seen, and from first to last held numerous inspections to gauge the morale and physical condition of his troops, and to dispense a little more of his magic among them. If he felt lessons were needed, he did not hesitate to administer them. At the outset in Italy, in 1796, when the Third Battalion of the 105th Regiment of the Line mutinied at Nice, he treated it to a withering harangue, forced it to march—then halted it, sent it to the rear in ignominy, ordered its major to be court-martialed, the officers disbanded, NCOs dismissed from the army and the rank and file dispersed in fives to other units. Even more celebrated was his handling of the Thirty-ninth and Eighty-fifth Regiments near Rivoli later in the same campaign. Assembling them in front of a hollow square formed by the rest of their division, he addressed them: "Soldiers, I am not pleased with you. You have shown neither discipline, nor constancy, nor bravery. No position could rally you. Men of the 39th and 85th, you are not French soldiers. Chief of staff! Have it inscribed on their colors—'They no longer belong to the Army of Italy.' "

On the other hand, his commendations were equally memorable. As General Desaix recorded, "Bonaparte never saw a demi-brigade without persuading it that he considered it the best in his army. He often spoke to them and always had something vigorous to say. He gave each demi-brigade magnificent flags, upon which, in large letters of gold, the names of the battles in which they had distinguished themselves were inscribed. They added the words of praise uttered by the general—'I know you well, the 18th—you will beat the enemy!'; whilst the 32nd called forth the words— 'I was easy in my mind for the brave 32nd were there' or 'The terrible 57th demi-brigade, whom none can stop.' "

In examining Napoleon's particular power of personality, his special brand of charisma, most of the examples will be taken from his earlier years, for it was then that these charcteristics emerged and developed, although some attention must be paid to the perversions and distortions that crept in as time progressed.

Almost every contemporary noted his dominating intellectual presence—the "halo of glory," as some described it—an impression that persisted to the end. We have already described (on page 62) the impression he made on the difficult General Vandamme. The dashing cavalry commander Auguste de Colbert, destined to be killed in 1809, wrote of this power: "It is a long time since, for the first time, he awakened in my soul the desire for glory. To merit his esteem will ever be my finest victory. The more I see of this man, the greater I have found him."

A second often-mentioned characteristic was Napoleon's intense curiosity and general alertness. Visitors to his office at the Tuileries or his headquarters in the field would often find themselves bombarded with queries. Thus the young Lieutenant Thiébault, a new *aide de camp* delivering a message from his chief, was "grilled with a thousand questions." Sometimes, though rarely, Napoleon received rather more than he expected. Shortly before the outset of the campaign of 1806, on first meeting Napoleon, the highly intellectual young Swiss soldier Jomini, staff aide to Marshal Ney and later one of the most important interpreters of Napoleonic warfare, found himself closely questioned about his published work on strategy. He astounded the emperor by prophesying that Napoleon would unite the French army at Bamberg in four days' time. "Who told you that I am going to Bamberg?" he was asked. "The map of Germany, sire!" replied the cocky young man with aplomb, " . . . and your operations before Ulm and Marengo. To mete out to the Duke of Brunswick the treatment you accorded Mack and Melas, you will need to march on Gera; and to march on Gera, you will have to pass by Bamberg." The emperor was impressed and ordered Jomini to mention this to nobody, not even Berthier. Usually, however, Napoleon dominated every interview, and even specialists were greatly impressed by his body of knowledge and his desire to add to it. As the Abbé Siéyès, his fellow consul, described it: "*Il sait tout; il fait tout; il peut tout.*" ("He knows all; he does all; he can do anything".)

Napoleon also knew how to create a mystique, both personal and corporate. Like Nelson, he could inspire a "Band of Brothers." Even if his methods were theatrical, they were no less effective. We have already mentioned his gift for oratory—the skill for finding the right word for the moment (and, sometimes, it must be admitted, finding it only after the moment had passed, and having it added to the official record subsequently). *His* "Army of Italy" was later transformed into *his* "Grand Army," and to have served under Napoleon's orders was encouraged to be regarded as a distinction in itself. "You will return to your homes, and your countrymen will say, as they point you out: 'He belonged to the Army of Italy.' " However, it is modern opinion that General Bonaparte's famous speech of March 27, 1796, was a later inspiration. At the camp of Boulogne in 1805 he exclaimed: "My army is formidable . . . once we had an Army of the Rhine, an Army of Italy, an Army of Holland; there has never been a *French* Army—but now it exists, and we shall soon see it in action." It is true that he adjusted *post facto* part of his message to the troops issued before battle on December 2, 1805, in order to fit in with events that had occurred, but he did not change its inspirational content. Thus: "You will only have to say: 'I was at the Battle of Austerlitz' to hear the reply: 'He is one of the brave!' "

He was not above resorting to moral blackmail to wring the utmost efforts out of his troops. The same message in 1805 also contained the following passage: "Soldiers, I shall in person direct all your battalions; I shall keep out of range if, with your accustomed bravery, you carry disorder and confusion into the ranks of the enemy; but if the victory is for a moment uncertain, you shall see your Emperor expose himself in the front rank." This type of appeal certainly worked on early-nineteenth-century Frenchmen. On May 22, 1809, at Aspern-Essling, the grenadiers of the Old Guard— alarmed by his exposure to enemy fire—threatened to down arms "if the Emperor does not retire." Of course, he built up a reputation based on personal example and deeds of courage and panache. In 1799, his visit to the plague hospital at Jaffa horrified his staff but earned the approval of his men. They knew he had almost been killed at

Napoleon at Wagram, July 6, 1809. (After Vernet.) During the great years, the emperor was always well forward on days of battle, seeing and being seen. In later years this activity occasionally diminished—as at Borodino in 1812, and at Waterloo three years later. As he remarked in 1805: "One has only a certain time for war."

the Battle of Arcola, tricolor in hand, leading an attack. They were aware that it was his custom to spend the eve of battle among them, "with mud up to the knees. . . ." Every soldier knew that the night before Jena in October 1806, Napoleon had taken part, lantern in hand, in the construction of a rough road up the Landgrafenberg; or that in July 1809 he had personally reconnoitered the enemy bank of the Danube at a proposed bridge site, disguised in a private's greatcoat, and with only a single companion, in full view of Austrian sentries. In the early 1800s he sported a distinctive uniform, but later, whether at court or in the field, he became even more distinguishable by the deliberate simplicity of his dress, contrasting with the splendor of those surrounding him. This was all the stuff of which legends were made—and deliberately so.

Napoleon also knew how to combine familiarity with severity, aloofness with approachability, stick with carrot. At his ceaseless reviews already referred to, he encouraged the men in the ranks to present petitions, even to suggest their own promotion or decoration. He would walk along the ranks, occasionally making a rough joke, allowing the men to use the familiar *tu* (even among the marshals only Lannes, who had saved his life at Arcola, was allowed that degree of intimacy)—these displays of friendliness and trust all being part of his avowed policy of "seeing and being seen."

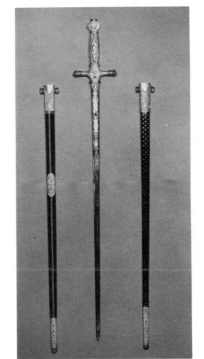

Napoleon in his undress uniform of colonel in the chasseurs à cheval *(far left). (By Arnold, after Dahling.) The emperor deliberately dressed simply to make a contrast with his sumptuously uniformed entourage. This green-coated uniform alternated with the blue and white of a colonel of grenadiers—both, of course, belonging to the Imperial Guard.*

Napoleon's court sword, with alternative scabbards (left). (Wellcome Trust.) This decorated weapon formed part of the booty found in Napoleon's traveling coach, captured after Waterloo. No doubt he intended to wear it for his triumphant entry into Brussels.

Rarely did he offer compliments on such occasions, *"Soldats, je suis content de vous"* being about as far as he would normally commit himself unless a truly theatrical gesture was deemed requisite.

As for the "stick," not even the highest in the army were immune. General Gouvion Saint-Cyr, who in 1806 left his command in Naples to visit Paris in order to complain of his treatment by Murat and Massena, was accorded short shrift once he was able to secure an interview with the emperor.

"You have doubtless received the permission of the minister of war?"

"No, sire, but there was nothing for me to do in Naples."

"If within two hours you are not on the road back to Naples you will be shot before noon."

The situation had been made quite clear as early as 1798 in Egypt. When a mutiny was threatened, General Bonaparte gave the following warning: "I know that several generals are dissatisfied and preach revolt. Let them take care. The distance between a general and a drummer boy is the same to me under certain circumstances, and if one of those circumstances presents itself I shall shoot one like the other." General Dupont, the hapless commander who surrendered his corps to the Spaniards at Bailén in 1808, was brutally victimized by Napoleon. Having been repatriated by General Cuesta, he was rash enough to appear at a military review the emperor was inspecting in Madrid. Once aware of his presence, Napoleon immediately canceled the review, almost had Dupont shot on the spot, but contented himself with publicly cashiering him, stripping him of all honors (he had served with great distinction on the Danube in 1805) and finally incarcerating him under a severe regime for six years. Little wonder that Dupont thereupon transferred his allegiance to the Bourbons (who appointed him minister of war in 1814 and later a minister of state and member of the Privy Council after Waterloo). Several marshals, Massena among them, suffered periods of disgrace, unemployment and exile from Paris.

However, the reverse of the coin has also to be taken into account. Rewards were showered on the faithful, the favorites or those fortunate enough to be regarded with approval. The celebrated Legion of Honor, with its four classes and sixteen "cohorts" of members, was awarded almost indiscriminately. Some forty-eight thousand crosses were bestowed between 1802 and 1814 (apparently, only twelve hundred went to civilian recipients). But this was only the tip of the iceberg of the Napoleonic honors system. Within the army orders, promotions, cash rewards and patents of nobility were distributed on a generous scale. Inevitably, the most senior men fared best. Joachim Murat, imperial brother-in-law through his marriage in 1800 to Caroline Bonaparte, became a prince of the blood, grand admiral of France, grand duke of Cleves and Berg, viceroy and then king of Naples, as well as being the "emperor's lieutenant" and arguably the senior appointee of the marshalate. Berthier, apart from his *bâton*, enjoyed the positions of vice-constable, grand master of the hunt, grand officer of the palace, duke of Vallengin, sovereign prince of Neuchâtel, Vice-constable of the Empire and prince of Wagram. Few refused the offer of honors; among those who did were two staunch republicans, Brune and Jourdan. Monetary grants, 1,261 in all, totaling sixteen million gold francs, were made to 824 general officers, some of the marshals inevitably doing particulary well, especially Berthier, Ney and Davout. Besides the six military princes (Poniatowski, the seventh, was a prince in his own right), the military aristocracy eventually comprised 23 dukes, 193 counts, 648 barons and 117 knights, many with monetary grants of between four thousand and fifty thousand francs *per annum*. Palaces, Parisian hotels and hunting lodges were also awarded to the great men of the new regime. Heiresses were married off to the fortunate few. Of course, the recipients had little time to savor these privileges, most of which were arranged at the expense of conquered provinces.

Nor did the rank and file go unrecognized. Many shared in the Legion of Honor from its institution, and before this received swords and other weapons of honor from the first consul in recognition of valorous deeds. Napoleon's phenomenal attention to detail in such matters was another facet of his charisma. Thus in 1800 he found time to write a personal letter to Sergeant Léon Aune of the Thirty-second Demibrigade, a veteran who could claim five wounds and as many battles, on the soldier's return from Egypt:

"To Brave Léon—I have received your letter, brave comrade. You have no need to tell me of your actions. Since the death of brave Benezette you are the bravest grenadier in the army. You possess one of the 100 swords which I am distributing to the army. All the soldiers agree you are the model of the regiment. I have a great desire to see you, and the Minister of War is sending you the order. I love you like my own son."

Other humble soldiers found themselves hauled out of the ranks when the emperor requested that a colonel produce his bravest man. After questioning the soldier on his experience, Napoleon would order his promotion, award him the Legion of Honor (sometimes taking the cross from his own breast—he kept a few spares in a pocket for replacement purposes), allot his children free places in state schools; on other occasions a soldier might receive a cash bonus. This was the kind of imperial largesse about which legends accrued, and it certainly helped raise morale in general as the stories went the rounds. At a review at Tilsit, in July 1807, Napoleon even awarded his personal Legion of Honor to the bravest Russian grenadier at a review shared with Tsar Alexander.

At other times, this same attention to detail could be less fortunate for the recipient. After a review at Cologne in 1805, Napoleon wrote to Berthier:

"You will note that the Emperor, having put the 58th through maneuvers at Cologne, was satisfied with the officers' and soldiers' appearance, but observed with chagrin that the major had no knowledge of his maneuvers. That consequently he has ordered that he be suspended for three months, and sent for that time to a camp to receive instruction; and that he will not be reinstated until he has shown that he knows the maneuvers in the greatest detail."

But, as we have seen, marshals and generals could also receive brusque treatment if it was deserved. In 1805 Murat was called "a stunned fool" for advancing on Vienna rather than pursuing the Russians over the Danube; Bernadotte was almost court-martialed after Auerstädt in October 1806 and was only spared this fate, some contemporary sources allege, because of his marriage to Desirée Clary, sometime girlfriend of Captain Buonaparte during his time at Marseilles in the early 1790s. In March 1814 Marmont was castigated for comporting hismelf "like a second lieutenant" at the Festieux defile, and Ney was likened disparagingly to "the last-joined drummer boy" for rash conduct at Jena (although in later years he would be called the "bravest of the brave" for his conduct during the retreat from Russia). Few matters escaped the emperor's keen eye (or the notice of his ubiquitous spies or informers).

Napoleon was also a master of theater, capable of wringing the utmost dramatic value out of a great occasion. In May 1803 the famous distribution of the Legion of Honor took place in a vast natural amphitheater not far from Boulogne. Over twenty thousand troops were present as the consul for life (the plebiscite creating the Empire still lay ahead) pinned the white enameled crosses to the breasts of deserving soldiers. The casque of Charlemagne had been brought from Notre Dame to hold the medals; the symbolism was clear: the deliberate link with the splendors of the Carolingian dynasty was evident to all participants. The coronation of December 2, 1804, was also made into an immensely splendid occasion, and planned to the last detail. The robes were gorgeous, much use being made of the symbol of the golden bee, the chosen insignia for the new emperor, denoting industriousness. The pope was brought from Rome to participate, and all the Bonaparte brothers, the marshalate and other great officers of state, sumptuously attired, played active parts. At the climactic moment, Napoleon took the crown from the hands of the pope and placed it on his own head—symbolizing that he would not accept it from any authority other than his own—before proceeding to crown Josephine empress. Napoleon's sisters were train bearers, together with Hortense Beauharnais, and gossip had it that the spiteful siblings did their best to trip Josephine up with it. Propaganda was much involved in the celebrated painting of this event by the artist David. Napoleon's mother is prominently shown in a box overlooking the scene, but in fact she did not attend, allegedly because of a

Napoleon in his coronation dress, 1804. (After Isabey.) The emperor possessed a sense of the dramatic and colorful and gave it full rein when grand occasions of state were involved. However, he also appreciated the greater impact that simplicity of dress could achieve.

serious disagreement between "Madame Mère" and her second son. According to the story, a euphoric Napoleon had stretched out his hand for his mother to kiss, but the spirited *dame* had sunk her teeth into it instead.

Later significant events were carefully stage-managed. Mack's surrender at Ulm in October 1805 was held in another natural amphitheater, with the French victors looking down on the Austrians marching in to surrender their arms. Napoleon received "the unfortunate General Mack" (the words the Austrian commander used to introduce himself) wearing his old gray overcoat, whose tails he was singeing before a vast bonfire. The next year, when taking possession of Berlin, Prince Hatzfeldt was required to tender the keys to Napoleon on bended knee. Napoleon then ordered him to be taken away and shot for some infraction of surrender terms and was only dissuaded when the princess (on carefully arranged cue) flung herself at his feet to plead for mercy. The greatest event of all was probably the meeting with Tsar Alexander on the raft moored in the Niemen near Tilsit. Every last detail of protocol was observed to the letter, and for two hot July weeks of that 1807 summer there were ceremonial parades, great banquets, concerts and other entertainments as Napoleon set out to impress his fellow potentate. Even the famous farewell in the Court of the White Horse at Fontainebleau in April 1814 was pure theater.

The favors of the great man could be capricious. There was no guarantee that the emperor would not adjust his view with no warning at all. Some deserving men were ignored or even written out of the record of historical events. Thus Kellermann the Younger was excluded from the Bulletin of June 14, 1800, and Carra-Saint-Cyr from the final official account of the Battle of Marengo. Others were lionized, such as Desaix after Marengo (after all, he was safely dead, killed at the moment of victory). After handsomely defeating the Russians on the River Alle shortly before Friedland in 1807, Ney was accorded the honor of marching at the head of his corps past the entire army, which was standing at attention. The year before, Davout's III Corps had been given the distinction of being the first troops to enter Berlin, in recognition of their superb fighting record at Auerstädt.

There can be no questioning Napoleon's power to inspire great and selfless efforts among his troops, but from 1812 this willingness began to wilt at the highest level of commanders as war-weariness and a desire to enjoy their privileges spread. A few marshals remained loyal to the end, but many opportunistically began to look to their own interests, demonstrating Napoleon's failure to institutionalize his position. Nevertheless, the rank and file remained loyal through 1814 and until after Waterloo the next year. And it is clear that his powers of persuasion survived aboard HMS *Bellerophon*: "Damn the fellow," exclaimed Admiral Lord Keith, "—if he had obtained an interview with His Royal Highness [the Prince Regent] in half an hour they would have been the best friends in England."

The real basis of Napoleon's charismatic power lay in his careful psychological study of human character in general and that of the Frenchman in particular. In Baron Meneval's opinion, "the study of the human heart had taught him the art of attaching men to him and subjecting them. His presence and words aroused enthusiasm. His eloquence was earnest and rapid; his words were energetic, profound, and often sublime. His simple exterior was heightened by an air of grandeur and the habit of command, and the fascination of his look, whose quiet and severe expression penetrated to the depths of the heart, inspired respect mingled with fear and affection. No leader was more popular, and yet never would he consent to humble himself to acquire that popularity."

As early as Toulon, at the age of twenty-four, he knew how to influence men, as the "batterie des hommes sans peur" incident, already recounted, illustrates. He had a distinct view of the French soldier, his strengths and weaknesses, and was aware of his power to sway his countrymen emotionally. "There is nothing one cannot obtain from Frenchmen by offering them the allurement of danger; it seems to put spirit into them; it is their Gallic heritage. Valor and a love of glory are with Frenchmen an instinct, a sort of sixth sense. How many times, in the thick of a battle, have I stopped to watch my young conscripts throwing themselves into the fight for the first time! Honor and courage issued from every pore." In this, the Corsican reflected the view of the Prussian Frederick the Great. "If I were in command of Frenchmen, I would make them the greatest soldiers in the world. To pass over a few thoughtless acts, never to worry them unnecessarily, to encourage the natural gaiety of their minds, to be scrupulously just towards them, and to inflict no *minutiae* upon them—such would be my secret in rendering them invincible."

Yet Napoleon's view of human nature was not basically optimistic. As Nietzsche observed, "Napoleon's being was certainly formed by faith in himself and in his star, and by the contempt of man which proceeded from it." The older and more disillu-

The Imperial Legend. (German engraving of early 1815.) Napoleon's rise and fall ends here with a period of undisturbed contemplation on the isle of Elba. In fact, there was one more chapter to add to the story—the dramatic events of the Hundred Days in 1815.

1817. Napoleon put on weight during the last years of the empire, and even more during his frustrating six years in exile (opposite page, left). As a student, in a notebook that still survives, he had described Saint Helena as "une petite île."

sioned he became, the more Napoleon was convinced that men were motivated only by fear or self-interest. "Fear and the hope of fortune and favors could alone exist between them and me. I was lavish with both. I have made courtiers—I have never pretended to make friends." And so, as we have seen, he played upon human fear and human greed to the full—the classic use of stick and carrot.

Consequently, he was unprepared to place great trust in humankind outside his family. In his servants, he came to prefer servility and sycophancy in later years. He played them off against one another, encouraging feuds and rivalries among them so as to retain control over them and discourage the formation of cabals against him.

Popularity in the ordinary sense meant nothing to him. He knew that his troops often felt for him a special brand of love/hate. They could curse him when he demanded great exertions from them, as when he drove them over the arid desert from Alexandria to the Nile in 1798, or over the icy Guadarrama Pass in pursuit of Sir John Moore's army on December 21, 1808. Vandamme, enraged at not being selected to receive a marshal's *bâton*, vituperated: "He is a mean-spirited fellow, a forger and a liar; and but for me, Vandamme, he would still be keeping pigs in Corsica." But usually the rank and file accorded the emperor an affection bordering on the idolatrous. He would ignore their occasionally hostile moods with a shrug of the shoulders; provided that they would produce the superlative performance when the situation required it, he would often overlook misdemeanors and complaints. They grumbled—but they followed him.

As might be supposed from such a master of propaganda, Napoleon was not averse to spreading a legend during his six years on the South Atlantic island of Saint Helena. With time on his hands, he began to dictate his memoirs to his companions in exile such as Las Cases and Baron Gourgaud. He was determined to leave a myth behind him. Inevitably, it was a blend of truth and falsehood, fact and romantic fiction. He asserted that he had been the champion of the oppressed peoples of Europe against the despotic power of the old monarchies, the promulgator of a new social order that would have brought peace, harmony and prosperity under constitutional rule. He even spoke of creating a form of United States of Europe. He represented enlightenment; he was the mediator between the harsher aspects of the French Revolution and the ordinary peoples of Europe. Above all, he had been forced to wage endless wars against his better instincts by the obdurate opposition, hostility and plotting of the ancient monarchies, especially Great Britain. As he declared in his last will and testament, his motto had always been "Everything for the French People." And the sufferings, real and imagined, of the heroic exile of Saint Helena, of Prometheus bound to his rock, lost nothing in the telling, and were widely believed throughout the European world.

The flood of memoirs that soon emanated from the pens of old soldiers, servants

Napoleon's tomb in Les Invalides, Paris. (Photograph by A. Moulin.) The final resting place of Napoleon's remains was dedicated and inaugurated by his nephew Napoleon III on December 2, 1861. They were placed in a special open crypt beneath the dome of Les Invalides within a sarcophagus fashioned out of a single block of pink porphyry. Guarded by two large statues representing civil and martial power, the sarcophagus is flanked by twelve statues of Victories, each bearing the name of one of the emperor's great battles. In December 1940, Hitler ordered the ashes of Napoleon II to be brought from Vienna and reburied nearby.

The author standing by the Prince Imperial's Memorial. (Photograph by Oliver Hemmerie.) Napoleon's great-nephew, the son of Napoleon III, after training at the Royal Military Academy Woolwich, joined the British Royal Artillery after accompanying his parents into exile in 1870. He was killed in 1879 during the Third Zulu War. The statue was subscribed by all ranks of the British army and now stands at the Royal Military Academy Sandhurst.

and statesmen, which the public avidly read, calling for more, inevitably heaped fuel upon the fires of emperor worship and reached a peak during the rule of his nephew, Louis-Napoleon (son of Louis Bonaparte, sometime king of Holland), as both prince-president and then as emperor from the middle of the nineteenth century to the great debacle of 1870. The pomp and ceremony surrounding the return of the emperor's remains from Saint Helena to rest amid the splendors of Les Invalides in 1840 encouraged the spread of the legend throughout Europe and the New World. The process had already been gathering momentum while the exiled Napoleon was still alive, and as the percipient Russian count Rostopchin observed just two years after the emperor's death in 1821, "The Napoleon who is popular today is the Napoleon of the Legend rather than that of History." It is debatable, however, whether the latter was one jot less impressive than the former. Almost 180 years after Napoleon's death, his name still inspires posterity, and is likely to do so for many more to come.

SELECT BIBLIOGRAPHY

Adye, Sir John. *Napoleon of the Snows.* London: Nash and Grayson, 1931

Aubry, Octave. *Napoleon.* London: Paul Hamlyn, 1964.

Bainville, Jacques. *Napoleon.* London, 1932.

Barnett, Corelli. *Bonaparte.* New York: Hill and Wang, 1978.

Becke, Archibald F. *Napoleon and Waterloo.* London: Kegan Paul, 1914. Reprint. 2 volumes. Salem: Ayer Co. Pubs.

Belloc, Hillaire. *Napoleon.* London: Cessell, 1932. Reprint. Norwood: Telegraph Books, 1986.

Brett-James, Antony. *The Hundred Days.* London: Macmillan, 1964.

Camon, Henri. *Génie et métier chez-Napoléon.* Paris: Berger Levrault, 1929.

Carlyle, Thomas. *Critical and Miscellaneous Essays.* London, 1843. Reprint. New York: Century, 1984.

Caulaincourt, Armand Auguste. *The Memoirs of General de Caulaincourt, Duke of Vicenza.* 1935. Reprint. New York: Greenwood, 1976.

Chandler, David G. *Austerlitz: 1805.* London: Osprey, 1990.

———. *The Campaigns of Napoleon.* New York: Macmillan, 1973.

———. *Dictionary of the Napoleonic Wars.* New York: Macmillan, 1979.

———. *Waterloo—the Hundred Days.* London: Osprey, Geo. Philips Ltd, 1980.

———, ed. *The Military Maxims of Napoleon.* New York: Macmillan, 1988.

———, ed. *Napoleon's Marshals.* New York: Macmillan, 1987.

Clausewitz, Carl von. *On War.* London: Kegan Paul, 1911.

Coignet, Jean-Roche. *The Notebooks of Captain Coignet.* Edited by J. Fortescue. London: Chetto and Windus, 1928.

Colin, Jean. *The Transformations of War.* London: Hugh Rees, 1912. Reprint. New York: Greenwood, 1977.

Connelly, Owen. *Blundering to Glory.* Wilmington: Scholarly Resources, Inc., 1987.

Cronin, Vincent. *Napoleon.* London: Collins, 1971.

Delderfield, Ronald F. *The March of the Twenty-Six.* London: Hodder & Stoughton, 1962.

Dodge, Theodore. *Napoleon: A History of the Art of War.* 1907. Reprint. 4 volumes. New York: AMS Press.

Duffy, Christopher J. *Borodino.* London: Seeley, Service and Co. Ltd, 1972.

Dupont, M. *Napoléon et ses grognards*. Paris: Hachette, 1945.

Esposito, Vincent J., and Elting, John R. *A Military History and Atlas of the Napoleonic Wars*. New York, 1965. Reprint. New York: AMS Press, 1987.

Faber du Four, Christian W. von. *La campagne de Russie, 1812*. Paris: Flammarion, 1895.

Fain, Agathon Jean Francois, Baron. *Mémoires*. Paris: Plon-Nourrit, 1908.

Fisher, Herbert A. *Napoleon*. Oxford: Home University Library, 1950.

Fuller, John F. *The Decisive Battles of the Western World*. London: Eyre & Spottiswoode, 1956.

Geyl, P. *Napoleon, For and Against*. London: Jonathan Cape, 1949.

Herold, J. Christopher. *The Age of Napoleon*. London: Weidenfeld & Nicolson, 1967.

———. *The Mind of Napoleon*. New York: Columbia University Press, 1955.

Horward, Donald. *Napoleonic Military History*. London: Greenhill Press, 1986.

Hudson, William Henry. *The Man, Napoleon*. London, 1915.

Jackson, William. *Attack in the West*. London: Eyre & Spottiswoode, 1953.

Jomini, Antoine-Henri. *The Art of War*. 1862. Reprint. New York: Greenwood, 1971.

Jones, R. Benjamin. *Napoleon, Man and Myth*. New York: Holmes and Meier, 1977. London: Hodder & Stoughton.

Lachouque, Henri. *The Anatomy of Glory*. London and New York: Lund Humphries, 1961.

Las Cases, M. J. Emmanuel, Count. *Memoirs of the Emperor Napoleon*. London: Bentley, 1836.

Lecestre, L. *New Letters of Napoleon I*. Translated by Lady Mary Lloyd. London: Heinemann, 1898.

Liddell-Hart, Basil. *The Ghost of Napoleon*. London, 1933. Reprint. New York: Greenwood, 1980.

MacDonnell, A. G. *Napoleon and His Marshals*. London: Macmillan, 1950.

Manceron, Claude. *Austerlitz*. London: Allen & Unwin, 1966.

Marbot, Marcellin Baron de. *Mémoires*. Paris: Librarie Plan, 1892.

Markham, Felix. *Napoleon*. London, Weidenfeld & Nicolson, 1963. New York: New American Library, 1966.

Marshall-Cornwall, Sir James. *Napoleon*. London: B. T. Batsford Ltd, 1967.

Napoléon. *Correspondence de Napoléon Ier*. 32 vols. Paris: 1858–69. Reprint. New York: AMS Press.

Odeleben, Ernst Otto Innocenz d'. *Relation de la campagne de Francais en Saxe de 1813*. Paris, 1817.

Petre, F. Lorraine. *Napoleon's Conquest of Prussia*. London: John Long, The Bodley Head, 1972.

Phipps, Ramsey W. *The Armies of the First French Republic & the Rise of the Marshals of Napoleon I*. Oxford, 1939. Reprint. New York: Greenwood, 1980.

Quimby, Robert W. S. *The Background of Napoleonic Warfare: The Theory of Military Tactics in Eighteenth-Century France*. New York: AMS Press, 1957.

Rose, J. Holland. *Life of Napoleon*. London: G. Bell, 1902.

Thompson, James M. *Life of Napoleon*. Oxford: Blackwell, 1952.

Tulard, Jean. *Napoleon, the Myth of the Saviour*. New York: Beaufort Books, 1984.

Vachée, A. *Napoleon at Work*. London: A. & C. Black, 1914.

Wartenburg, Yorck von. *Napoleon as a General*. London: Kegan Paul, 1902.

Wilkinson, Spencer. *The Rise of General Bonaparte*. Oxford: Oxford University Press, 1930.

Young, Peter. *Napoleon's Marshals*. Reading: Osprey, 1973.

INDEX